BESS BRADFIELD
CAROL LETHABY

Series editors:
BEN GOLDSTEIN & CERI JONES

The BIG Picture

B1 PRE-INTERMEDIATE Student's Book

CONTENTS UNITS 1–6

	GRAMMAR	VOCABULARY	READING & LISTENING	PRONUNCIATION
1 SPEAKING THE SAME LANGUAGE *page 4*	• Present simple & present continuous • Questions	• Languages & countries • Free time • Communication	Ⓡ Being bilingual • An article about the SETI Ⓛ An Earth Speaks message	• Final *-s*

page 12 **FUNCTIONAL LANGUAGE:** CHECKING UNDERSTANDING   *page 13* **SPEAKING TASK:** PLANNING YOUR LANGUAGE LEARNING
page 152 **WRITING BANK:** LEARNING JOURNALS

2 BACK TO NATURE *page 14*	• Past simple • Past continuous • Past simple & past continuous	• Geography • Animals	Ⓡ Three newspaper articles Ⓛ An interview with a wildlife photographer • Encounters with animals	• Past simple endings

page 22 **FUNCTIONAL LANGUAGE:** CHECKING IN   *page 23* **WRITING TASK:** A HOLIDAY REVIEW

3 ICONS *page 24*	• Relative clauses • Articles: *a/an, the,* no article	• Landmarks • Cultural icons	Ⓡ Will the real Taj Mahal please stand up? • A blog post • The legend of Bob Marley Ⓛ Describing a photo • Three opinions • Discussing fictional characters	• *a & an*

page 32 **FUNCTIONAL LANGUAGE:** EXPRESSING PREFERENCE   *page 33* **SPEAKING TASK:** DESIGNING A LOGO
page 153 **WRITING BANK:** COMMENTS ON A WEBSITE

page 34 **REVIEW A,** UNITS 1–3   *page 37* **BRING IT TOGETHER** 1, 2 & 3

4 AGES AND CHANGES *page 38*	• Present perfect • Present perfect & past simple • Present perfect with *for* & *since* • Comparatives & superlatives	• Life stages • Activities • Home life	Ⓡ Act your age! • Young achievers Ⓛ A video appeal • A report about a lost property office in Paris	• Auxiliary verbs

page 46 **FUNCTIONAL LANGUAGE:** CATCHING UP   *page 47* **WRITING TASK:** AN INFORMAL EMAIL

5 LIVE AND LEARN *page 48*	• Present continuous & *going to* • *Must(n't)* & *(don't) have to* for obligation	• Education & learning • *-ed/-ing* adjectives • Adjectives & prepositions	Ⓡ Degrees with a difference • The school of fun • A museum brochure Ⓛ Talking about university studies • A museum audio guide	• Stress in two-syllable words

page 56 **FUNCTIONAL LANGUAGE:** SOUNDING POLITE   *page 57* **SPEAKING TASK:** A TELEPHONE ENQUIRY
page 154 **WRITING BANK:** WRITING TO SAY SORRY

6 HELP! *page 58*	• Modal verbs: *can/can't, should/shouldn't* • Predictions: *will, may, might*	• Jobs & services • Adjective suffixes *-ful* & *-less* • Senses • Health problems	Ⓡ The homeless world cup • Introduction to a web article • An information leaflet Ⓛ Discussing a film • Discussing problems and giving advice • Four conversations	• Word stress

page 66 **FUNCTIONAL LANGUAGE:** ADVICE   *page 67* **WRITING TASK:** A FORMAL EMAIL

page 68 **REVIEW B,** UNITS 4–6   *page 71* **BRING IT TOGETHER** 4, 5 & 6

	GRAMMAR	VOCABULARY	READING & LISTENING	PRONUNCIATION
7 SWITCHED ON page 72	• The -ing form & to + infinitive • Countable & uncountable nouns, some & any • Quantifiers	• Science & research • Make & do • Cities • Technology	® An article about brain training • The perfect city? ⓛ Three opinions	• Three- and four-syllable words
	page 80 **FUNCTIONAL LANGUAGE:** AGREEING AND DISAGREEING page 81 **SPEAKING TASK:** DISCUSSING AN ISSUE page 155 **WRITING BANK:** A REVIEW			
8 REAL OR FAKE? page 82	• If + present simple • Modal verbs: must, can't, may, might	• True or false adjectives • Look & see • Common collocations with say & tell	® Travel tip no. 75 • A film review • Urban legends ⓛ Conversation between two tourists • Advertisement for a radio show	• /ə/
	page 90 **FUNCTIONAL LANGUAGE:** WARNINGS AND PROMISES page 91 **WRITING TASK:** A BLOG POST			
9 MAKING ENDS MEET page 92	• If + past simple • So & such • Some-/any-/no- + -one/-body/-thing	• Money verbs • Money nouns	® An article about a freeconomist ® An article about the Lavigueur family • Get-rich-quick adverts ⓛ Four opinions • What happened next?	• Would
	page 100 **FUNCTIONAL LANGUAGE:** MONEY TRANSACTIONS page 101 **SPEAKING TASK:** SPENDING YOUR MONEY page 156 **WRITING BANK:** WRITING TO SAY THANK YOU			
	page 102 **REVIEW C**, UNITS 7–9 page 105 **BRING IT TOGETHER** 7, 8 & 9			
10 A GLOBAL MARKET? page 106	• Passive (1): present simple • Passive (2): past simple	• Advertising • Expressing your opinion • Describing clothes • Adjectives	® A brand transformed • A factual document ⓛ A sports journalist talking about football shirts • Describing photos	• Was/were strong and weak forms
	page 114 **FUNCTIONAL LANGUAGE:** DESCRIBING A LOCAL DISH page 115 **WRITING TASK:** A LOCAL STREET FOOD GUIDE			
11 NICE TO MEET YOU page 116	• Reported speech: say • Reported speech: tell	• Making friends • Adjectives to describe personality • Relationships	® How we met • Tips about arguing • Staying single? ⓛ A radio phone-in • An argument • Talking about relationships	• Stress to change meaning
	page 124 **FUNCTIONAL LANGUAGE:** TELEPHONE MESSAGES page 125 **SPEAKING TASK:** GIVING AN UPDATE page 157 **WRITING BANK:** MAKING ARRANGEMENTS			
12 ENTERTAIN ME page 126	• Modal verbs review • Used to	• Entertainment • Music • The internet	® A music-lover's blog post • A minute of your time ⓛ Four website messages • Discussing TV • Describing an online slideshow	• Used to
	page 134 **FUNCTIONAL LANGUAGE:** MAKING RECOMMENDATIONS page 135 **WRITING TASK:** A DESCRIPTION OF A TV SERIES			
	page 136 **REVIEW D**, UNITS 10–12 page 139 **BRING IT TOGETHER**, 10, 11 & 12			

page 140 **GRAMMAR REFERENCE**   page 152 **WRITING BANK**   page 158 **COMMUNICATION BANK**
page 162 **TRANSCRIPTS**   page 168 **IRREGULAR VERBS**

1 SPEAKING THE SAME LANGUAGE

1 a 💬 Work in pairs. Look at the welcome signs. How many different languages can you see? Do you know what they are?

b Match signs a–f to the places where they could appear.

on a beach   on the side of a building   on a motorway
at a port   at a shopping centre   at a zoo

2 💬 Work in pairs. How many languages can you say 'hello' and 'goodbye' in? Which country/countries do you associate with each language? Complete A in the KEY VOCABULARY PANEL ▦.

3 a 🔊 1.1 Listen to Ellen and Ernesto talking about the languages they speak. Note the languages they mention.

Ellen: _Welsh_
Ernesto: _Guaraní_

b What similarities did you notice about the two speakers?

4

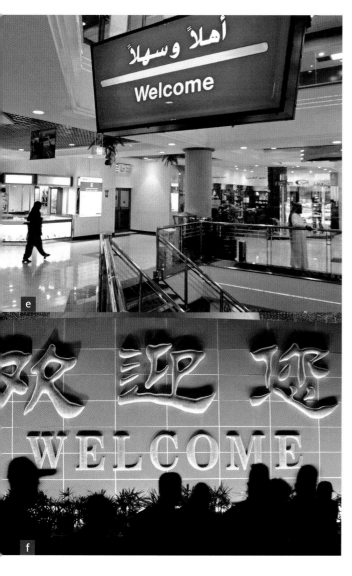

KEY VOCABULARY

Languages

A Languages & countries

- Match the language to the country/countries.
  One country has two languages.

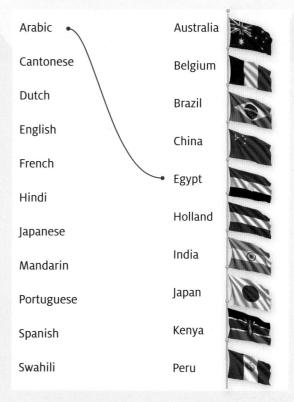

Arabic	Australia
Cantonese	Belgium
Dutch	Brazil
English	China
French	Egypt
Hindi	Holland
Japanese	India
Mandarin	Japan
Portuguese	Kenya
Spanish	Peru
Swahili	

- Can you think of more countries and languages?

B Words to describe languages

1 to speak two languages fluently and comfortably
   to be ....

2 the language the government uses on forms,
   on road signs and in school books

   ....

3 the language you spoke as a child OR the language
   you speak at home

   .... OR ....

4 the language of government and business in the
   country where you live, which is not the same as
   your language

   ....

5 a language which is spoken in a different country

   ....

---

4 a Listen again and match the statements to Ellen,
   Ernesto or both.

   1 There are two **official language**s. ....
   2 I have two **first language**s. ....
   3 Guaraní is my **mother tongue**. ....
   4 A lot of people are **bilingual** in my country. ....
   5 I learnt Spanish as a **second language**. ....
   6 I learnt French as a **foreign language**.

   b Match the words in **bold** with definitions 1–5
   in B in the KEY VOCABULARY PANEL ▇ .

5 a 💬 Work in groups. Discuss the questions.
   - What is your first language? Do you have a second
     language? Do you speak any other languages?
   - What are the official languages in your country? Are
     any other languages popular? Are people bilingual?
   - Which languages would you like to learn? Why?
   - Which language would you not like to learn? Why?

   b Share your answers with the class.

READING

1 💬 Work in pairs. Look at the photos. Discuss the questions.

- Which countries do you think the photos show?
- Which languages do the people speak there?
- Can you think of three countries which have more than one official language?

2 a Read the article *Being bilingual*. Match the people to the photos.

b Read the article again. Complete the sentences with the correct name: Marcela, Robert, Wotoro or Brad.

1   *Robert*   lives in a country where French is an important language.
2 .... is working as a teacher at the moment.
3 .... goes to school five days a week.
4 .... lives and works in two different countries.
5 .... uses French when he/she is teaching.
6 .... is learning a new language.
7 .... regularly travels to a different part of the same country.

Being bilingual

What's it like to be fluent in two or more languages? We interviewed four bilingual people to find out.

Marcela: 'I live in Tijuana in Mexico, but I work in San Diego in the USA five days a week. I speak English and Spanish well and I'm taking weekly Japanese classes at the moment. Sometimes I don't know how to say what I want to say in English, so I say it in Spanish. Luckily most people I know speak both languages.'

Robert: 'I live in Belgium and I speak Flemish (which is like Dutch) and French. I live in Flanders and almost everyone here speaks Dutch and French. A lot of people also speak English, like me – I'm speaking English now! I visit the French-speaking part of Belgium every month, because my grandmother lives there. A lot of people there don't know Flemish or English.'

Wotoro: 'There are over 60 languages in Kenya and there are two official languages, so it's common for people to speak at least three different languages – their mother tongue and English and Swahili. I speak Gikuyu with my family, English on Monday to Friday mornings when I go to school, and Swahili or Gikuyu when I buy things at the market. I think in all three languages. Right now I'm thinking in English, because I'm speaking English.'

Brad: 'I'm American, but I work at a French immersion school. I'm teaching beginner's French at the moment. I started to learn French when I was four and a half and then I majored in French at college and lived in France for a few years. Some people think that being bilingual makes you smarter. I don't know if that's true, but it's fun to know two languages.'

d

3 🗨 Work in groups. Discuss the questions.

- Are you bilingual?
- What would you enjoy/not enjoy about being bilingual?
- Do you know someone who is bilingual? Describe how he/she uses the two languages.

GRAMMAR

1 Look at the sentences in READING 2b again. Underline the verbs. Which are a) in the present simple? b) in the present continuous?

2 a Look at the GRAMMAR PANEL ▪️. Complete 1–3 with a–c.

a   general truths or situations
b   regular habits/routines
c   things that are happening right now

b Find one more example of each of the uses 1–3 in the sentences in READING 2b. Write the examples in the GRAMMAR PANEL ▪️.

3 Complete the email with the correct form of the verbs. Explain your choice.

Hi Misha,

How are you? I'm really busy this term, I (1)*study / 'm studying* Arabic. It's really interesting, but it means I'm quite busy! I (2)*go / 'm going* to class every day for three hours. We (3)*work / 're working* on the alphabet at the moment. I love the Arabic script, it's so beautiful, but it's really difficult too! I (4)*spend / am spending* three hours every night practising my handwriting. It's like being at primary school again!

(5)*Do you do / Are you doing* that online course at the moment? We really must meet up soon for a chat. Me and Toni usually (6)*meet / are meeting* for coffee every morning at about 10 o'clock. Do you want to join us? Tomorrow maybe?

Text me! Corinne

4 a Write true sentences about you.

1   live / with my family
2   study / a foreign language / at the moment
3   take / a summer holiday / every year
4   like / Italian food
5   work / at the moment

b 🗨 Find one person in the class who wrote the same as you for each of 1–5.

▪️ PRESENT SIMPLE & PRESENT CONTINUOUS

We usually use the **present simple** to talk about:

(1) *general truths or situations*
  I live in Tijuana.

(2) _____
  I go to class on Saturdays.

We use the **present continuous** to talk about:
(3) _____
  Right now, I'm studying English.

We often use these time expressions with the present simple:
usually, often, every day, every night

We often use these time expressions with the present continuous: *at the moment, (right) now, these days*

See page 140 for grammar reference and more practice.

▪️ NOTICE   *RIGHT NOW*

Use *right now* to talk about things happening at the time of speaking. *I'm reading this right now.*

PRONUNCIATION: final -*s*

1 🔊 1.2 Listen to four people talking about learning a language. Which skill does each speaker think is most important?

listening   reading   speaking   writing

2 a 🔊 1.3 Listen to the verbs. How do we pronounce -*s*? Match 1–3 to a–c.

1 /s/	2 /z/	3 /ɪz/
a writes speaks	b practises uses watches notices	c reads listens

b Add the verbs to 1–3.

changes   helps   loves   makes   needs
plays   puts   teaches   thinks   wants

3 🔊 1.4 Listen and check.

SPEAKING

1 a Match photos a–d to situations 1–4.

1 interviewing someone for a job
2 going on a first date
3 talking to a good friend
4 meeting someone for the first time

b What do people usually talk about in situations 1–4? Think of three ideas for each situation.

2 a 1.5 Listen and match conversations e–h to the situations.

b Listen again. Tick the things people talk about in conversations e–h.

	e	f	g	h
Name				
Age				
Nationality				
Languages you speak				
Hobbies				
Recent events				
Skills and experience				
Personality				
People you both know				
Family				

GRAMMAR

1 a Read the questions from the conversations in SPEAKING 2. Can you remember the answers?

1 When do you play squash?
2 Who do you play with?
3 Why do you want to work here?
4 How many languages do you speak?
5 Are you a student?
6 What kind of music do you like?
7 Do you like going to concerts?
8 How often do you go?

b 1.5 Listen again and check.

2 Which two questions in 1 have the answer 'yes' or 'no'?

3 a Underline six question words and expressions (e.g. *When*) in 1a.

b Complete 1–6 in the GRAMMAR PANEL ▪▪ .

4 a Circle the main verbs and the auxiliary verbs (*Do/Does*) in 1a.

b Choose the correct option for 7 and 8 in the GRAMMAR PANEL ▪▪ .

"Intonation in questions"

🔊 1.6 Listen to four questions. Does the person's voice go up ↗ or down ↘ at the end of

1 yes/no questions?
2 questions with a question word?

Listen again and repeat.

5 Write questions for the answers.

My favourite actor is Johnny Depp.
Who is your favourite actor?

1 I like horror films and comedies.
2 My favourite singer is Shakira.
3 My birthday is on 11 May.
4 I live on Calle de la Cruz in Vigo, Spain.
5 I watch TV every night.
6 I want to learn English because it is useful for my job.
7 I speak two languages, English and Spanish.

6 Write four more questions you would like to ask the person sitting next to you.

7 **a** 💬 Work in pairs. Ask and answer your questions.

b What did you learn about your partner?

■ QUESTIONS

Types of questions

• *Yes/No questions*
We answer the questions with 'yes' or 'no'.
Are you a student? (Yes, I am./No, I'm not.)
Do you work here? (Yes, I do. /No, I don't.)

• **Question words/expressions (*Wh-* questions)**
We form other questions with question words or expressions.

   Where (places),
(1) W_____ (people)
(2) W_____ (kind of) (things)
(3) W_____ (time)
(4) W_____ (reason)
(5) H_____ o_____ (frequency)
(6) H_____ m_____ (number)

Who is your teacher?   *Where do you live?*

Word order in questions

In present simple questions, we put *do* or *does*
(7) *after / before* the subject, and the main verb
(8) *after / before* the subject.

Do you like your job?   *Where does he live?*

We don't use *do* or *does* in questions with *be*.

Are you English?   *Who is that man?*

See page 140 for grammar reference and more practice.

VOCABULARY: free time

1 💬 Work in pairs. Look at the photos. Discuss the questions.

- Which of the things do you enjoy doing?
- Is there anything you don't enjoy doing? Why?

2 **a** Complete the activities. Use a dictionary to help you.

1 l*i*stening to m u s i c
2 going t___ the gy___
3 s___rfing the int___net
4 pl___ying f___tb___ll
5 having friends r___nd
6 eating ___ut at rest___r___ts
7 going clu___ing
8 r___ding the n___sp___er
9 sho___ing in town

b Match six activities to the photos.

3 Read the questions and make notes for your answers.

- What do you usually do in your free time in the evenings?
- What do you usually do in your free time at the weekend?

4 **a** 💬 Ask the questions in 3 to students in your class. Make notes of their answers.

b Who is the most similar to you? What are the most popular free-time activities?

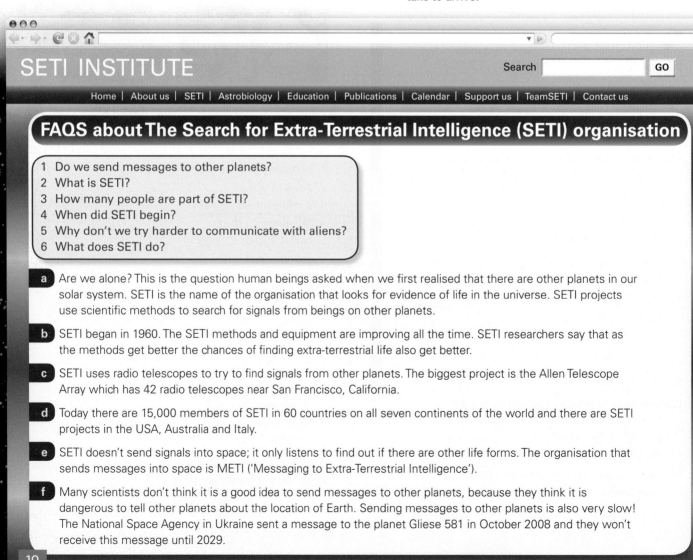

READING & SPEAKING

1 a Look at the photo. Where is it and what can you see there?

b Quickly read the online article about SETI and check your answer.

2 Read the article again. Match the Frequently Asked Questions (FAQS) about SETI to the answers.

3 Read the article again and answer the questions.
1. What is SETI looking for?
2. Are SETI methods the same now as in 1960?
3. What is the Allen Telescope Array?
4. Where are there SETI projects?
5. What is the difference between SETI and METI?
6. How long will the message from Ukraine to Gliese 581 take to arrive?

SETI INSTITUTE

Search [＿＿＿＿＿＿＿] **GO**

Home | About us | SETI | Astrobiology | Education | Publications | Calendar | Support us | TeamSETI | Contact us

FAQS about The Search for Extra-Terrestrial Intelligence (SETI) organisation

1. Do we send messages to other planets?
2. What is SETI?
3. How many people are part of SETI?
4. When did SETI begin?
5. Why don't we try harder to communicate with aliens?
6. What does SETI do?

a Are we alone? This is the question human beings asked when we first realised that there are other planets in our solar system. SETI is the name of the organisation that looks for evidence of life in the universe. SETI projects use scientific methods to search for signals from beings on other planets.

b SETI began in 1960. The SETI methods and equipment are improving all the time. SETI researchers say that as the methods get better the chances of finding extra-terrestrial life also get better.

c SETI uses radio telescopes to try to find signals from other planets. The biggest project is the Allen Telescope Array which has 42 radio telescopes near San Francisco, California.

d Today there are 15,000 members of SETI in 60 countries on all seven continents of the world and there are SETI projects in the USA, Australia and Italy.

e SETI doesn't send signals into space; it only listens to find out if there are other life forms. The organisation that sends messages into space is METI ('Messaging to Extra-Terrestrial Intelligence').

f Many scientists don't think it is a good idea to send messages to other planets, because they think it is dangerous to tell other planets about the location of Earth. Sending messages to other planets is also very slow! The National Space Agency in Ukraine sent a message to the planet Gliese 581 in October 2008 and they won't receive this message until 2029.

4 💬 Work in groups. Discuss the questions.

- Do you think SETI or METI is a good idea? Why/Why not?
- Do you think there is life on other planets? Why/Why not?
- Do you know about any theories or research into life on other planets?
- Would you like to talk to beings from other planets? What would you ask them?

VOCABULARY: communication

1 Complete the sentences with the correct form of the verbs in the box.

receive   listen   send   tell

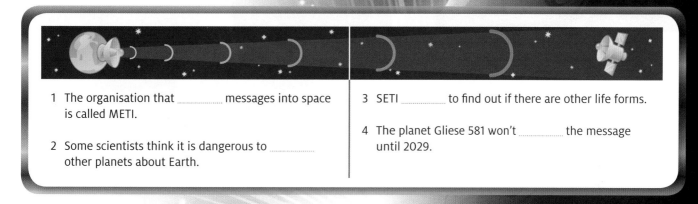

1 The organisation that .... messages into space is called METI.

2 Some scientists think it is dangerous to .... other planets about Earth.

3 SETI .... to find out if there are other life forms.

4 The planet Gliese 581 won't .... the message until 2029.

2 a 💬 Work in pairs. What is the difference between the expressions?

1 I usually tell *the truth / lies*.
2 I like talking *about / to* other people.
3 I like to write *about / to* my friends.
4 I like *listening to / hearing about* interesting news stories.

b Which option in each sentence describes you?

LISTENING & SPEAKING

1 Read about the *Earth Speaks* project. Answer the questions.

1 What is the purpose of the project?
2 What can people send?

2 🔊 1.7 Listen to this *Earth Speaks* message. Are the statements true or false? Correct the false statements.

1 They like living on Earth.
2 People are very selfish.
3 People on Earth like to know about other places.
4 They don't expect to hear from the other planet.

3 a 💬 Work in pairs. What do you want to tell aliens about Earth? Make your own message for the *Earth Speaks* project and record it or write it.

b Listen to or read all the messages. Which messages were the most serious/funniest and why?

Hello!

Earth Speaks

Welcome to **Earth Speaks**, a research project that investigates this question:

'If we discover intelligent life beyond Earth, should we reply, and if so, what should we say?'

We invite people from around the world to send pictures, sounds and text messages that they want to send to other worlds. The project aims to answer two questions: Can we talk to aliens? What can we tell them?

TUNE IN

1 💬 Work in pairs. Look at photos a–d. Where are the people and what are they doing?

2 🔊 1.8 Listen and match conversations 1–4 to the photos.

3 What is the problem in each conversation?
- speaking too quietly
- the person doesn't understand a word
- the person doesn't know how to say the word in English
- speaking too quickly

4 Listen again and complete the sentences.
1 Could you _____ more _____, please?
2 I'm _____. I didn't _____ you.
3 What _____ 'deposit slip' _____?
4 How _____ you _____ it in _____?

FOCUS ON LANGUAGE

5 Match the responses in 4 with a similar way of saying the same thing.
1 Can you repeat that, please?
2 Can you say it again, please?
3 What did you say?
4 I don't know what … means.
5 What do you call this in English?

6 💬 Match the two parts of these five conversations. Work in pairs. Practise saying them.

1 What do you call the things you use to read with?
2 What does 'Dutch' mean?
3 What did you say?
4 Sorry, I didn't hear you.
5 Could you say that again, please?

a Sorry. Is this better? Where are you from?
b I said – Do you want whipped cream with your coffee?
c Oh, do you mean 'glasses'?
d Sure. I asked if you would like a sandwich.
e It's the language of the Netherlands.

OVER TO YOU

7 💬 Work in groups. Choose a new word. Get your group to describe it without saying the word.

What do you call it when someone is saying things that are not true?

8 💬 Work in pairs. Student A, imagine you are staying with an English-speaking friend. You need one of the items in photos e–h. Explain what you need to student B, without saying the name of the item.

Student B, you have a friend staying with you. He/She needs one of the items in photos e–h. Listen and try to identify the item. Check your answer on page 158.

TUNE IN

1 Look at the advertisement. Do you think it's possible? How?

2 💬 Work in groups. Discuss your own language-learning experiences.

- What languages have you tried to learn and why?
- When did you start? How successful were you?
- Which things made it easier/harder for you?

PREPARE FOR TASK

3 a Read the questionnaire extract. Which things are true for you? Which are not?

b 💬 Work in pairs. Compare your answers with your partner.

4 Read the list of study skills and say how each one can help you. Which ones do you do?

- study outside class
- watch films in English
- listen to music in English
- check your notes before/after class
- do your homework
- memorise vocabulary
- organise your lesson notes
- read books and magazines in English
- use a dictionary
- speak to English-speaking people

5 🔊 1.9 Listen to Sandra and Max talking about learning English this year. Complete the form.

	SANDRA	MAX
I plan to spend ... hours a week outside class practising English.		
I plan to...		
• watch films and TV		
• listen to music		
• read my notes before/after class		
• do homework		
• write down and study new vocabulary		
• read books and magazines		
• use a dictionary		
• practise exercises online		

6 Work in groups. Compare your answers and decide who you think has the best plan.

Learn a language in just six weeks with our new system. You'll be speaking French, German, Spanish or Japanese in just six weeks or your money back! No boring classes, no hours of grammar study – just learn to speak.

---

1 I'm learning English:
    to get a better job / more money
    to pass an exam
    because I'm interested in language
    to understand films and music
    because my parents want me to
    other reasons _____

2 I'm interested in
    speaking   listening   reading   writing

3 I plan to study 2–4, 5–10, 11–15 hours a week outside class.

TASK

7 Complete the form with your own answers.

Name: _____	
I plan to spend ... hours a week outside class practising English.	
I plan to...	
• watch films and TV	
• listen to music	
• read my notes before/after class	
• do homework	
• write down and study new vocabulary	
• read books and magazines	
• use a dictionary	
• practise exercises online	

8 💬 Work in pairs. Talk about what you have written with your partner.

REPORT BACK

9 💬 Work in groups or as a class. Compare language-learning plans. Who has the best plan?

➡ Go to Review A, Unit 1, p. 34   ➡ Go to Writing bank 1, p. 152

2 BACK TO NATURE

a

b

c

d

1 💬 Work in groups. Look at the photos. What are the people doing?

2 Use the phrases in **A** in the KEY VOCABULARY PANEL ■ to describe the photos. Use a dictionary to help you.

3 a 🔊 2.1 Listen to four people describing a place. Match each speaker to one of the photos.

Roxanne ☐   Sunee ☐
Juan ☐   Mohammed ☐

b Listen again and complete the sentences with words from **A**.

1 Roxanne's favourite place is a Chinese ....
2 Juan goes to the .... most weekends.
3 Sunee lives on the .... of Phuket in Thailand. She often goes to the .... to meet friends.
4 Mohammed thinks that the .... can be dangerous, but it's very beautiful, especially in the ....

4 Complete **B** in the KEY VOCABULARY PANEL ■ . Listen again. Which point of the compass does each speaker mention?

5 a 💬 Work in groups. Can you remember who said these sentences?

1 'It's a really peaceful place.'
2 *'It's very friendly.'*
3 'This place is unique – there's nowhere quite like it.'
4 'It's noisy and dirty!'

b Read transcript 2.1 on page 162. Underline other adjectives to describe places. Which adjectives describe your hometown?

6 💬 Work in pairs. Discuss the questions.

• Which of the places in the photos do you like the most? Why?
• What is your favourite outdoor place? Why do you like it?

e

f

■ KEY VOCABULARY

Geography

A Outdoor places

far from everywhere   in a field   in a forest
in a rainforest   in the country   in the desert
in the mountains   near the sea   on an island
on the banks of a river   on the beach   on the coast

B Points of the compass

● Label the compass using *north*, *south*, *east*, *west*.

1 ....

2 ....

3 ....

4 ....

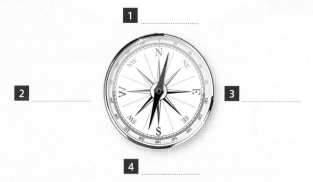

● Match the places on the map to the phrases in the box.
(There are more phrases than places).

near the capital   in the centre   in the east
inland   on an island   in the north
in the south   on the west coast

Coimbra is in the centre.

PORTUGAL

Vila Real
Porto
Coimbra
Castelo
Branco
SPAIN
NORTH
ATLANTIC
OCEAN
Lisbon
Setúbal
Évora
Madeira
Funchal
Faro
Golfo de Cadiz

● Where is your hometown? Use the words above to
describe exactly where you live.

I live in a small town in the north. It's on the coast, near the capital.

READING

1 💬 Work in pairs. Look at the photos and newspaper headlines. What do you think is similar about these three stories?

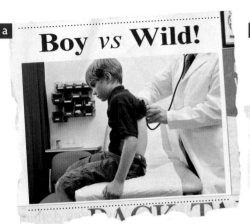

a **Boy *vs* Wild!**

b **A COLD WALK HOME**

c **River Rescue**

2 **a** Read newspaper articles 1–3 and match them to headlines a–c in **1**.

b Read the sentences. Are they true or false? Correct the false sentences.

1 Christopher used his mobile phone to call for help.
2 Christopher was walking somewhere cold.
3 Grayson did not have anything to eat.
4 Grayson was wearing something bright.
5 Rory thinks that TV can sometimes be useful.
6 Rory was lost for more time than Christopher and Grayson.

1
A few years ago, Rory and Chiara Maddocks and Rachel Hodson lost their way in a rainforest in central Malaysia. They didn't have any food or drink, and they were tired and scared. The forest was beautiful, but it was dangerous, with many wild animals and rainy weather.

How did the three friends survive? They followed tips from Ray Mears's *Extreme Survival* programme on TV. They walked to a river until they saw the sea. They swam and they tried to find help. Luckily, some boys on a boat rescued them. After two nights in the forest, they were safe. When he got home, Rory said he wanted to watch more *Extreme Survival*. 'You never know when you might need it!'

                                                                                    Mar

2
In 2009, nine-year-old Grayson Wynne spent 18 hours alone in a forest in eastern Utah, USA. He survived – thanks to TV adventurer Bear Grylls.

Grayson and his family were on a camping holiday. On Saturday, Grayson went for a walk by himself. He put some food in his rucksack before he left. But he didn't take a map!

Grayson was a big fan of Bear Grylls's books and TV shows, and he knew what to do. Bear said that it was important to help people to find you, so Grayson left pieces of his yellow jacket on paths and in trees. Rescuers found Grayson after they noticed the yellow material.

3 Find words/phrases in the articles that mean:

1 did not know where they were (3 words)
2 felt unhappy about something bad (1 word)
3 advice, useful ideas (1 words)
4 with no other people (two items: 1 word / 2 words)
5 safe places to sleep (1 word)
6 the beginning of the day (1 word)

3
When Christopher Traverse's snowmobile broke last winter, the Canadian was worried. He didn't know where he was, and he didn't have a mobile phone with him. Luckily, he remembered a TV show called *Survivorman*. As part of the show, a man called Les Stroud stayed in many wild, dangerous places. Christopher decided to use some of Les's ideas. He slept in shelters which he made out of trees, and he drank snow. He got up each day at dawn, and he walked until it grew dark. Four days later, he found a road, and a way home.

4 💬 Work in groups. Discuss the questions.

● Which story did you find the most interesting? Why?
● Are survival television shows popular in your country?
● Would you be good at surviving outdoors? Why/Why not?

GRAMMAR

1 a 💬 Work in pairs. Find the sentences in the articles.

1 They **noticed** the yellow material.
2 He **didn't have** a mobile phone with him.
3 How **did** the three friends **survive**?

b Complete 1 and 2 in the GRAMMAR PANEL ▪.

2 Underline the past simple verbs in one of the articles. Which verbs are a) regular? b) irregular?

3 Look at the highlighted words in the articles. Complete 3–7 in the GRAMMAR PANEL ▪.

4 a Look at the photo of Bear Grylls. What do you remember about him from the article?

b Complete the text using the past simple form of the verbs.

Q How (1)*Bear / become* a famous adventurer?

A • He (2)*climb* Mount Everest aged only 23.
• In 2003, he (3)*go* across the Arctic Ocean. He (4)*not travel* on a big ship, but on a tiny boat!
• Two years later, he (5)*fly* over Angel Falls in Venezuela in a paraglider.

Q What (6)*he / do* on his first show?

A • On *Man vs Wild*, Bear (7)*sleep* outside in many wild places. He (8)*not stay* in warm hotels!
• He (9)*not take* any food with him. On the show he (10)*eat* many strange things, like snakes and sheep's eyes!

5 a Think about the last time you visited the countryside. Make questions. Then note your answers.

1 When / go   What / weather like
2 Where / go   What / place like
3 What / do   anything interesting happen

b 💬 Work in pairs. Discuss with a partner.

PAST SIMPLE

We use the **past simple** for completed past actions.

(+) They ___visited___ wild places.
(–) They (1)_____ any cities.
(?) Which countries (2)_____ they _____?

Some verbs have an irregular affirmative form (+).
make → made, do → did, etc.

Time expressions

We often use time words with the past simple, such as:
a.*g o*, (3) a..., (4) i..., (5) l......, (6) o..., (7) w........ .

She went there **last** week.   They left **at** half past ten.
He left two hours **ago**.   We found her **on** June 9th.
I lived there **in** 2003.   It was cold **when** we left.

See page 141 for grammar reference and more practice.

PRONUNCIATION: past simple endings

1 a Complete the table with the past simple form of the regular verbs.

Infinitive	Past simple	Infinitive	Past simple
decide		stay	
follow		stop	
need		walk	
notice		want	

b 🔊 2.2 Look at the infinitive forms. Which verbs have two syllables? Listen and check.

2 a 🔊 2.3 Listen to both the infinitive and the past simple forms. For which three verbs do we pronounce the *-ed* ending as an extra syllable /id/ ? Listen again and repeat.

b Complete the rule.

When the infinitive form of the verb ends in a /___/ or /___/ sound, the *-ed* ending is pronounced as an extra syllable /id/.

3 a Read the sentences. Which past simple endings are pronounced as an extra syllable?

1 We went camping last weekend. It rained and rained. I hated it!
2 I visited my grandparents last Sunday. We sat in the garden and talked about the weather.
3 We went on a long walk. We started at nine and we didn't get back until half past six!

b 🔊 2.4 Listen and repeat.

4 Write three sentences about last weekend. Use at least one regular past simple verb in each one.

lion zebra elephant frog monkey

a b c d

SPEAKING & LISTENING

1 💬 Work in pairs. Look at the photos. Discuss the questions.
- Where were the photographers when they took the photos?
- How often do you take photos?
- Do you use a camera or your mobile phone? Which do you prefer?

2 💬 Work in pairs. Look at jobs 1–3. Discuss the questions.

1 news photographer
2 wildlife photographer
3 wedding photographer

Which job
- do you think is the most difficult? Why?
- would you like to do the most/least?

3 🔊 2.5 Listen to a radio interview with a wildlife photographer. Which three animals in the photos does he talk about?

4 Read the questions. Listen again and circle the answers.

1 When did Steve win the photography competition?
   a this morning
   b a few days ago
   c last year

2 Steve took his winning photo when he was
   a sailing on a river.
   b walking beside a river.
   c sitting next to a river.

3 Steve got his first camera when he was
   a seven.
   b eight.
   c nine.

4 While he was travelling last year, Steve visited
   a Africa.
   b Australia.
   c North America.

5 Steve's favourite animals are
   a lions.
   b snakes.
   c birds.

6 Which animal took Steve's food?
   a a bird
   b a monkey
   c a crocodile

GRAMMAR

1 **a** Read the sentences. Which photos (a–d) is Steve talking about?

1 My girlfriend and I **were travelling** through Bolivia.
2 I **was working** in Africa.

b Look at the verbs in **bold** in 1a. Complete 1 and 2 in the GRAMMAR PANEL ▪ .

2 Read transcript 2.5 on page 162. Find five more examples of the past continuous.

3 **a** What were the animals in photos a–d doing when Steve took the photos?
Write sentences using the verbs in the box.
More than one answer may be possible.

The zebra was running.

> chase climb jump run
> sit stand swim watch

b Work in pairs. Compare your answers with a partner. Did you use the same verbs?

4 Look at photos e–h. What do you think the photographer was doing at the time?

I think he/she was travelling in a helicopter.

5 💬 Work in pairs. Try to guess what your partner was doing at these times. Ask and answer. Were you right?

What were you doing:
1 ten minutes ago?
2 yesterday evening?
3 last summer?
Were you:
4 studying English this time five years ago?
5 living in the same place in 2000?

▪ PAST CONTINUOUS

We use the **past continuous** to talk about an action that was in progress at a specific time in the past.

He was working in Africa at the time.

We form the past continuous with *was/were* + verb + *-ing*.

(+) *It* (1) .... *swimming.*
(–) *It wasn't moving.*
(?) *What* (2) .... *they doing?*

See page 141 for grammar reference and more practice.

SPEAKING

1 💬 Work in pairs. Look at the photo. Discuss the questions using the words in the box.

> have/party laugh
> swim walk watch

- What was the bull doing just before the photo?
- What were other people doing?
- What do you think happened afterwards?

2 🔊 2.6 Listen to a woman talking about what happened. Check your ideas.

SPEAKING & VOCABULARY: animals

1 a Look at the photos. Can you name the animals? If not, find their names in the box. Use a dictionary to help you.

> cat   cow   deer   dog   fox   giraffe
> horse   lion   monkey   pig   polar bear
> rabbit   sheep   snake

b What are the animals doing in each photo? Which situation would worry you most?

2 a Match the animal names in **1a** to the categories. Use a dictionary to help you. Some animals can go in more than one category.

1 Common pets _rabbit_ ....

....

2 Zoo animals ....

....

3 Wild animals _rabbit_ ....

....

4 Common farm animals ....

....

b Can you add at least one more animal to each category?

3  Work in pairs. Discuss the questions with a partner.

● Is there a particular animal that is associated with your country or region?
● If yes, what is it?
● Why is this animal important?

I'm from Wales. Two animals are important in my country. The first is a mythical animal, the dragon – it's on our flag. The second is a sheep – there are more than 20 million sheep in Wales!

LISTENING

1 a 🔊 2.7 Listen to Jan and Lucia talking about an encounter with animals. Match their conversations to two of photos a–d.

b Listen again. Match the statements to the people, Lucia (L), Jan (J) or both (B).

1 It was the first night of the holiday.   _J_
2 It was the last day of the holiday.   ....
3 She enjoyed the holiday.   ....
4 They went to look at some animals.   ....
5 Some animals came to look at them.   ....
6 The experience scared her at first.   ....
7 The experience made her laugh.   ....

2 Check your answers in transcript 2.7 on page 162.

3 a Look at the pairs of sentences. Choose the correct option, a or b, for each one.

Conversation 1
1 a The cows were in the campsite.
  b The tent wasn't in the campsite.
2 a The cows sounded human.
  b The cows didn't sound human.
3 a One of the campers opened the door of the tent.
  b One of the cows opened the door of the tent.

Conversation 2
4 a They were driving past a zoo.
  b They were driving through a safari park.
5 a They were following some animals.
  b Some animals were following them.
6 a They chased the monkeys away.
  b Some men chased the monkeys away.

b Listen again and check your answers.

4 💬 Work in pairs. Discuss the questions with a partner. Whose story do you think is

● more interesting? Why?
● more amusing? Why?

GRAMMAR

1 a Complete the sentences with the correct endings in the box.

> some monkeys jumped on the car
> took my sunglasses
> Agata opened the door of the tent
> a cow put its head inside the tent

Conversation 1

1 While we **were talking** about what to do,

....

2 She **opened** the door and

....

Conversation 2

3 We **were driving** through a safari park when

....

4 One of the monkeys **climbed** through the window and ....

b Work in pairs. Answer the questions.

1 Look at the verbs in **bold** in **1a**. Which are in
   a the past simple?
   b the past continuous?
2 Look at the second verb in each sentence. Which describe
   a an action that happened while the first action was in progress?
   b an action that happened immediately after the first action?

2 Choose the correct options to complete 1–4 in the GRAMMAR PANEL ■ .

3 Choose the correct form of the verbs to complete the story.

> We ⁽¹⁾ *walked / were walking* along a quiet country road when we ⁽²⁾ *heard / were hearing* a noise in the trees. We ⁽³⁾ *stopped / were stopping* and ⁽⁴⁾ *were listening / listened* carefully. Suddenly a fox ⁽⁵⁾ *jumped / was jumping* into the middle of the road. It ⁽⁶⁾ *carried / was carrying* a bird in its mouth. It ⁽⁷⁾ *looked / was looking* at us, then ⁽⁸⁾ *was turning / turned* and ⁽⁹⁾ *was running / ran* away.

4 a Work in pairs. Look at the pictures. Write a short story about what happened.

b 🔊 2.8 Listen to Alison talking about her experience. Compare her story with your own. Were there any differences?

5 a 💬 Work in groups to discuss the questions.

- Have you ever seen an animal in the wild?
- If yes, where were you?
- What were you doing?
- What happened?

b Report the most interesting story to the class.

■ PAST SIMPLE & PAST CONTINUOUS

We often use the **past continuous** and the **past simple** in the same sentence. This shows that an action happened while a longer action was in progress:

*We **were driving** through a safari park (a) when some monkeys **jumped** on the car (b).*

```
                    (a)              (b)
        ~~~~~~~~~~~~~~~~~~~~~~~~~~~~~~●────────▶
Past                              Now      Future
```

The ⁽¹⁾ *past continuous / simple* describes the shorter, completed action. The ⁽²⁾ *past continuous / simple* describes a longer action that was in progress at the time.

We often use the ⁽³⁾ *past continuous / past simple* with **while**:

*While we **were talking** about what to do, Agata **opened** the door of the tent.*

We can use two verbs in the **past simple** to show that one action followed another:

*Agata **opened** the door (a) and a cow **put** its head in (b).* (= first Agata opened the door and after that, the cow put its head in.)

```
                         (a) (b)
        ─────────────────●○●────────────────▶
Past                            Now      Future
```

We often use linkers like **and**, **then** and **so** with the ⁽⁴⁾ *past continuous / past simple* to introduce the second action.

*So we **put** the tent up quickly, then we **went** to bed.*

See page 141 for grammar reference and more practice.

TUNE IN

1 a Look at the photos. Where are the people? What is the connection with the title of the lesson?

a

b

b Match the words to the situations in the photos. Some words go with both situations.

	a	b
1 Boarding pass		✓
2 Passport	✓	✓
3 Reference number		
4 Connection		
5 Internet		
6 Breakfast		
7 Boarding gate		
8 Suite		
9 Bags		

2 a 🔊 2.9 Listen to two conversations. Match them to the photos in 1a. Underline the words you hear in 1b.

b Listen again. Mark the statements true (T) or false (F). Correct the false statements.

Conversation 1
1 The passenger is late for her flight.
2 The airline worker asks her three questions.
3 They don't know how long the delay is.

Conversation 2
1 The couple have booked the room for two nights.
2 The room price doesn't include breakfast.
3 The receptionist has given the guests a better room.

FOCUS ON LANGUAGE

3 a Match extracts 1–9 from the conversations to people a–c.

a airline worker   b hotel receptionist   c hotel guest

1 Is breakfast included?
2 Here's a free pass to our business lounge.
3 Can I check in, please?
4 I'm afraid there's a delay to your flight.
5 I'm pleased to tell you, you have a suite!
6 I'm afraid there's an extra cost for internet. Here are the details.
7 How many bags do you want to check in?
8 Do you have your booking reference number?
9 Can I have your passports, please?

b Match responses a–i to extracts 1–9.

a Just this one.
b Yes, of course, here they are.
c Yes, here it is, we booked online.
d Let me check, sir...
e Of course, do you have your booking reference number?
f Oh, that's a shame.
g Oh, that's a surprise. Thanks very much.
h Oh, that's great... thank you!
i Oh, dear... how long is it?

4 Listen again and check.

> **❝ Intonation: sounding surprised and disappointed ❞**
>
> 🔊 2.10 Look again at the last four responses in 3b. Which speakers are a) happy? b) unhappy?
>
> Listen to the four responses. What do you notice about the intonation? When does it a) go up? b) go down?
>
> Practise saying the responses sounding surprised or disappointed.

OVER TO YOU

5 a 💬 Work in pairs. Act out the first situation (at an airport check-in desk). Student A, turn to page 158. Student B, turn to page 160.

b Act out the second situation (at a hotel reception). Student A, turn to page 158. Student B, turn to page 160.

TUNE IN

1 Work in pairs. Look at the photos on a travel website. Discuss the questions.

1 Where did the woman go on holiday?
2 What did she do on holiday?
3 Do you think she enjoyed it? Why?

2 Quickly read the holiday review and check your answers to **1**.

3 The website has a 'rate this review' feature, where readers decide how useful a review is. How would you rate this review? Why?

Holiday company: Wild Travel
Reviewer: Sally Castle

Rate this review:

very useful ☆☆☆☆☆
quite useful ☆☆☆
not useful ☆

HOLIDAY REVIEW

a When we booked our holiday, my husband and I were really excited. We are both quite adventurous people, so trekking on the island of Borneo seemed like our dream holiday. Unfortunately, it was more like a nightmare!

b We travelled in summer, so we were expecting hot, sunny weather. But when we arrived at the airport, it was raining. It rained for fourteen days! We walked for more than 10 kilometres every day, but we didn't see any interesting wildlife – only dangerous snakes! Our tour guide, Azman, wasn't very reliable. On the first day he was two hours late. Then he lost our map while we were following a river. We were walking until midnight that night!

c By the end of the holiday, we were tired and fed up. Borneo was beautiful. But the best part of our holiday was going home!

PREPARE FOR TASK

4 Match paragraphs a–c to descriptions 1–3.

1 giving a conclusion
2 setting the scene
3 describing what happened

5 Read the review again. Find and <u>underline</u> two examples of

1 past tenses
2 time expressions
3 adjectives
4 linkers

TASK

6 Imagine you are going to write about a holiday experience for the website. Choose one of the following:

- an amazing holiday experience
- a terrible holiday experience

7 Think of an experience to describe. You can use your own ideas, or describe an experience from the news or TV. Answer the questions in the paragraph plan.

Paragraph	Content ideas
1	Where did you go on holiday? When did you go? Who did you go with?
2	What happened on the holiday? Why was it good/bad?
3	How did you feel after the holiday?

8 Now write a short description of your holiday experience. Remember to:

1 follow the paragraph plan in **7**.   2 use a variety of language as in **5**.

REPORT BACK

9 a Compare your reviews in groups.

b What are the two most interesting things about each story?

10 Decide as a group which was your favourite holiday review. Why?

→ Go to Review A, Unit 2, p. 35   23

3 ICONS

1 a 💬 Work in groups. Look at the photos. Do you recognise the landmarks? Where are they?

b 🔊 3.1 Listen to two radio presenters talking about the landmarks. Check your answers to a and answer the questions.

1 What are the Seven Wonders of the Modern World?
2 When was the list announced?
3 Which photo is not one of the seven? Why?

2 💬 Work in groups. Discuss the questions.
• Have you ever visited any of the landmarks?
• If yes, when? What was your impression?
• If no, which one would you most like to visit? Why?

3 💬 Work in pairs. Complete A and B in the KEY VOCABULARY PANEL ▪. What are the most famous landmarks in your country? Do you know why and when they were built?

4 a 🔊 3.2 Listen to short extracts from audio guides for tourists at two of these landmarks. Which landmarks are they describing?

b Listen again and complete the extracts.
1 It is almost .... metres tall – one of the tallest sculptures ever made of the Christ figure.
2 A .... **engineer**, Heitor da Silva Costa, drew up the **design**s for the statue.
3 It took the .... **sculptor** Paul Landowski .... years to build it.
4 It was designed by a team of local **architect**s in the traditional style of .... architecture of the time.
5 It took .... years to complete.

24

KEY VOCABULARY

Landmarks

A Types of landmarks

- Match words from the box to the photos. Which don't match any of the photos?

  arena   bridge   city   palace   ruins
  sculpture   statue   temple   tower   wall

B Reasons for building landmarks

- Match the reasons for building the landmarks to photos a–h. Check your answers on page 158.
  - as **a defence** against invasion
  - **in memory of** a loved one
  - **to hold** competitions
  - **to bury** the dead
  - **to protect** an important source of water
  - as a religious **monument**
  - as a **capital city**
  - for an **emperor**

C Word families

What it is	Person who does it
architecture	....
building	builder
....	designer
engineering	....
sculpture	....

- 🔊 3.3 Listen to the words and mark the stress. Listen again and repeat.

---

5 💬 Work in pairs. Do you know anything else about these two landmarks or any of the others in the photos? Share your information with the class.

6 Use the words in **bold** in 4b to complete C in the KEY VOCABULARY PANEL ▪.

7 a Work in groups. Think of a landmark in your country. Write a short description for a tourist audio guide. Use the KEY VOCABULARY PANEL ▪ and include information about

- where it is.
- what it looks like.
- when and why it was built.
- anything else you know about it.

b 💬 Read your description to the class without giving the name of the landmark. Can they guess what it is?

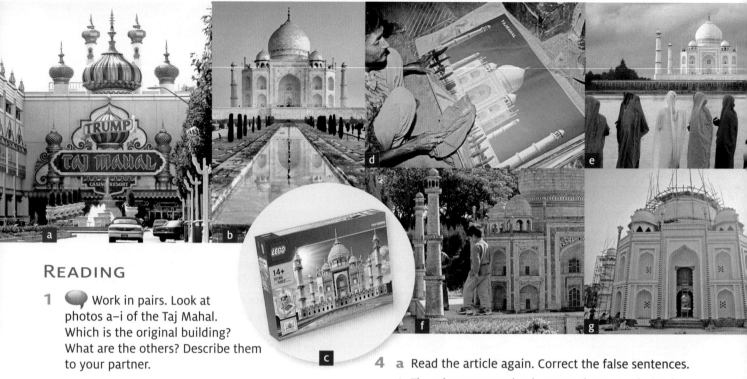

READING

1 💬 Work in pairs. Look at photos a–i of the Taj Mahal. Which is the original building? What are the others? Describe them to your partner.

2 Look at the title of the article. What do you think it will say about the Taj Mahal?

- There are so many imitations that there's no reason to see the real thing.
- There are so many imitations that you have to see the real thing.
- We cannot tell the difference between real things and imitations any more.

3 Read the article and check your answer to 2. Underline the parts of the article that refer to photos a–i and match them to the photos.

4 a Read the article again. Correct the false sentences.

1 There is no connection between the Mona Lisa and the Taj Mahal.
2 Westerners see the building as being very familiar.
3 The Taj Mahal casino in Atlantic City is an exact copy of the original building.
4 Many Chinese restaurants in the world are called the Taj Mahal.
5 You can't get much Taj Mahal merchandising.
6 You realise that the real Taj Mahal is different as soon as you see it.

b 💬 After reading the article, are you more or less interested in visiting the Taj Mahal? Why/Why not?

Will the **REAL** Taj Mahal **please stand up?**

Writer Salman Rushdie said that the Taj Mahal sits at the top of the West's shortlist of images of the Exotic and Timeless Orient. Like the Mona Lisa, mass reproduction has sterilised it.

The fact is, there are fake Taj Mahals all over the world. The most famous is in Shenzen, China, in the Window of the World theme park. Then there is Donald Trump's luxury Taj Mahal casino in Atlantic City that uses the original building for exotic inspiration. But the building which has caused most controversy is an exact copy made in Bangladesh. Indian authorities are angry with Ahsanullah Moni, a millionaire film maker, who thought up the replica. However, Moni has been quick to defend the building: Everyone dreams about seeing the Taj Mahal, but very few Bangladeshis can make the trip as it's too expensive.

But it's not just the building itself. There are lots of Indian curry restaurants which are called the Taj Mahal and use it as their logo. Children can build Lego models of it, you can get T-shirts and buy posters and, of course, take your own photos.

That's why, at the moment when you're standing in front of it, you can't believe it is real. And this is why you have to see the original, in the place where it truly stands in Agra, India. As Rushdie said, the beauty of beautiful things can still transcend imitations... And the Taj Mahal is a lovely thing, perhaps the loveliest of things.

h i

GRAMMAR

1 a Work in pairs. Cover the Taj Mahal article. Match the two parts of the sentences.

1 There are lots of Indian curry restaurants	a **which** are called the Taj Mahal.
2 Indian authorities are angry with a millionaire film maker	b **that** uses the original building for exotic inspiration.
3 There is the Taj Mahal casino in Atlantic City	c **who** thought up the replica.

b Check your answers in the article.

2 What do the second half of the sentences (a–c) add to the first half (1–3)? Complete 1–4 in the GRAMMAR PANEL ■ .

3 a Look at the sentences. Replace *that* with either *who* or *which*.

1 The Taj Mahal is one of the buildings that I'd most like to visit in the world.
2 I've never met anybody that has been to the Taj Mahal.
3 I hate buildings that are just imitations of the original.
4 I know the place that most people in the world want to go to.

b 💬 Work in pairs. Which ones are true for you? Change the ones which are not true. Compare your answers with your partner.

■ RELATIVE CLAUSES

Look at these sentences.

There are lots of Indian curry restaurants. They are called the Taj Mahal.

There are lots of Indian curry restaurants which are called the Taj Mahal.

When we join two sentences together in this way, the first part is the **main** clause and the other part is the **relative** clause.

There are lots of Indian curry restaurants is the (1) .... clause.

which are called the Taj Mahal. is the (2) .... clause.

We use *who*, *which* and *that* to link the two clauses. They replace nouns or pronouns in the original sentences.

This is the photo. I took it at the Taj Mahal. → *This is the photo **that** I took at the Taj Mahal.*

This is the man. He built the casino. → *This is the man **who** built the casino.*

We use (3) .... or *that* to refer to things.

We use (4) .... or *that* to refer to people.

See page 142 for grammar reference and more practice.

LISTENING & SPEAKING

1 Look at the photo. Guess who and where the people are.

2 a 🔊 3.4 Listen and check your answers. Identify the people in the photo.

b Listen again and complete the sentences.

This is the Alhambra taken from the Plaza San Nicolas, (1) .... is in the Albaicín, the Arab quarter. This is the place where I was happiest on my trip to Europe last year. There were five of us on that trip. You can see David sitting on the left, and next to him, Rod is playing the guitar. That's the guitar (2) .... he bought in Granada, in fact, he learned to play on that trip! But I love the photo because Neil looks so silly. He's the one (3) .... is taking a picture of the wrong thing! I'm not there of course, I'm the one (4) .... took the photo.

READING

1 💬 Work in groups. Look at icons a–k and answer the questions.

1 What do these icons mean and where do you see them?
2 Can you think of other icons we use and recognise in different parts of the world?

2 Read the blog post. Which icon is it discussing?

ARTICLES | ABOUT | CONTRIBUTE | SUBSCRIBE | CONTACT

ICON DESIGN

There are lots of icons used in technology that are clever and creative. I like the house icon on the internet to represent a 'homepage'. It looks just like the houses that children draw! I like the bin, too – that's the place where you put the things you don't want. It's a very clear icon. The symbols and the icons that Messenger, Twitter and Facebook use are also fine because they're attractive and everyone recognises them. But there is one icon which just doesn't work these days: the floppy disk icon for 'save'.

Computers don't use floppy disks anymore. They stopped using them in 2002! Young people don't know what they are. I think they should design a new icon. There must be an icon out there that's more modern. Here are some ideas I came up with. What do you think? Which do you like best? Or do you have a better idea?

---

3 **a** Read the blog post again. Are the sentences true or false?

1 The writer likes some icons used in technology.
2 The last new computers to use floppy disks were in 2002.
3 Children know what a floppy disk is.
4 The writer wants a new icon for 'save'.

b Do you agree with the blog post? Why/Why not?

4 **a** Look at the new icons for 'save'. Which do you like best? Why? Can you think of any others? Draw your own version.

b Compare with other groups. Who has the best one?

GRAMMAR

1 **a** Work in pairs. Cover the text in REARING 2. Complete the sentences with the words in the box.

> bin children floppy disks
> icon (x2) internet technology

1 There are lots of icons used in .... that are clever and creative.
2 I like the house icon on the .... to represent a 'homepage'.
3 It looks just like the houses that .... draw!
4 I like the .... , too – that's the place where you put things you don't want.
5 Computers don't use .... anymore.
6 I think they should design a new ....
7 There must be an .... out there that's more modern.

b Check your answers in the text.

2 a <u>Underline</u> all the examples of *a/an* and *the* in the sentences in **1a**. Which nouns do they refer to? Can you find six nouns that don't have an article?

b Complete 1–6 in the Grammar panel ■ with examples from **1a**.

3 Read the reply to the blog post. Complete it with *a/an*, *the* or no article.

> I agree with you. (1)........... icon for 'save' is ridiculous. I have (2)........... 12-year-old child and I asked her if she knew what it was. She said it was (3)........... blue square! If we want to use (4)........... icons, not (5)........... words, then we must use (6)........... icons that everyone recognises.

4 💬 Work in pairs. Talk about an icon or logo that you like or dislike. Complete the sentences.

1 I like/don't like the icon/logo for…
2 Icons are a good form of communication because…
3 I think tattoos are interesting icons. The most common tattoos are…
4 Gestures can also be icons. For example, we have a gesture here which…

■ ARTICLES: *A/AN*, *THE*, NO ARTICLE

A/an

We use *a/an* to talk about a person or thing in a general way.
*We need **a** new icon.* (we don't know which specific icon)
(1) _____

Use *a* and *an* with singular countable nouns.

Use *a* before a consonant sound and *an* before a vowel sound.
a (2) _____ , *an* (3) _____

The

We use *the* to talk about a specific person or thing.
The houses <u>that children draw</u>.
(4) _____

We also use *the* when there is only one example in our world or experience.
the moon, the world, (5) _____

No article

We can't use *a/an* with uncountable nouns or plural nouns.

If we want to talk about uncountable or plural nouns in a general way, we don't use an article.
There are lots of icons (NOT ~~the icons~~) *in technology* (NOT ~~the technology~~)
(6) _____

See page 142 for grammar reference and more practice.

PRONUNCIATION: *the & a*

1 a Complete the phrases with *a* or *an*.

.... unusual icon	.... new icon
.... interesting icon	.... international gesture
.... confusing gesture	.... universal gesture
.... Asian icon	.... European gesture

b 🔊 3.5 Listen and check.

2 Look at the phrases in **1a** again. Complete the rules using *a* or *an*.

1 We use .... before a consonant sound.
2 We use .... before a vowel sound.

Some words that start with a vowel are pronounced with a semi-vowel sound, e.g. /j/: *universal, university, European*

3 We use .... before a word that starts with /j/.

3 a 🔊 3.6 Complete the sentences with *a* or *an*. Listen to the pronunciation of *a/an*. Is it weak or strong?

1 I'm .... only child.
2 My brother's .... university student.
3 My eyes are .... unusual colour.
4 I drive .... European car.

b Listen again and repeat.

SPEAKING

1 a Look at the photos. What do the gestures mean?

b 🔊 3.7 Listen and match the speakers to the photos.

2 What gestures do you use to indicate these ideas?

- how tall someone is
- eating
- I don't know
- money
- drinking
- what time is it?

LISTENING & VOCABULARY: cultural icons

1 a Read the definition.

> **cultural icon** A *cultural icon* can be an image, a logo, picture, name, face, person or building that people recognise immediately. It usually represents an object or concept with great meaning to a large cultural group.

b 💬 Work in pairs. Look at the photos of 'cultural icons'. Do you agree with the definition? Why/Why not?

2 a 🔊 3.8 Listen to three people giving an opinion about some of the icons above. Which icons do they mention? What do they think of them?

b Match the speakers to the points they make.

1 It represents a particular country.
2 It's a cultural icon for some parts of the world.
3 It can show that people have money or are important.

3 a Look at the adjectives. Which speaker uses these adjectives? Listen again to check.

> familiar   famous   iconic
> legendary   popular   well-known

b Rank the words in order of fame.

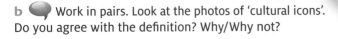

MOST FAMOUS   1 ....   2 ....   3 ....

4 ....   5 ....   6 ....   LEAST FAMOUS

4 Look at the nouns which can refer to famous people. Which can also be used to refer to objects?

> a celebrity   a household name   an icon
> a legend   a (super)star

5 a Complete the sentences using words from 4.

1 Nelson Mandela is ....
2 Che Guevara is ....
3 Levi's is ....
4 Rubik's Cube is ....
5 James Bond is ....
6 Mickey Mouse is ....

b Work in pairs. Compare your ideas with your partner. Do you have similar answers?

6 💬 Work in pairs. In your country or culture, which people or things are iconic? Why?

7 a 💬 Work in groups. Who and what do you think are global cultural icons? Make a list of six people or objects.

b Report back to the class with your list. Compare your list with other groups.

READING

1 a You are going to read about Bob Marley. Make a list of things you know already about him.

b Now read and check. Are the things you wrote mentioned in the article? Write down at least one thing that you did not know about him.

The Legend of Bob Marley

Few singers have had the influence on music that Bob Marley has had. He was born in a small village in Jamaica as Nesta Robert Marley in 1945 to a young black mother and an older white father.

In 1963, Bob Marley formed a group, who became the famous Wailers. In 1966, Marley became a member of the Rastafarian movement, and started to wear his famous dreadlocks hairstyle. Their first album came out in 1973, but it was in 1975 that Marley became an international star with his first hit outside Jamaica, 'No Woman, No Cry'. Marley was suddenly a celebrity.

Marley was important around the world as a musician, but in Jamaica he was more than just a singer, he was a huge cultural icon. Some said he was even more important than the Jamaican government in the 1970s. On December 5, 1976, Marley was going to give a free 'Smile Jamaica' concert, to help to unite the people of his country. Just before the concert, gunmen attacked Bob Marley and his friends. He was injured, but he amazed the crowd of 80,000 people when he appeared to play at the concert two days later. He really seemed to be superhuman, and this helped to make him the legend that he is today.

In 1977, doctors found that Marley had cancer, and he died on 11 May 1981 at the age of 36. Bob Marley's music lives on and he has become the symbol of reggae music all over the world.

2 a Read the article again and complete this timeline about Bob Marley's life.

1945 *He was born.*
1963 ....
1966 ....
1973 ....
1975 ....
1976 ....
1977 ....
1981 ....

b Which do you think was the most important event in his life and why?

3 a Imagine you want to describe Bob Marley to someone who doesn't know him. Complete the sentences.

Bob Marley is the person who ....
He is famous for ....
What people don't know is that he ....

b Work in pairs. Compare your sentences.

4 Do you, or any of your friends, listen to Bob Marley's music? Is reggae popular in your country?

LISTENING

1 💬 Work in pairs. Look at the photos. Do you know anything about these iconic fictional characters?

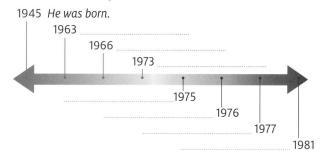

2 a 🔊 3.9 Listen to two people discussing the characters. Who does Karina like? Who does Simon like?

b Listen again. Complete the sentences with Karina (K) or Simon (S).

1 .... thinks *The Simpsons* is about serious things.
2 .... likes shows using real actors.
3 .... thinks *House* is not a perfect character.
4 .... thinks *The Simpsons* makes you think and laugh.
5 .... says Dr House and Homer Simpson are both unreal.

3 Do you agree with Karina and Simon? Are there other fictional characters that you consider to be 'cultural icons'? Why?

4 a 💬 Work in groups. Choose four iconic characters, real or fictional, to invite to a party.
I'd like to invite... because...

b Compare your list with another group. Who has the most interesting party?

TUNE IN

1 Look at the photos of laptop 'skins'. Do you think they are a good idea? Which one do you like best?

2 🔊 3.10 Listen to four people talking about laptop skins. Which one do they prefer?

Jake: _____ Carly: _____ Dave: _____ Sal: _____

3 Listen again. Which of the opinions is not mentioned?

1 Nature scenes are not interesting.
2 A laptop skin needs to say something about the owner.
3 Laptop skins help to keep a laptop clean.
4 A laptop skin is better if it's not in fashion.
5 A laptop skin should show your interests.
6 It's better to have your own design.
7 Laptop skins are not necessary at all.

FOCUS ON LANGUAGE

4 Listen again and complete the sentences.

1 Which is your _____ , Jake?
2 Personally, I _____ the ones that show beautiful scenery.
3 I _____ have one that says something about me and who I am.
4 I _____ something more classic, like a piece of art.
5 I _____ to have something that shows one of my hobbies or interests.
6 Wouldn't _____ to have a custom design?

NOTICE *PERSONALLY*

We use *personally* to emphasise that what you are saying is your personal opinion.

Personally, I prefer laptops to desktop computers.

5 Complete the table of ways to ask about and express preferences. Use your answers from 4 to help you.

Asking about preferences	Expressing preferences
• What's your _____ ?	• I (much) _____ ...
• Which is better?	• I'd (much) prefer...
• Which do you _____ ?	• I'd (much) _____ ...
• Would(n't) it be _____ to... ?	• I like _____ best (of all).
	• I like _____ better than _____

❝ Intonation: adding emphasis ❞

🔊 3.11 Listen and <u>underline</u> the word which adds emphasis in these sentences.

1 *I'd rather have something modern.*
2 *I'd much rather have something modern.*
3 *I'd prefer a piece of art.*
4 *I'd much prefer a piece of art.*

Practise saying the sentences with the same emphasis.

6 💬 Work in groups. Which laptop skin would you prefer? Why?

OVER TO YOU

7 💬 Turn to pages 158–159. Imagine you want to choose a template for a blog about your English class. Which of the five templates would you prefer? Discuss with your group. Consider

• design   • colours   • style   • use of images

8 Compare your choice with other groups and choose one for the whole class.

TUNE IN

1 a 💬 Work in groups. Look at the logos. What do they say about the companies that they represent?

b Which of the values do the logos suggest about the company?

active creative dynamic exciting fast
fun modern reliable serious traditional

PREPARE FOR TASK

2 a Read the article about designing a good logo. Do the logos in **1** have these features? Complete the table with a tick (✓) or a cross (✗).

Logos are the icons of your business. A logo is a visual icon that identifies a company or product. Logos are very important and can bring success or failure, so you must understand the qualities of good logo design. Here are four easy points to remember:

1 Make an impact – attract attention and make people look at it.

2 Keep it simple.

3 Limit the colours to a maximum of three to keep printing costs low.

4 Represent the company. For example, if it's a serious company, the logo should be serious.

	1	2	3	4
Close Up Photography				
Circumference Travel				
Eden & Lithgow				
Happy Days Nursery				
Creature Comforts				
Hayes & Co				

b 💬 Compare in groups. Did you agree on all of the logos?

3 Which logo did you like best and why? Do you think you could improve any of the logos?

TASK

4 💬 Work in groups. Think of a company and a company name. Complete the table about your company.

Name	
Product or service	
Values of the company	
Logo	

5 Design a logo to represent the company. Use **2a** to help you.

REPORT BACK

6 💬 Present your logo to the class. Explain about your company using the table in **4**.

7 Listen to the presentations. Does the logo follow the four points in **2a**? What do you think about the company? Which logo and company is your favourite?

➜ Go to Review A, Unit 3, p. 36   ➜ Go to Writing bank 2, p. 153

VOCABULARY
Languages & countries

1 💬 Work in pairs. Answer the questions.

1 Name four countries where English is an official language, but is not a language people speak as a mother tongue.
2 Name four countries where there are lots of bilingual people.

2 💬 Work in groups. Which languages do you speak fluently? How many languages does your group speak in total?

Free time

3 **a** 🔊 R1 Look at the photos. Listen and answer the questions.

1 Where are the people from and what languages do they speak?
2 What do they do?
3 What do they do in their free time?

b Listen again and compare your answers.

Communication

4 Correct the mistakes in **bold**.

Hannah knew that Joe was not (1) **telling truth**. He talked for ten minutes, but she stopped (2) **listening him**. 'You're (3) **telling lie!**' she said finally. He stopped (4) **talking her** and he (5) **told she** that he was leaving. After he left she sent a text message (6) **at** her friend, but she couldn't think about anything except Joe. She needed to (7) **talk about** him, so she called his mobile.

GRAMMAR
Present simple & present continuous

1 **a** Complete the sentences with the correct form of the verbs.

1 At the moment I .... (learn) French.
2 I .... (want) to go to the USA on holiday.
3 I .... (not eat) fruit, because
  I .... (not like) it.
4 I .... (not live) in my hometown at the moment.

b 💬 Work in pairs. Are the sentences in 1a true about you? Compare your answers with your partner.

Questions

2 **a** Write the words in the correct order.

1 do do you What weekend the at ?
2 live you parents Do with your ?
3 moment What you studying the are at ?
4 work Who with do you ?
5 saw last film What the was you ?
6 like Did it you ?

b 💬 Work in groups of three. Ask and answer the questions.

3 **a** Write one question you would like to ask students in your class.

b 💬 Ask students your question and make a note of the answers. Report back to the rest of the class.

FUNCTIONAL LANGUAGE
Checking understanding

1 Complete the questions using the words in the box.

| call   repeat   say (x2) |

1 Can you .... it again, please?
2 What did you ....?
3 Can you .... that, please?
4 What do you .... this in English?

2 **a** Work in pairs. Think of a reply to each question in 1 and write it down.

b 💬 Ask and answer the questions.

▪ LOOKING BACK

- What is easy about learning English? What is difficult?
- Which activity or lesson in this unit did you enjoy most? Why?
- Write down three new things you can say about yourself.

VOCABULARY
Geography

1 Complete the words.

1 Not f_____ from means 'near'.
2 A f_____ is a place with lots of trees.
3 A place on the c_____ is near the sea.
4 The c_____ of Spain is Madrid.
5 In the c_____ means 'in the middle'.
6 Great Britain, Iceland and Cuba are all i_____ .

2 a Use two of the words in **1** to describe two different places in your country.

b Describe your favourite part of the country to your partner. Why do you like it?

Animals

3 a Name animals 1–8.

1 _____ 2 _____ 3 _____ 4 _____
5 _____ 6 _____ 7 _____ 8 _____

a _____ b _____ c _____ d _____

b Label each pair of animals a–d using the categories in the box. Can you name any more animals in each category?

zoo animals   wild animals
common pets   common farm animals

4 Is there a particular animal which is important/significant to you? If yes, why is it important?

GRAMMAR
Past simple

1 a Complete the sentences with the correct form of the verbs.

1 I _____ (watch) a TV nature documentary last night.
2 I _____ (do) something to help the environment yesterday.
3 I _____ (not be) interested in nature when I was young.
4 I _____ (not visit) the countryside last year.
5 I _____ (have) a pet when I was a child.
6 I _____ (not travel) anywhere on holiday last summer.

b 💬 Work in pairs. Are the sentences true for your partner? Take turns to ask and answer questions.

> *Did you watch a TV nature documentary last night?*

> *Yes, I saw a programme about wildlife in Africa. It was really interesting!*

Past continuous & past simple

2 Complete the sentences with the correct form of the verbs.

1 While he _____ (swim), he _____ (see) a crocodile.
2 We _____ (cook) dinner on a fire when they _____ (find) us.
3 It _____ (not rain) in the forest when we _____ (arrive).
4 I _____ (walk) along the path when I _____ (stand) on a snake!
5 What _____ (you / eat) while you _____ (wait) for the rescue team?

FUNCTIONAL LANGUAGE
Checking in

1 a Complete the conversations.

1 A How many bags do you want to _____ in?
  B Just these two, please.

2 A Do you have your _____ reference number?
  B Yes, here it is... GB458Q.

3 A I'm afraid breakfast isn't included. There's an extra _____ of $10.
  B Oh, that's a shame.

b 🔊 R2 Listen and check.

2 💬 Work in pairs. Look at the picture and act out the conversation.

◼ LOOKING BACK

- Which story in this unit did you find the most interesting? Why?
- How many irregular past tenses can you remember?
- Think of three interesting things that happened to you recently. Can you describe what happened?

VOCABULARY
Landmarks

1 a Name as many different types of landmarks as you can.

b 💬 Work in pairs. Describe a landmark from your town or country.

2 💬 Find out how many people in your class have visited a famous landmark. What is that landmark and where is it?

Word families

3 a Write the name of the person who does each thing.

1 architecture   3 sculpture
2 engineering   4 design

b 💬 Work in groups. Do you know a person who does each thing in a?

Cultural icons

4 a Name five celebrities in your country. Are any of them icons? If yes, why?

b 💬 Work in pairs. Tell your partner about the celebrities. Does he/she know them? Does he/she think they are icons?

GRAMMAR
Relative clauses

1 a Choose five items from this unit. Write a definition for each item using *who*, *which* or *that*.

b 💬 Work in pairs. Read your definitions to your partner. He/she must guess what they are.

Articles: *a/an*, *the*, no article

2 a Complete the text with definite articles, indefinite articles or no article.

(1)............ mobile phone case is (2)............ good way to protect your mobile phone. (3)............ case you choose depends on (4)............ type of phone you have and what you want to say about yourself. If you choose (5)............ bright colour you are (6)............ outgoing person. If you choose (7)............ dark colour you are (8)............ shy person. So (9)............ mobile phone cases are very important accessories.

b Do you agree with the text? What kind of mobile phone cover do you have? What do you think it says about you?

FUNCTIONAL LANGUAGE
Expressing preference

1 a Match the questions to the answers.

1 Who's your favourite actor?
2 Do you prefer classic or modern art?
3 Which do you prefer?
4 Wouldn't it be better to see the Eiffel Tower first?

a I'd prefer to do that later.
b I like Cate Blanchett best of all.
c I usually like modern art better.
d I'd much rather have this one.

b 🔊 R3 Listen and check.

2 💬 Work in groups. Discuss your preferences for

1 places to go at the weekend.
2 things to do on your birthday.
3 programmes to watch on TV.
4 food to eat for breakfast.

▪ LOOKING BACK

- Think of three things you learned in this unit.
- Is there anything you want to look at again?
- Tell a partner three preferences you have.

LISTENING

1 🔊 R4 Listen to three people introducing themselves on *English Chat*, an online chatroom. Complete their profiles.

Name: Xian
Country: (1) ....
Languages: (2) ....
Started learning English (when?): (3) ....

Name: Natasha
Country: (4) ....
Languages: (5) ....
Started learning English (when?): (6) ....

Name: Tati
Country: (7) ....
Languages: (8) ....
Started learning English (when?): (9) ....

2 a 💬 Work in pairs. Look at these 'key words' from the listening. What do you remember about them?

1 Violin
2 Restaurant
3 India
4 The USA
5 Computer games
6 Sister

b Listen again and check.

3 Work in pairs. Discuss the questions.
- Do you write down key words when you listen?
- Can you think of any more listening tips?

READING

4 a Read the description of a good listener. Do you think the *English Chat* moderator was a good listener? Why/Why not?

> When someone is speaking, a good listener:
> - asks questions if he/she doesn't understand something.
> - asks questions to find out more information.
> - sounds interested.
> - is always polite.

b 💬 Work in pairs. Can you think of one more idea to add to the list?

SPEAKING

5 a 💬 Work in pairs. Take turns to be Student A and Student B.

Student A, you are a new member of *English Chat*. Introduce yourself to the group. Say four things about yourself.
Student B, you are the chatroom moderator. Welcome Student A to the chatroom, and remember to be a 'good listener'.

b What was the most interesting thing you learnt about your partner?

◼ QUICK CHECK

Complete the checklist below.

Can you...	Yes, I can.	Yes, more or less.	I need to look again.
1 name ten countries and ten languages?	☐	☐	☐
2 talk about your hobbies and interests?	☐	☐	☐
3 talk about what is happening right now?	☐	☐	☐
4 describe places?	☐	☐	☐
5 talk about what you do on holiday?	☐	☐	☐
6 talk about things that happened in the past?	☐	☐	☐
7 describe an interesting building?	☐	☐	☐
8 talk about your preferences?	☐	☐	☐

💬 Compare your answers with a partner.
- What else do you know now after studying units 1–3?
- Do you need to look again at any of the sections?
- Do you need any extra help from your teacher?

4 AGES AND CHANGES

a

b

1 💬 Work in pairs. Look at the photos. How old are the people in each photo? What are they celebrating?

2 a 🔊 4.1 Listen and check. Match extracts 1–3 to photos a–c.

b What one thing do all three celebrations have in common?

3 💬 Work in groups. Discuss the questions.
- How do young people in your country celebrate their 'coming of age'?
- What was the last birthday party you went to? Whose birthday was it? How and where did you celebrate it?
- How many weddings have you been to? Do you like weddings? Why/Why not?

4 a Work in pairs. Order the words in A in the KEY VOCABULARY PANEL 🔲 from the youngest to the oldest. What age, more or less, does each category cover?

baby – 0 to 2 years

b 💬 Work in groups. Discuss the questions.
- Do you know someone in each age category? How do you know them? Do you spend a lot of time together? What do you usually do together?
- Do you think it's possible to say which is the 'best time' of your life? Why/Why not?

C

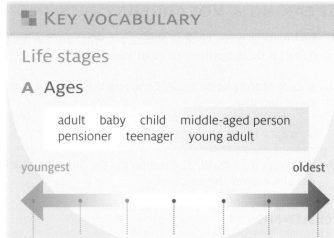

KEY VOCABULARY

Life stages

A Ages

adult   baby   child   middle-aged person
pensioner   teenager   young adult

youngest   oldest

B Stages

- be born
- learn to walk and talk
- become independent
- come of age
- fall in love
- finish school
- get a job
- get divorced
- get married
- go to school for the first time
- go to university
- have children
- leave home
- learn to drive a car
- retire
- vote
- die

NOTICE *GET*

We can use *get* with nouns to talk about something which somebody gives to you, or something you obtain: *He got a job. She got a new car.*
We can use *get* with adjectives to mean *become*.
They got married. They got divorced. NOT *They married*.

---

5 a 💬 Work in pairs. Look at B in the KEY VOCABULARY PANEL ▇. Which age/ages do you associate with each stage? Can you think of other stages to add to the list?

b 💬 Work in small groups. Discuss the questions.
- How many of the stages have you done?
- How old were you when you did them?
- What, if possible, do you remember about them?

6 a People don't always do the stages in the same order. Do you know someone who's done them in an unusual order? Tell your group about that person.

My sister went to university after she got married.

b Share your stories with the class. Whose story was the most unusual?

SPEAKING & VOCABULARY: activities

1 💬 Work in pairs. Look at photos a–f. What are the people doing? Is there anything unusual about them?

2 a Look at the photos again. Complete the activities with *do*, *go* and *play*.

    b 🔊 4.2 Listen and check.

3 💬 Work in pairs. What question did the interviewer ask? Ask and answer the question.

READING

1 Work in pairs. Think about your own country. Which hobbies are usually more popular with

- young people?
- old people?
- young and old people?

2 Read the article and answer the questions.

   1 What are Ela and Marco's main hobbies?
   2 What other hobbies can you find?

3 a Read the article again. Decide if these sentences are true or false.

   1 Ela only recently started getting interested in adventure sports.
   2 Surfing is a relatively old sport.
   3 Ela is not the only older person who enjoys surfing.
   4 Marco's friends don't like knitting.
   5 Marco thinks knitting is more interesting than yoga.
   6 Yarn-bombers paint graffiti on buses.

   b Compare your answers with a partner. Correct the ones that are false.

4 💬 Work in pairs. What hobbies are popular with you and your friends and family? Do you know anyone who has an unusual hobby? What do they do?

a .... karate   b .... fishing

d .... golf

f .... skateboarding

Act your age!

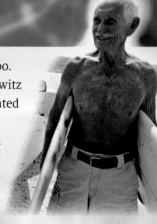

The media loves stereotypes. How many photos have you seen which show teenagers playing computer games, or grandparents doing the gardening? In real life, of course, we enjoy all kinds of hobbies, at all ages. We've interviewed two people who don't want to 'act their age'.

Ela, 79

I've always liked adventurous sports. Paragliding, skydiving – you name it, I've tried it. On the day I retired, I went surfing. I've never liked taking it easy, 'acting my age'. I haven't lost my love of excitement, just because my hair's gone grey! Surfing has a young image now, but it's an old, old sport – did you know that James Cook first saw people surfing in Tahiti in 1769? For me, it's a great way to stay fit, as well as to meet friends. It can

help people in difficult times, too. In 1997, a man called Don Paskowitz took surfboards to Gaza. He wanted people there to experience happiness and freedom, even in war time. He was 86! Compared to him, I'm still pretty young.

Marco, 15

I'm a knitter. I've knitted hats and scarves, as well as a cover for my iPod. They don't look like things your granny knits! I've used dark colours and added skull and crossbones logos*. They look pretty good! I'm not the only one. In my school in Manhattan, we're allowed to knit in class. Studies have shown that knitting is good

GRAMMAR

1 **a** Complete the sentences using the words in the box. Which part of the article do they come from, Ela's or Marco's?

> adventurous sports   a cover for my iPod   excitement
> graffiti   knitting   skydiving   taking it easy

1 I**'ve knitted** hats and scarves, as well as ....
2 I**'ve** always **liked** ....
3 **Have** you ever **seen** .... on city streets?
4 Paragliding, ... – you name it, I**'ve tried** it.
5 I**'ve** never **liked** ....
6 I **haven't lost** my love of ....
7 Studies **have shown** that .... is good for stress.

b Look at the verbs in **bold** in the sentences above. Which are describing

1 an action that happened in the past, but we don't know exactly when?
2 a situation or feeling that started in the past and continues in the present?

2 Complete 1–10 in the GRAMMAR PANEL 🔲.

3 Complete 11 and 12 in the GRAMMAR PANEL 🔲. Are any of the example sentences true for you? Then complete 13–16.

c .... the electric guitar

e .... crafts

*skull and crossbones logo

for stress, so it helps us to learn. I'd definitely rather knit than do yoga! Knitting can be fun, too. In the USA and Canada, there's a craze for 'yarn-bombing'. Have you ever seen graffiti on city streets? Well, it's a bit like that. People cover signs, walls, even buses, in colourful wools. But you can take the knitting off afterwards – not like graffiti!

PRESENT PERFECT

Form

To form the present perfect simple we use *have / has* + past participle (*done, tried, seen*).

(+) I'⁽¹⁾ .... *tried a lot of different sports.*

(–) *She* ⁽²⁾ .... *lost her love for life.*

(?) ⁽³⁾ .... *you tried knitting?*

(Y/N) *Yes, I* ⁽⁴⁾ ..../*No, I haven't.*

Past participles

Regular verbs: infinitive + *-ed*
like →⁽⁵⁾ .... , *play* → *played,*
knit →⁽⁶⁾ .... , *try* →⁽⁷⁾ ....

Many verbs have irregular past participles.
do → *done, go* → *been,*
see →⁽⁸⁾ .... , *show* →⁽⁹⁾ .... ,
lose →⁽¹⁰⁾ ....
(See Irregular verbs, page 168.)

See page 143 for grammar reference and more practice.

Some common uses

To talk about actions that happened at some time in the past, but we don't say when. ⁽¹¹⁾ ....

To talk about situations or feelings that started in the past and continue to be true in the present.
⁽¹²⁾ ....

Time expressions

ever/never
We often use *ever* and *never* to talk about our life experiences.
Have you ⁽¹³⁾ .... *tried skydiving?*
I've ⁽¹⁴⁾ .... *done karate.*

always/never
We often use *always* and *never* to talk about feelings or beliefs we've had for a long time.
I've ⁽¹⁵⁾ .... *wanted to try paragliding.*
I've ⁽¹⁶⁾ .... *lost my love for playing games.*

4 **a** Write *Have you ever... ?* questions about the hobbies in the photos, and other hobbies. *Have you ever been skateboarding?*

b 💬 Ask other students in your class your questions. Make a note of their answers. Which hobby was the most popular?

LISTENING

1 💬 Work in pairs. Look at the webpage and answer the questions.

1 Who are you going to hear?
2 Who is this person going to talk about?
3 What is Missing People?

2 a 🔊 4.3 Listen to the video. Complete the sentences.

1 Ceri last saw Alun .... months ago.
2 Bethan is Alun's ....
3 Alun disappeared on Friday the .... of ....
4 He was going to meet his friends at the ....
5 Since Alun left, Ceri hasn't been able to ....
6 The Missing People telephone number is ....

b How is Ceri going to spend Christmas? What would she like to happen?

3 💬 Work in groups. Look at the webpage and the photos. Discuss the questions.

● Have you ever seen any notices like these?
● Can you think of any other ideas to help find missing people?
● Do you know any stories about missing people in your country?

home · missing people · campaigns · Message From Mum · Ceri Padarn for Alun

Message From Mum – Ceri Padarn for Alun

0:06 / 3:25

Video appeal for missing Alun Padarn
From: missingpeople

Missing People is the only UK charity that works with missing people, their families and others who care for them.

Please help us find more missing people. Visit our website at www.missingpeople.org.uk. Thank you for your support.

GRAMMAR (1)

1 a Underline the verbs in the sentences. Are they present perfect or past simple?

A Have you seen Alun?
B Yes, I've seen him. I saw him last week.

b Choose the correct options for 1–3 in the GRAMMAR PANEL ■.

2 a Write present perfect and past simple questions.

you   ever   be   lost   ?   what   happen   ?
Have you ever been lost?   What happened?

1 you   ever   stay   out all night   ?
   how   you   feel   ?
2 you   ever   argue   with your parents   ?
   why   you   argue   ?
3 you   ever   give   money   to a charity   ?
   what   the money   for   ?
4 you   ever   help   a stranger   ?
   what   you   do   ?
5 you   ever   say   goodbye   to someone for a long time   ?
   what   you   say   ?

b 💬 Ask and answer the questions.

PRESENT PERFECT & PAST SIMPLE

We can use both the **present perfect** and the **past simple** to talk about things that happened in the past.

When we use the (1)*past simple / present perfect* we don't say exactly when something happened. This is not important.

I've seen him. NOT ~~I've seen him last week.~~
They've found him.

When we use the (2)*past simple / present perfect* we often use a past time expression, e.g. *two days ago, last week.*

I saw him six months ago.
They found him yesterday.

We often use the (3)*past simple / present perfect* to add extra details about a specific past event.

Where did they find him? They found him at the train station.

See page 143 for grammar reference and more practice.

PRONUNCIATION: auxiliary verbs

1 a 🔊 4.4 Listen to three short conversations. What have the people lost?

b Listen again and complete the questions.

1 .... you like to wait here while I get it?
2 .... you looking for this?
3 .... you seen my mobile phone?

2 a Listen again and notice the pronunciation of the auxiliary verbs.

1 Would /wəd/   2 Are /ə/   3 Have /həv/

b Practise saying the questions in 1b.

LISTENING

1 💬 Work in pairs. Have you ever lost something on public transport? What did you lose? Did you get it back?

2 a 🔊 4.5 Listen to a report about the Lost Property office in the centre of Paris. Answer the questions.

1 How long has the office been open?
2 What objects do people lose most frequently?
3 What four strange objects does the reporter mention?

b Listen again. How long has each object been in the lost property office?

1 .... : since last Sunday.
2 .... : for almost a year.
3 .... : since last May.
4 .... : for about five weeks.

3 💬 Discuss in pairs. How do you think these things got lost?

GRAMMAR (2)

1 Look at how the words *for* and *since* are used in LISTENING 2b. Choose the correct option for 1 and 2 in the GRAMMAR PANEL █ below.

2 Look at the time expressions in the box. Which can you use with

1 for?   2 since?

> 2010   a long time   I was a child   last night
> three years   two weeks

3 a Think of things you haven't done for each of the time expressions in 2. Write sentences using the present perfect and a time expression.

I haven't seen snow for a long time.

b 💬 Work in pairs. Share your sentences with a partner. Do you have anything in common?

4 a Look at the categories below and write the first four answers you think of.

● Two people (other than my family) who are important in my life:
  my best friend, my boyfriend
● Two possessions which are important to me:
  my mobile, my diary

b 💬 Work in pairs. Talk about your answers.
● How long have you known/owned them?
● Why are they special to you?

PRESENT PERFECT WITH *FOR* & *SINCE*

When we use the **present perfect** to talk about a situation that started in the past and continues in the present we often use the question *How long... ?* and time expressions with *for* and *since*.

How long have you known her?

We use:

(1)*for / since* to talk about a period of time.

(2)*for / since* to talk about when something started.

I've known her   *for years.*
             since 2009.

See page 143 for grammar reference and more practice.

READING

1 Quickly read the article. Who are Libby, Rosemeri and Ciro? Write summary sentences like the one below. Change the **bold** words.

*Libby is a **13-year-old Australian girl** who is a **teenage carer**.*

Youngachievers

For millions of teenagers, responsibilities begin early.

The carer

A carer looks after an elderly or sick person at home, often a relative. We do not know how many teenage carers there are worldwide, but there are over 180,000 in Australia alone.

Spotlight on:
Libby, 13, Australia

Mum's illness started getting worse a few years ago (she's got multiple sclerosis), and now she needs my help. Dad died when I was young, and I'm the oldest child, so I do most of the housework. I make the breakfast, do jobs around the home, that sort of stuff. I've got four younger sisters, so I'm always busy! The oldest child always does more work, I think.

The mum

Every year, more than 13 million teenage girls have a child.

Spotlight on:
Rosemeri, 16, Brazil

Life is certainly easier without kids. Now I've become a mum I look after Angela, do the shopping, pay the bills, adult things – I don't have a lot of time for myself. Sometimes I feel jealous of my friends. Going to the beach is much more fun than staying at home with a baby! But I wouldn't change places for anything. Seeing Angela grow up is amazing. It's hard, but being a mum is the best thing I've ever done.

The worker

About 158 million under-14-year-olds work. In Latin America, about 16% of children work. The figure is about 22% in Asia and 41% in Africa.

Spotlight on:
Ciro, 12, Bolivia

I've always worked – when I was little I did the gardening at home and grew vegetables. Now I'm older, I work for much longer hours, sometimes ten or more a day. I work with my father and brothers in the fields. I'm the youngest worker, but I'm faster than my dad! Younger workers are quicker, I think. I left school early. Sometimes I miss it. Having a job is a lot more difficult than studying. But I want to help my family.

NOTICE   *ABOUT* + NUMBERS

We can use *about* with numbers, ages and times to mean *approximately*, *a little* or *more/less than*.

She's about 50. (She may be a little older or younger than 50.)
I'll arrive at about 10 o'clock. (I may arrive a little before or after 10 o'clock.)

2 Read the article again. Choose the correct answer.

1 Which one of the sentences is true about Libby's family?
   a She doesn't have a father.
   b Her mum became ill a few months ago.
   c There are four children in her family.

2 How does Rosemeri feel about being a mum?
   a She does not enjoy it.
   b She thinks it can be hard.
   c She loves everything about it.

3 What does Ciro say about work?
   a He prefers having a job to going to school.
   b He enjoys working with his family.
   c It is more difficult now than it was in the past.

4 Which of the facts is correct?
   a There are more teenage mums than child workers.
   b The biggest number of teenage carers is in Australia.
   c A bigger percentage of children work in Africa than in Asia.

3 💬 Work in small groups. Do you know any 'young achievers' like Libby, Rosemeri or Ciro? What have they done/are they doing?

VOCABULARY: home life

1 Find the expressions in the article and write the missing verbs.

1 .... jobs around the home
2 .... the breakfast
3 .... the shopping
4 .... after children/other people
5 .... the housework
6 .... the bills
7 .... the gardening

2 🔊 4.6 Listen to Nico talking about the things he does at home. What does he *often*, *sometimes* and *never* do?

3 **a** 💬 Do you help at home? What do you do? How often do you do it? Tell your partner.

b Who helps the most/least?

GRAMMAR

1 Which of the people in the article agrees with the statements? Do you agree?

1 Working is **more difficult** than studying.
2 Life is **easier** without kids.
3 The **oldest** child in a family usually has the **most difficult** time.
4 **Younger** workers are **better** than **older** workers.

2 Complete 1–5 in the GRAMMAR PANEL ▪.

3 **a** Complete the questions about family and home life.

1 Do you have any (**old**) or (**young**) brothers and sisters? How old are they?
2 Who is the (**good**) and the (**bad**) person for doing housework in your family? What do they do?
3 What is the (**busy**) time in your house? Why is it busy?
4 Is your family (**big**) or (**small**) than Libby's? Is it (**easy**) to live in a big or a small family?
5 Who do you think has the (**interesting**) job in your family? What do they do?

b 💬 Work in pairs. Ask and answer the questions. Are your families very similar or very different? Share your answers with the class.

4 **a** Add *than* or *the* to the sentences below.

1 My family is one of biggest families in the class.
2 My family is smaller most of the other families in the class.
3 Biggest family is the teacher's family.
4 The person with most interesting job is my partner's father.
5 Most people think it's easier to live in a big family in a small one.
6 Busiest time in most families is breakfast time.

b Change the sentences to make them true for your class.

COMPARATIVES & SUPERLATIVES

We use **comparative adjectives** to compare and contrast two things.

We use **superlative adjectives** to compare and contrast something with all the other items in a group.

	Adjective	Comparative	Superlative
One syllable	old	*older*	(1)
Two syllables ending in -y	easy	(2)	easiest
Two or more syllables	difficult	(3)	(4)
Irregular	good	(5)	best

We often use **than** with comparative adjectives.
*I'm much faster **than** him.*

We usually use **the** or a possessive adjective (**my**, **his**, etc.) before a superlative adjective.
*I'm **the** youngest child.   She's **my** best friend.*

See page 143 for grammar reference and more practice.

SPEAKING

1 **a** Make notes comparing your family members. Use the words in the box or your own ideas.

annoying   childish   lazy   friendly
funny   intelligent   helpful   noisy

My sister's the laziest. She's lazier than my brothers!

b 💬 Work in groups. Ask and answer questions about your family members.
Who's the laziest person in your family? Why?

2 💬 Tell the rest of the class about the families in your group. Whose family would you most like to live in? Why?

NOTICE SAY/TELL

We use an object after *tell*, but we don't use an object after *say*.

He had something to say.
He had something to tell us.

❝Intonation: sounding enthusiastic ❞

4.8 Listen to the expressions. Pay attention to the way the speakers say the **bold** words.

1 I've **missed** you.
2 It's **great** to see you.
3 We **must** meet up again **soon**.
4 I've got **lots** to tell you.

For each of 1–4, decide which speaker sounds the most enthusiastic, a or b.

Practise saying sentences 1–10 in **3a**. Be enthusiastic!

TUNE IN

1 💬 Work in pairs. Look at the three photos. Discuss the questions.

- What is the relationship between the people?
- Do you have any family or friends who live a long way away? How do you stay in touch?
- When was the last time you met these friends or relatives? What did you do?

2 🔊 4.7 Listen to three conversations and answer the questions.

1 How do the people know each other?
2 How long ago did they last see each other?

FOCUS ON LANGUAGE

3 a Read these extracts from **2**. Choose the correct options.

1 Welcome *back / again*!
2 I've *lost / missed* you.
3 So *say / tell* me, how are things?
4 It's great to *see / look* you again.
5 It's been a long time *for / since* we last met.
6 It's good to catch *down / up*.
7 We must meet up again *quickly / soon*.
8 How *are / do* your sons?
9 So, Mum, how's it *doing / going*?
10 I've got lots to *say / tell* you.

b Listen again and check.

4 💬 Work in pairs. Answer the questions.

1 What other questions do people often ask when they're catching up?
2 How do people usually answer these questions?

5 🔊 4.9 Listen to the questions from 3a and write the answers.

OVER TO YOU

6 Imagine you are at a class reunion party. You haven't seen the students in your class for five years! Think of five things you would like to ask them.

7 💬 Work in groups.

- Take turns to talk to each person in the group and ask your questions.
- Use the expressions from 3.
- Remember – you're excited to see each other, so sound enthusiastic!

TUNE IN

1 Read three emails sent through a networking website called *Link Up*. How do the people know María?

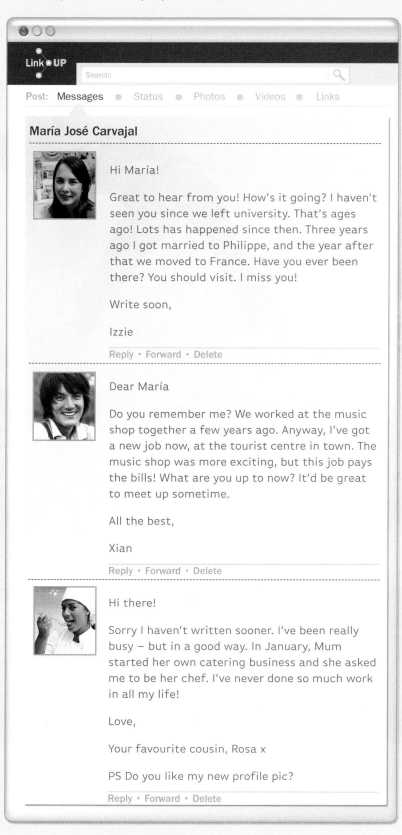

Link UP

Search:

Post: **Messages** • Status • Photos • Videos • Links

María José Carvajal

Hi María!

Great to hear from you! How's it going? I haven't seen you since we left university. That's ages ago! Lots has happened since then. Three years ago I got married to Philippe, and the year after that we moved to France. Have you ever been there? You should visit. I miss you!

Write soon,

Izzie

Reply • Forward • Delete

Dear María

Do you remember me? We worked at the music shop together a few years ago. Anyway, I've got a new job now, at the tourist centre in town. The music shop was more exciting, but this job pays the bills! What are you up to now? It'd be great to meet up sometime.

All the best,

Xian

Reply • Forward • Delete

Hi there!

Sorry I haven't written sooner. I've been really busy – but in a good way. In January, Mum started her own catering business and she asked me to be her chef. I've never done so much work in all my life!

Love,

Your favourite cousin, Rosa x

PS Do you like my new profile pic?

Reply • Forward • Delete

2 Why do people use websites like *Link Up*? Have you ever used a website like this? Why/Why not?

PREPARE FOR TASK

3 Read the emails again. Find three ways of
1 beginning an email
2 ending an email

4 💬 Work in pairs. Which expressions would you use in an email to a friend?
1 Yours sincerely,
2 Hiya
3 Give me a call sometime!
4 I look forward to hearing from you.
5 Take care,
6 See you soon.
7 I am writing to…
8 Dear Sir / Madam,
9 Best wishes,
10 What's up?

5 Read the emails again and answer the questions.
1 Can you find any more useful informal expressions?
2 Do we use full forms (*I have been*) or short forms (*I've been*) in informal writing?

TASK

6 Think of a friend that you haven't seen for a long time. Make notes about
1 who your friend is.
2 when you last met your friend.
3 what you have done since you last met/ spoke to your friend. Think of at least four things.
4 what you would like to know about your friend now.

7 Imagine you have seen your friend's profile on the *Link Up* website. Write an email to him/her. Use informal expressions.

REPORT BACK

8 Swap your email with another student. Imagine you wrote to each other. Write a short reply (50–100 words).

→ Go to Review B, Unit 4, p. 68

5 LIVE AND LEARN

1 💬 Work in pairs. Look at the photos of different learning situations and discuss the questions.

- Who is the teacher?
- Who are the students?
- Where are they?
- What are they studying?

2 a 🔊 5.1 Listen and answer the questions.

1 Who's speaking, the teachers or the students?
2 What's special about each teaching situation?

b Listen again. Complete the statements with Professor Quarashi (PQ), Matthew Sanford (MS) or Phil Higgins (PH).

1 .... thinks classrooms are ugly places.
2 .... believes everyone can do something special.
3 .... teaches IT.
4 .... teaches at secondary school.
5 .... teaches at a university.
6 .... teaches Science.
7 .... flies to class.
8 .... teaches in the USA.

3 a 💬 Work in pairs. Think about a teacher who made an impression on you. What was special about him/her? Tell your partner.

b Share your experiences with the class. Do you think any of the teachers could be 'Teacher of the Year'?

4 a Look at A in the KEY VOCABULARY PANEL ▪. Put the subjects in the correct category. Can you add any more subjects?

b 💬 Look again at the list in A and answer the questions.

● Which of these subjects have you studied? Are you studying any now?
● Are there any you would like to study in the future? Why?

5 a Look at B in the KEY VOCABULARY PANEL ▪. Do these types of school exist in your country? Use a dictionary to help you. What is the age group for each one?

b Match the qualifications to the types of school.

6 💬 Work in pairs. Tell your partner about the schools you have attended and the qualifications you have.

7 a 🔊 5.2 Listen to Keira talking about a course she is doing. What makes her course different from the ones in the photos? Is she enjoying it? Why/Why not?

b 💬 Work in groups. Have you ever done a course online? If yes, what did you think of the experience? If not, would you like to? Why/Why not?

▪ KEY VOCABULARY

Education & learning

A Academic subjects

Art   Biology   Business Studies
Chemistry   Drama   Economics
Geography   History
IT (Information Technology)
Languages   Literature   Mathematics
Music   Philosophy   Physics
Politics   Psychology   Sport

Arts: ....
Sciences: ....
Social Sciences: ....
Other: ....

B Schools & qualifications

SCHOOLS

high school   kindergarten
pre-school   primary school
secondary school   technical college
university

QUALIFICATIONS

degree   masters
professional diploma
school leaving certificate
vocational qualification

NOTICE *CAREER, COURSE, STUDIES*
Use *career* to talk about someone's professional life.
Use *course* or *studies* to talk about education.
During his long career as a teacher, he lived in the USA.
I've just finished a course at university.
As part of his university studies, he travelled to India.
How do you say *career*, *course* and *studies* in your language?

SPEAKING & READING

1 💬 Work in pairs. Look at the photos. What does each photo show?

2 **a** Match photos a–d to the university courses.

1 Sports Science   2 Equine Studies   3 Social Networking Studies   4 Forensic Science

b 💬 Discuss the questions with your partner.

- What's the link between these courses and the title of the article?
- What are 'traditional' subjects?
- Would you like to study any of the subjects in the photos? What do you think the course would include?
- Can you think of any other 'non-traditional' subjects which are popular in your country?

3 Look at the expressions highlighted in ▮red▮ in the article. Can you guess what they mean?

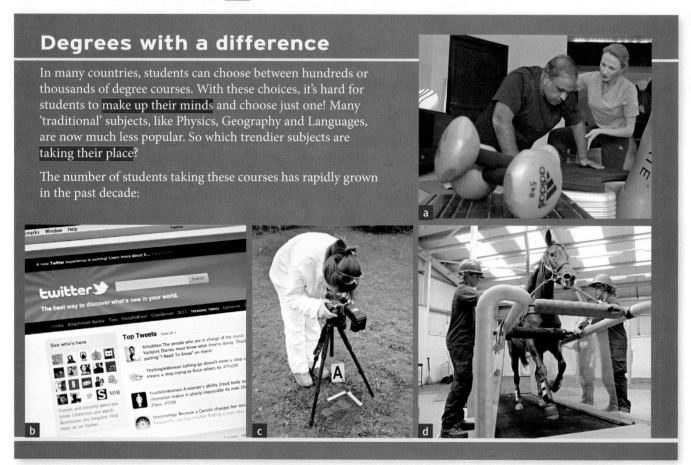

Degrees with a difference

In many countries, students can choose between hundreds or thousands of degree courses. With these choices, it's hard for students to make up their minds and choose just one! Many 'traditional' subjects, like Physics, Geography and Languages, are now much less popular. So which trendier subjects are taking their place?

The number of students taking these courses has rapidly grown in the past decade:

LISTENING

1 **a** 🔊 5.3 Listen to three people talking about their university studies. Match the people to three of the photos.

b Listen again. Choose the correct answer, a or b, for each speaker.

1 Ilaria chose her course because
   a it will be easy to get a job with this degree.
   b the subject looked interesting in TV shows.
2 Raushan's very interested in learning more about
   a health.
   b psychology.
3 Lee chose his subject because
   a he already knows a lot about it.
   b his parents think it's a good idea.

2 **a** Complete the statements with the correct name, Ilaria, Raushan or Lee.

1 .... lives in a country where horses are important.
2 .... likes police dramas.
3 ....'s parents don't approve of his/her choice.

b Read transcript 5.3 on page 164 and check your answers.

3 Do you think some degree subjects are more useful than others? Which ones? Why?

GRAMMAR

1 **a** Look at the sentences. Who is speaking, Ilaria or Lee?

1 **I'm taking** my final exam next month.
2 **I'm working** really hard for this exam.
3 **I'm starting** the course next year.
4 **I'm getting** excited about it already.

b Which sentences refer to a) the future? b) the present? Underline the future time expressions. Then complete 1 and 2 in the GRAMMAR PANEL .

2 **a** Write the verbs in brackets in the present continuous. Use the affirmative or negative to make the sentences true for you. Which sentences refer to the future?

1 I .... (work) really hard at the moment.
2 I .... (go) shopping after class.
3 I .... (stay) in tomorrow night.
4 I .... (cook) dinner for friends at the weekend.

b Compare your sentences with a partner. Then write two more about

a things you're doing at the moment.
b plans you have for the near future.

3 **a** Read transcript 5.3 on page 164. What other verb form is used to describe future plans?

b Complete 3 in the GRAMMAR PANEL .

4 **a** Look at the questions. Which can you rewrite using *going to*?

1 Are you studying for an exam at the moment?
2 What are you doing next weekend?
3 How are you getting home tonight?
4 Are you reading a book at the moment? If yes, are you enjoying it?

b 💬 Ask and answer the questions in pairs.

SPEAKING

1 💬 Work in small groups. You are going to design a new university course. Follow the instructions.

1 Think of a subject that isn't offered at universities in your country.
2 Decide why it might be useful or interesting. (Is it going to help students get a job? Is it related to youth culture? Is it related to new technologies?)
3 Decide what kind of information and skills the course is going to cover and how long it's going to last.

2 💬 Present your course to the class. Which course is

a the most unusual? Why?
b the most useful? Why?

PRESENT CONTINUOUS & *GOING TO*

Present continuous

We use the **present continuous** to talk about

1 the present (what we are doing now or around now):
I'm working really hard for this exam.
(1) ....

2 plans and arrangements for the future (with a fixed time or date).
I'm starting the course next year.
(2) ....

Going to

We also use *going to* to talk about future plans and intentions.

There is very little difference between the present continuous and *going to* for future plans and arrangements.
What are you studying next year? OR *What are you going to study next year?*

I'm starting a degree in September. OR
(3) ....

We often use the **present continuous** for fixed (diary) arrangements & *going to* for more general plans or intentions:
I'm starting French classes next Tuesday.
I'm going to study French one day.

See page 144 for grammar reference and more practice.

NOTICE *GONNA*

In very informal writing, e.g. in emails to friends, text messages and online chats, we often write *gonna* instead of *going to*.
Gonna study after class today. Speak tomorrow!
We're gonna miss you! Have a good trip.

It's also common to see *gonna* in song lyrics and advertising slogans.
Never gonna give you up...
It's gonna be big!

Savage Chickens by Doug Savage

VOCABULARY: *-ed/-ing* adjectives

1 a 💬 Work in pairs. Choose the options which best describe your experience of school.

1 I usually felt *bored / interested* in class.
2 Maths lessons were *confusing / exciting*.
3 Homework was usually *boring / interesting*.
4 I was always *depressed / excited* on Sundays. School started on Monday morning!

b 🔊 5.4 Listen. <u>Underline</u> the best option. How do the speakers feel? Who likes/doesn't like school?

2 Look at the pairs of adjectives in **1**. Which ones describe

1 how somebody feels?
   I am...
2 something that makes a person feel a certain way?
   My lessons are...

3 Write sentences with the correct adjectives.

> annoyed / annoying   fascinated / fascinating
> pleased / pleasing   tired / tiring

1 This subject   2 These students

....

3 I've passed! I / really   4 Stop it! You / really

....

4 a Think about your English lessons. Make the questions.

1 What was the most *interesting / interested* thing you learnt last week?
2 Which lessons are the most *tired / tiring*: morning lessons or afternoon lessons?
3 What do you do when you are *confused / confusing* in class?

b 💬 Ask and answer the questions.

READING

1 Look at the photos and answer the questions.

1 What country do you think they show?
2 What is the boy doing in each one?
3 Where do you think he is in the first one?

2 Read the article quickly and check your ideas. Who is Anselmo? What do the photos tell us about his life?

3 Read the article again. Find and correct the false sentences.

1 Ester thinks Anselmo is an annoying student.
2 Students with low marks can't go to the school.
3 Ester thinks that the most important thing students learn is that life can be difficult.
4 Students don't pay any money to the school.
5 Anselmo didn't enjoy his job.
6 Anselmo wants to work in the circus.

4 Would you like to go to this school? Why/Why not?

THE SCHOOL OF FUN

At school yesterday, Anselmo rode a bicycle in the classroom. Then he stood on his head. But his teacher wasn't angry. 'Excellent, Anselmo! I'm really pleased!' Ester da Silva said.

Anselmo goes to an unusual school in Rio de Janeiro, in Brazil. At the school, students aged 4 to 24 learn how to dance, sing and do acrobatics in a circus.

That sounds exciting, but it isn't easy. 'Students have to work hard,' says Ester. 'We say that all students at Circus School have to study 'normal' school subjects like Languages and Maths as well – that's very important. They don't have to get the highest marks, but they do

GRAMMAR

1 a Read the sentences. Are they true for Anselmo's school?

1 All the students **have to** work hard.
2 They **don't have to** study Languages and Maths.
3 They **mustn't** be late for class.
4 They **must** always be polite to their teachers.

b Check your answers in the article in READING 1.

2 a Look at the sentences in 1a again. Which talk about

a rules the students always need to follow?
b things it isn't necessary for the students to do?

b Look at the verbs in **bold** in 1a. Use them to complete 1–4 in the GRAMMAR PANEL ▓ .

have to try their best. They mustn't be late for classes, and they must always be polite.'

Ester thinks that Circus School teaches students many useful things. 'Students learn how to work with other people, and they learn about themselves, too. They see that some things in life can be difficult, but if you work hard they can get better. Best of all, they learn that school – and life – can be exciting and enjoyable!'

Circus School is a charity, and all the classes are free. Most of the students come from *favelas* (poor parts of town), where many children leave school without any qualifications. Anselmo lives in a tiny room with his mother and three brothers. He left secondary school when he was 12, and he washed cars for money. 'It was tiring, and many drivers didn't pay.' Now, thanks to Ester, he's hoping for a better future. 'I'm probably not going to be a circus star!' he smiles, 'but I might be a teacher one day, like Mrs da Silva. I'm very happy I don't have to clean cars any more!'

3 a Read the information and choose the correct option. Sometimes both options are correct.

> **In Japanese schools, there are many rules. They are called *Kosaku*. Here are some examples:**
>
> • Students [1]*must / have to* wear a uniform. They can't even choose their own socks!
> • Boys [2]*mustn't / don't have to* grow their hair longer than their ears. They can only have short hair. Girls [3]*mustn't / don't have to* have short hair. They can have it long or short.
> • Students [4]*must / mustn't* be on time. Late students can't go into class.
> • Students [5]*must / mustn't* have jobs. Teachers think that students who work are too tired to study.
> • Students [6]*mustn't / don't have to* stay in every night, but if they want to go out, they [7]*must / have to* ask their teacher – even at the weekend!

b Are any of these rules true for schools in your country? Write three more sentences about schools in your country using *have to, must, mustn't* or *don't have to.*

▓ MUST(N'T) & (DON'T) HAVE TO FOR OBLIGATION

Must & have/has to

We use **must** and [1]................................ to talk about rules and obligations.

Have to is more common than [2]................................ .
*We **must**/**have to** be at school at 8 a.m.*
*Anselmo **must**/**has to** work hard at school.*

Mustn't & don't/doesn't have to

We use [3]................................ to talk about prohibition – about things that are against the rules.

We use [4]................................ to explain that there is no obligation or rule.

*You **mustn't** be late for school.* (= this is one of the rules, you don't have a choice)

*Anselmo **doesn't have to** wash cars anymore.* (= it isn't necessary for him to wash cars now)

See page 144 for grammar reference and more practice.

SPEAKING

1 💬 Work in groups. Imagine you are going to write the rules for your English class next week. Discuss your ideas.

Students don't have to do any exams. Great idea!

2 Make a poster with your five best ideas.

SPEAKING & READING

1 💬 Work in pairs. Look at this photo.
Discuss the questions.

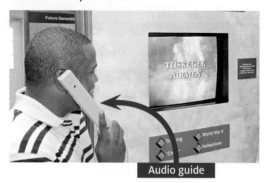

Audio guide

- Do you enjoy visiting museums?
- When was the last time you went to
  a museum? What did you learn?
- Have you ever used an 'audio guide'?
  Do you think they're a good idea?

2 a Read part of a museum brochure. Where is the museum and
what can visitors learn about?

b Have you got any museums like this in your town?

The Museum of Romany Culture isn't
a big museum, but it's a fascinating one.
At the museum you can learn about the
history of the Romany people in the
Czech Republic and around the world.
You can also learn about Romany
culture and art – and buy some amazing
souvenirs in the shop!

You can find the museum in Brno, in
the centre of the city's Romany district.

LISTENING

1 🔊 5.5 Listen to the audio guide. In what order do you learn about

- language? • crafts? • music?

2 Listen again. Complete the summaries in the museum brochure.

A Romany musicians prefer to play instruments like
the accordian or the (1) .... , rather than the
(2) .... Romany music has inspired musicians
like the (3) .... player Django Reinhardt (Belgium)
and the punk band Gogol Bordello ((4) ....).

B Today, most Romany people live in (5) .... or
(6) .... , but not in wagons. Traditional Romany
crafts and clothes are (7) .... , because this is
a lucky colour. At the museum, (8) .... can learn
these crafts.

C A lot of Roma people speak Romany, but they don't
(9) .... or (10) .... the language. In the past,
many Romany people told stories about their (11) ....
and tradition. At the museum, we teach visitors these stories.
You can also buy (12) .... in the gift shop!

SBÍRKY
MUZEA
ROMSKÉ
KULTURY

Tradiční
řemesla,
profese
a zaměstnání/
traditional crafts,
professions
and employment

3 💬 Work in pairs. Discuss the questions.

- In your region, what are the traditional:
  a) foods? *(pasta, wine...)* b) hobbies or activities? *(music, story-telling...)*
- What traditional things can you do or make?

PRONUNCIATION: stress in two-syllable words

1 ◀))) 5.6 💬 Work in pairs. Complete the table with words from the audio guide. Listen and check.

children enjoy goodbye guitar language lucky ~~music~~ people prefer stories

.●	●.
	music

2 a Is the word stress more often on the first or the second syllable?

   b Can you think of two more words for each category?

VOCABULARY: adjectives + prepositions

1 Read the museum's activity programme. How many activities are there?

Museum Activity Programme

All activities are free, and everyone is welcome!

Lectures

Romany culture – 1900 to present day

Workshops

Written and spoken Romany – beginners
Music – all levels
Romany dancing – all levels
Romany crafts – make your own basket!

Other events

Film night

---

2 ◀))) 5.7 Listen to six museum visitors. Choose the best activity for each visitor.

3 a Match 1–7 to a–g.

   1 I'm **bad**
   2 I'm quite **good**
   3 I'm really **interested**
   4 Flamenco is quite **similar**
   5 I always get **excited**
   6 Japanese is quite **different**
   7 I'm **bored**

   a **from** Romany.
   b **about** the cinema.
   c **with** reading.
   d **in** history.
   e **at** art.
   f **at** music.
   g **to** some Romany dances.

   b Listen again and check.

4 a Complete the sentences about you. Use the correct preposition after each adjective.

   I'm completely different from my sister.

   1 I'm really good ....
   2 One person who's quite similar .... me is ....
   3 I sometimes get quite bored ....
   4 My best friend and I are both interested ....
   5 I always get excited ....
   6 When I was young, I was bad ....

   b 💬 Compare your answers with your partner. Give extra details.

   I'm completely different from my sister. She works hard at school. I don't!

5 a Imagine you are visiting the museum. You only have time to go to <u>one</u> event. Which one would you choose?

   b 💬 Find another student who would like to go with you.

   Would you like to go to the… ?
   Yes, I'd love to. I'm (really) interested in… / (quite) good at…
   Sorry, I'm not interested in / not very good at…

A

NOTICE REQUESTS WITH CAN, COULD & WOULD

We often use the modal forms *can*, *could* and *would* in polite questions and requests.

Can/Could I have some more, please?
I'd like some more, please.

Could and *would* are more formal than *can*.

" Intonation: sounding polite "

🔊 5.9 Listen and write three requests. You will hear each request twice.

Listen again. For each request, decide which speaker sounds more polite, a or b.

Do the polite requests have rising (⤴) or falling (⤵) intonation?

Work in pairs. Practise the polite conversations in the transcript on page 164.

TUNE IN

1 Look at the photo. What do you notice about it? Do you have a café at your school, university or workplace? Is it similar or different to this?

2 🔊 5.8 Listen to five conversations. Which students were polite?

3 💬 Work in groups. Discuss the questions.
- Do you think most people are polite?
- Can you think of any times when you heard someone being impolite? What happened?

FOCUS ON LANGUAGE

4 Are these expressions from the conversations polite (P) or impolite (I)?

1 I want a hamburger.
2 I'd like some curry, please.
3 Give me that too.
4 What would you like?
5 Can I have the lasagne, please?
6 Please could I have some curry?
7 What can I get you?
8 I'll have some chips.

5 a Look at five ways people answered requests. Which reply is NOT polite?

1 Of course.   4 I'm afraid...
2 I'm sorry, but...   5 Whatever.
3 Certainly.

b Complete the table with the polite replies.

Positive (+)	.... , ...
Negative (−)	.... , ...

OVER TO YOU

6 💬 Work in pairs. Choose two of the photos. What are the people doing?

a
b
c
d

7 For each photo, think of a question or request someone might ask in this situation.

8 Write a short conversation for each photo. Use polite questions and replies.

9 💬 Work in pairs. Practise your conversations.

TUNE IN

1 Look at the extracts from advertisements for three different language schools. Which countries are they in? Discuss which course you'd like the most and why.

Language school in Dublin
40 hours a week – choose from a number of languages
Small classes

a

Study English and other subjects in Sydney
Full programme of after-class activities
Relax while you learn!

b

c
Come to the beautiful Colorado Mountains
Learn about American culture   Good value!

PREPARE FOR TASK

2 🔊 5.10 Listen to a student asking about one of the courses and answer the questions.

   1 Which course is he asking about?
   2 Do you think he will go on the course? Why/Why not?

3 a Listen again and complete the first column in the table.

Name of school: **Adventures in English**	Question
1 Accommodation?	
2 Courses – which subjects?	
3 Class size?	
4 Activities?	
5 Price?	

b What questions did the student ask? Complete the second column with the questions. Check your answers in the transcript on page 164.

TASK

4 💬 Work in pairs. Student A, turn to page 159. Student B, turn to page 160. Have your conversations. Remember to be polite.

REPORT BACK

5 💬 Now that you have more information about the schools, which course would you choose? Is there a favourite course in the class?

➡ Go to Review B, Unit 5, p. 69   ➡ Go to Writing bank 3, p. 154   **57**

6 HELP!

1 a 💬 Work in pairs. What's the connection between the photos and the title of the unit? What do you think is the problem in each photo?

b Look at A in the KEY VOCABULARY PANEL ■.
Which words in the box can you see in the photos? Which words don't match with any of the photos? Which refer to people and which to services? Use a dictionary to help you.

2 a 🔊 6.1 Listen to three people talking about three of the situations in the photos. Match the situation to the photo.

b Listen again and answer the questions.
● Who's teaching someone? What are they teaching?
● Who phoned the firefighters? Why?
● What did the boy do? Why?

3 💬 Work in groups. Discuss the questions.
● Which person in the photos do you think was most grateful for the help? Why?
● Do you know anyone who does voluntary work for a charity or works for the emergency services? What do they do?
● When was the last time you helped someone with a problem? What was the problem? How did you help them?

4 Look at B in the KEY VOCABULARY PANEL ■.
Complete the table. Use a dictionary to help you.

KEY VOCABULARY

Help

A Jobs & services

ambulance driver   breakdown service
charity worker   doctor
emergency services   firefighter   helpline
passer-by   police officer   rescue worker
volunteer

- Can you think of any more people or services to add to the list?

B Adjective suffixes -ful & -less

Root word	-ful	-less
care	(1) _____	careless
end		endless
gratitude	grateful	
help	(2) _____	helpless
home		(3) _____
hope	(4) _____	hopeless
use	(5) _____	(6) _____

NOTE
-ful means that there's a lot of the quality.
  hopeful – with a lot of hope
-less means that there's nothing of that quality.
  homeless – without a home
Not all root words can take both suffixes.

NOTICE THE & A/AN + ADJECTIVE
We can use the + adjective to talk about a group of people in general terms.
the young, the elderly, the homeless
But you cannot use a/an + adjective.
a young, an elderly, a homeless
With a/an + adjective you need a noun.
a young woman, an elderly man, a homeless person

5 a Complete the sentences with adjectives from B. Sometimes there is more than one adjective.

1 I'm _____ when it comes to repairing cars. I really don't know anything about engines.
2 I can be very _____ sometimes. I'm always dropping or breaking things!
3 I'm very _____ to my parents and my family for all they've done for me.
4 I feel really sorry for _____ people. It must be very scary not having a roof over your head.
5 The list of things I have to do today is _____ ! I don't think I'll be able to do them al!
6 I find exercises like this very _____ .

b Work in pairs. Are any of the sentences true for you? Share your answers with your partner.

READING

1 a Work in groups. Look at the photos and read the headline. What do you think the article is about?

1 People playing football in a competition to make money to give to homeless people.
2 Homeless people from all over the world watching a football tournament.
3 Homeless people playing football in a tournament.

b Read the article. Were you right?

THE HOMELESS WORLD CUP

Most people think that we **should** try to get homeless people off the streets and back to work. But few people have good ideas about how they **can** help.

Mel Young from Scotland and Harald Schmied from Austria had a great idea. They are the founders of the Homeless World Cup (HWC). The HWC is an international football tournament for people who are homeless. The event is held every year and began in 2003 in Austria. At first people said things like 'homeless people **can't** play football' or 'they **shouldn't** waste time and money organising football matches, they **should** help the homeless find work'. But Young and Schmied saw football as a way to change people's lives and to help them feel good about themselves and get out of poverty. Thirty-one of the original 141 players from the 2003 tournament had a job one year after the tournament.

The impact is getting stronger each year and today about 73% of players make a positive change in their lives after taking part in the HWC. After playing in the HWC players come off drugs and alcohol. They move into jobs. They get training and education. They get in contact with their families again and they get somewhere to live. Some have even become professional or semi-professional football players or coaches.

So perhaps we **should** all think again about how to help the homeless instead of thinking that we **can't** do anything. We **can** make a difference. Sometimes it seems that finding a passion such as playing sport **can** help homeless people to find their way in life again.

2 Read the article again. Mark the statements true (T) or false (F). Correct the false ones.

1 Mel Young and Harald Schmied are from the same place.
2 The first HWC was in Austria.
3 There were fewer than 150 players in the first HWC.
4 Players from the HWC usually stay homeless.
5 All players in the HWC become professional football players.

3 Work in groups. Discuss the questions.

● Do you think the writer is in favour of or against the Homeless World Cup? How do you know?
● Do you think the Homeless World Cup is a good idea? Why/Why not?

GRAMMAR

1 a Look at the article in READING 1 again. Underline phrases which mean:

1 It's a good idea to help homeless people get off the streets.
2 Homeless people don't know how to play football.
3 It isn't a good idea to waste time and money organising football matches.
4 It's possible to make a difference.

b Look at the verbs in **bold** in your answers to 1a. Complete 1–4 in the GRAMMAR PANEL ■ with the correct sentence.

> **NOTICE** *THE THING IS*
> *The thing is...* is a useful phrase to introduce the main point or problem that we want to talk about.
> *The thing is, I would like a higher salary.*

2))) 6.2 Listen to the conversation and answer the questions.

1 How do the speakers know each other?
2 Why does Jason want time off?
3 Does Natalie say yes or no?

3 a Listen again. Match 1–5 to a–e.

1 Can I take
2 You should
3 I can
4 I can't
5 You shouldn't

  a ask for time off on the same day.
  b say no, can I?
  c finish the report this evening.
  d finish that report for the presentation tomorrow.
  e this afternoon off as holiday?

b Check your answers in transcript 6.2 on page 165. Find more examples of *can('t)* and *should(n't)*.

4 a Work in pairs. Do you agree with Jason or Natalie? Why/Why not?

b What else should/shouldn't you do at work? Share your ideas with the class. Which ones do you agree/disagree with?

You shouldn't surf the internet.

◼ MODAL VERBS: *CAN/CAN'T, SHOULD/SHOULDN'T*

Can/Can't

We use *can* or *can't* to talk about

1 ability

  (+) *I can speak three languages.*

  (–) (1) ....

2 possibility

  (+) (2) ....

  (–) *I'm sorry, I can't come to the meeting today.*

Should/Shouldn't

We use *should* to say you think something is a good idea, or the right thing to do.

(3) ....

We use *shouldn't* to say you think something is a bad idea, or the wrong thing to do.

(4) ....

Both *can* and *should* are modal verbs. We use them

1 with the infinitive without ~~to~~
2 to make negative sentences and questions:

  I can't swim. Can you?
  I shouldn't eat any more. Should we order coffee?

See page 145 for grammar reference and more practice.

LISTENING & SPEAKING

1 a))) 6.3 💬 Work in pairs. Listen to the people discussing a film and complete the advert.

The PURSUIT of HAPPYNESS

Starring Will Smith and Jaden Smith

The true story of Chris Gardner, who loses everything and becomes (1) ....

He has to sleep in a shelter with his young (2) .... He finally gets a (3) ...., but he has to do (4) .... months of training first.

See this on (5) .... at 9 p.m.

b Why should you see the film according to Sameera? More than one answer is correct.

1 The story's good.
2 It's romantic.
3 It's quite sad.
4 It has a happy ending.

2 Would you like to see the film or read the book? Why/Why not? If you have already seen it, what did you think?

3 Think about another film or story that you know and give two reasons why someone should see it or read about it.

You should see it because...

VOCABULARY:
senses

1 💬 Work in pairs. Look at photos a–e. Match the sense verbs and adjectives to make sentences.

feel	look	smell	sound	taste

delicious	loud	soft	stunning	terrible

Oysters taste delicious when they're fresh!

2 **a** Make more phrases with the ten words in **1a**. What can you describe?

Fresh baked bread smells delicious!

b Add other adjectives to the verbs to make five more sentences. Use a dictionary to help you.

His voice sounds very quiet…

3 💬 Work in pairs. Use the verbs in **1a** to describe

1 your favourite dinner.
2 someone you met recently.
3 a pet/animal you like.
4 your favourite music.
5 a place you've visited.

4 💬 Work in pairs. Student A, turn to page 159. Student B, turn to page 160. Take turns to describe and guess what the image shows.

> ❝ **Intonation:**
> **positive or negative** ❞

🔊 6.4 Listen to six expressions. Is the speaker saying something positive or negative?

🔊 6.5 Listen again. Write what they say.

Work in pairs. Practise saying the expressions. Your partner says if you sound positive or negative.

LISTENING

1 💬 Work in pairs. Look at the pictures. What problem do you think each person has?

2 🔊 6.6 Listen and check your ideas. Match the speakers' problems 1–4 to pictures a–d.

3 **a** Match advice i–iv to problems 1–4.

i leave him / talk to him   iii get more training / change jobs
ii stay at home / leave home   iv talk to her / don't tell her

b 🔊 6.7 Listen and choose the correct advice for each problem.

4 💬 Work in pairs. Discuss the questions.

● Which is the most serious problem?
● Do you agree with the advice?
● What do you think the people should do?

GRAMMAR

1 **a** Work in pairs. Read the predictions using *will, may* and *might*. Match 1–7 to a–g.

1 He may not	a a problem with her sense of smell.
2 They might be	b if they want you to leave.
3 They'll tell me	c angry, because she's your friend.
4 She'll give you	d have another girlfriend.
5 You may need to	e some ideas.
6 She might not be	f happy that you still live there.
7 She may have	g talk to your boss.

b 🔊 6.7 Listen again and check.

2 a Answer the questions.

1 Which sentences show the speaker is sure about the prediction?
2 Which show the speaker is talking about a possibility?
3 What is the negative form of *may* and *might*?

b Complete 1–4 in the GRAMMAR PANEL .

3 a Write predictions about your future with the prompts and *will/won't* and *may/might (not)*.

1 travel / all over the world
2 pass / my exams
3 get / my dream job
4 make / lots more friends
5 be / rich or famous

b Write two more predictions about yourself.

■ PREDICTIONS: *WILL, MAY, MIGHT*

USE

We use *will*, *may* or *might* + infinitive (without *to*) to make predictions about the future.

We use (1) .... when we are sure.

We use (2) .... or (3) .... when we are not completely sure.

FORM

+ subject + *will/might/may* + verb: *I might lose my job.*

− subject + (4) .... */might not/may not* + verb: *He may not come tonight.*

NOTE:

We never say or write *may not* as a contraction. We sometimes say *mightn't* but it isn't very common.

We also use *I think* or *I don't think* in predictions with *will*.

I don't think he will do well, NOT *~~I think he won't~~ do well.*

See page 145 for grammar reference and more practice.

Have you got what it takes to be a life coach?

If you are a friendly, active person who wants to help people, life coaching might be the right career for you.

a Life coaches are trained professionals who help their clients with a problem in their life. They will help people improve their lives in specific ways.

b They may meet with their clients in person, on the telephone or even online and by email. Life coaches work with clients in many ways and help them to have less stress, use time better and to have goals for the future.

c You should first decide what kind of life coach you want to be. You may want to work in finance or relationships. Or you might want to work in careers or how people spend their time. Then you should talk to a person who is already a life coach and discuss your ideas. Then you can sign up for a course at a college and start your new career!

READING

1 Look at the illustration and read the introduction to the web article. Do you know anything about this type of career? What do you think it involves?

2 Read the article. Match questions 1–3 to paragraphs a–c.

1 What does a life coach do?
2 How can I become a life coach?
3 What is a life coach?

3 Read the questions in 2 again. Answer each question in your own words.

SPEAKING

1 a Work in groups. Think about a time when you gave someone advice. Discuss the questions.

● Who was the person? (*friend, family member, co-worker, partner*)
● What kind of advice was it? (*relationship, finance, study, job*)
● What did you say? (*You should..., You shouldn't..., This will/might happen.*)
● Do you think you helped the other person?

b Compare your answers with other groups.

■ PRACTISE VOCABULARY TO DESCRIBE AILMENTS
■ DISCUSS GOOD HEALTH & CHINESE MEDICINE

a

b

c

d

VOCABULARY: health problems

1 💬 Work in pairs. Look at the photos. What is wrong with the people? Match the statements to the photos.

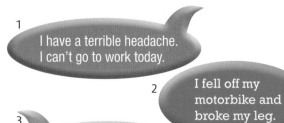

1 — I have a terrible headache. I can't go to work today.

2 — I fell off my motorbike and broke my leg.

3 — My ear hurts. I think I have an ear infection.

4 — My daughter has a sore throat. We're going to the doctor this afternoon.

2 What should you do when you have the problems in 1? Choose from the list.

- see a doctor
- see a dentist
- rest
- have an X-ray
- take a painkiller
- drink liquids
- stay in bed

> **NOTICE** *HURT/ACHE*
> *Hurt* and *ache* are verbs (*my stomach aches/hurts*), but *ache* is also a noun (*I have a stomachache.* NOT *I have a stomach hurt*).

PRONUNCIATION: word stress

1 a 🔊 6.8 Listen and complete the words and phrases.

backache, a ⁽¹⁾............., toothache,
an ⁽²⁾............. infection,
indigestion, my ⁽³⁾............. hurts,
my ⁽⁴⁾............. hurts,
a sore ⁽⁵⁾.............

b Listen again and <u>underline</u> the word stress.

2 Listen and repeat with the correct word stress.

LISTENING & SPEAKING

1 a 🔊 6.9 Work in pairs. Listen to the conversations. Where are the people?

b Listen again and complete the table.

What is wrong	What to do
(1)	
(2)	
(3)	
(4)	

2 💬 Look at the photos. What health problems might the people have? Describe what is wrong with the people and what they should do.

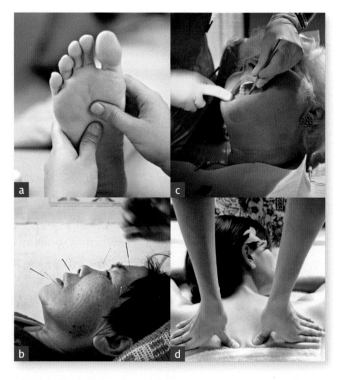
a
c
b
d

3 💬 Work in groups. Describe the problems. Who has the worst problem? Who gives the best advice?

READING

1 Read the first part of the information leaflet. Label the four parts of the face in **bold**.

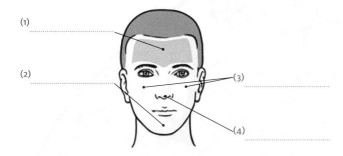

(1) ....
(2) ....
(3) ....
(4) ....

What do you see when you look in the mirror? According to Chinese medicine, your face can give you information about your health. Your **forehead**, **nose**, **chin** and **cheeks** can tell you what is happening inside your body.

2 Read the second part of the information leaflet. Complete the chart.

Problem on face	What it might mean
1 red forehead	• heart problem or .... problem
2 a spot on your nose	• ....
3 red nose	• ....
4 dark skin around chin or mouth	• problems with the .... or ....
5 skin problem on right cheek	• illness in the ....
6 red right cheek	• getting a ....
7 red left cheek	• a .... problem
8 problems with cheeks	• .... illness

Read on to find out what your face says about you.

FOREHEAD ☯ According to Chinese medicine, the forehead is connected to the heart, as well as the mind and spirit. If your forehead looks red it may show that you have a heart problem or it might be because you have recently had a difficult relationship problem.

NOSE ☯ Your nose has a connection to the stomach. If you have a spot on your nose your choice of food may be the problem. As a result, you may suffer from stomachache.

If the top of your nose is red it may mean stress. You shouldn't eat chocolate or drink alcohol if you have a lot of stress. Try deep breathing instead.

CHIN ☯ The chin area is connected to the kidney and bladder. If the skin around the chin and mouth is dark this may show problems with the kidneys or bladder.

RIGHT CHEEK ☯ Your right cheek is connected to the lung. If you have skin problems on your right cheek this might mean illness in the lung. If your right cheek is a little red it may be that you are getting a cold.

LEFT CHEEK ☯ Your left cheek is connected to the liver. If you are red on your left cheek and next to your nose you may have a problem with your liver. Problems in this part of the face can also show emotional illness, such as anger and depression, because the liver network is connected to the nervous system.

SPEAKING

1 💬 Work in groups. Which is most important to health? Rank in order.

- don't drink alcohol ....
- eat good food ....
- don't drink fizzy drinks ....
- have good relationships ....
- don't eat junk food ....
- have regular check-ups ....
- don't smoke ....
- manage stress ....
- don't watch TV ....
- sleep well ....
- take regular exercise ....
- take vitamins ....

2 💬 Compare your order with another group. Explain your reasons for the order. Work together to agree on a new order.

You should sleep well and then you will feel good the next day, you won't want junk food and you will want to take exercise. So it's number one!

TUNE IN

1 💬 Work in pairs. Look at the photos. What is the situation? Why is it stressful?

2 a 🔊 6.10 Listen. Which three conversations go with the photos?

b Listen again. Match each of the six situations to a piece of advice.

1 ....   a Call the emergency number.
2 ....   b Go home and go to bed.
3 ....   c Call and let someone know.
4 ....   d Ask someone for help.
5 ....   e Call a doctor.
6 ....   f Talk to a professional.

FOCUS ON LANGUAGE

3 Listen again and complete the phrases.

1 Why .... go home and go to bed?
2 You .... call the emergency number.
3 What .... I do?
4 Why .... speak to your teacher?
5 Do .... I should talk to my boss?
6 What .... calling your friend?
7 You .... call a doctor.

4 💬 Work in groups. Discuss whether you agree with the advice they gave.

5 Complete this table of ways to ask for and give advice. Use the phrases in 3 to help you.

Asking for advice	Giving advice
What .... I do?	You ....
Do you think I .... ?	You shouldn't ....
	Why .... you... ?
	What .... ?
	You .... to...

NOTICE *ADVICE*
The noun *advice* is uncountable.
We can't say *He gave me some ~~advices~~*.
We can say *a piece of advice*.
This is countable.
My mother gave me two pieces of advice.

OVER TO YOU

6 💬 Work in groups. Look at the photos. What problems can you see here?

7 Make notes on what advice you could give.

8 💬 Take turns to ask for advice and to give advice for each photo.

TUNE IN

1 Read the email from a teacher to a funding agency (an organisation that gives money). What is the teacher asking for?

To:	request@edufund.co.uk
From:	bmarshall@WestleaCS.edu

I am a teacher at a school in London. I am a new teacher to the school and we do not have enough money for all the things we need.

Teaching English literature to teenagers is an interesting task because they often enjoy writing and they have great stories to tell. I have found that they become very interested in stories about young people like themselves who go through a lot of problems.

I would like them to have their own copies of *Romeo and Juliet* and 30 books for my students would cost £289.

I would be delighted if you could help us with this.

Thank you very much.

Brad Marshall

2 Read the email again. Answer the questions.

1 Where does he work?
2 What does he teach?
3 Why does he like teaching teenagers?
4 How many books does he want?

3 💬 Imagine you work for the funding agency. You have twenty people a day who ask for money and you have £500 a day to give away. Should you give the money to this teacher? Why/Why not?

PREPARE FOR TASK

4 💬 Work in pairs. Read about the different organisations. Imagine you work for a funding agency that wants to donate some money. Which one would you give money to and why? How much money would you give?

Teens in Need is an organisation that works with homeless young people. We go out on the streets and give them the help they need to stay clean and safe and help them to plan their future.

Save the Animals is an organisation that protects animals from cruelty and extinction in different parts of our planet.

Research Doctors is a group of doctors who are looking for a cure for HIV/AIDS. The money you donate gives hope to millions of people in all parts of the world.

Girls First supports young women around the world by giving them access to education. Your money helps to pay for a young woman's education.

Planet in Danger helps you to help the environment by educating people about ways to clean and protect our world.

TASK

5 💬 Work in groups of three. Choose a local organisation (e.g. a school or hospital in your hometown). Write an email to a funding agency. Say

1 who you are.
2 what the money is for. Describe the organisation and why it needs money.
3 how much money you need.

6 a Read other groups' emails. Choose one you would like to give the money to and say why.

b Think about how much money they need, if it is a good cause and how it will help.

REPORT BACK

7 💬 Tell the others in the class which organisation you chose to give money to and why.

➡ Go to Review B, Unit 6, p. 70

VOCABULARY

Life stages

1 Write the name of a person you know who

- got a new job this year.
- was born before 1970.
- has got married.
- has gone to university.

2 💬 Work in pairs. Ask and answer the questions.

- How do you know the people in **1**? (e.g. friend, aunt, grandmother)
- How old are they?
- How often do you see them?

Activities

3 **a** Complete the table with the activities.

computer games	crafts	fishing	football	karate	skateboarding

do	go	play

b 💬 Work in pairs. Which ones a) do you do? b) do your friends do?

Home life

4 **a** Choose the correct words to complete the sentences.

1 My mum never *does / makes* the housework.
2 I prefer to *bring / do* the shopping online.
3 I often look *after / for* my sister's children.
4 I *make / do* dinner for the family every night.
5 We usually *pay / spend* our bills online.

b 💬 Work in pairs. Are the sentences true for you? What is the same/different?

GRAMMAR

Present perfect & past simple

1 **a** Complete the text using the correct form of the verbs.

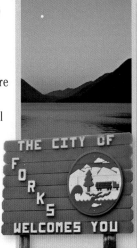

(1) .... you ever .... *(read)* any of the *Twilight* books by Stephenie Meyer? (2) .... you ever *(see)* any of the films? Stephenie Meyer (3) .... *(wrote)* her first novel about a girl, Bella, who meets her vampire boyfriend in the town of Forks, USA.

It (4) .... *(become)* a best-selling novel in 2005. Since that time, the town of Forks (5) .... *(change)* completely. In 2009, over 8,000 people (6) .... *(visit)* the town. In the same year, many new shops and restuarants (7) .... *(open)*. Since *Twilight*, sales in the town centre (8) .... *(grow)* by nearly 1,000%!

THE CITY OF FORKS WELCOMES YOU

b 💬 Work in pairs. Do you know any places which have changed? Tell your partner about them.

Present perfect with *for & since*

2 Complete the sentences with your own ideas. Add one more sentence about yourself with *for* or *since*.

- I have lived in this town since
  ....
- I have known the teacher of this class for
  ....
- I have had this hairstyle since
  ....
- I haven't been to the cinema for
  ....

Comparatives & superlatives

3 Write six sentences about people in your family. Use comparatives and superlatives.

1 old
2 difficult
3 easy
4 young
5 busy
6 small
7 interesting
8 good at cooking

young – The youngest person in my family is Faustina. She's only two!

FUNCTIONAL LANGUAGE

Catching up

1 **a** Complete the sentences with the words in the box.

back	going	missed	see	soon	tell

1 We must meet up again ....
2 I've got lots to .... you.
3 It's great to .... you again.
4 Welcome ....
5 I've .... you.
6 How's it .... ?

b 🔊 R5 Listen and check. Then choose one of the sentences and continue the conversation.

■ LOOKING BACK

- How many people live in your home? Can you describe them using language from this unit?
- Are you similar to your family? Compare yourself to a member of your family.
- Have you ever had an experience similar to a person in this unit? What happened? How did you feel?

VOCABULARY
Education & learning

1 Add as many words as you can to the word maps.

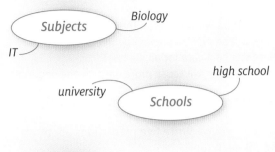

2 💬 Take turns to describe three words from 1. Can you guess which words your partner is describing?

'2 + 2.' 'Is it Maths?'
'Study of plants and animals.' 'Is it Biology?'

-ed/-ing adjectives

3 Choose the correct words. Complete the sentences with your ideas.

1 .... is a really *fascinated / fascinating* subject.
2 I felt *pleased / pleasing* when ....
3 One of the most *interested / interesting* things I've done is ....
4 I usually feel *tired / tiring* when ....
5 I think my .... is *confused / confusing* because ....

Adjectives + prepositions

4 Match adjectives 1–6 to prepositions a–f.

1	bored	a	about
2	different	b	at
3	excited	c	from
4	good	d	in
5	interested	e	with
6	similar	f	to

5 a Choose four adjectives + prepositions from 4. Use them in four different sentences about people or things connected with school.

Mrs Green is different from my other teachers. Her lessons are really funny!

b 💬 Work in pairs. Compare your sentences. Explain why these things or people are important to you.

GRAMMAR
Present continuous & *going to*

1 a Fill in the diary with your plans for the weekend.

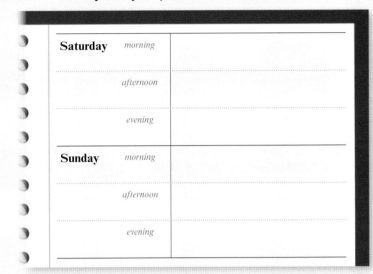

b 💬 Work in pairs. Tell your partner about your plans. Use the present continuous and *going to*.

Must & *have to*

2 a Complete the sentences with *must, mustn't, have to* or *don't have to* so that they're true for your country.

1 All children .... go to school.
2 Most school students .... wear a uniform.
3 Students .... stay at school until they're 16.
4 University students .... study for three years.
5 Primary school students .... study English.

b 💬 Work in groups. Discuss the sentences. Do you agree with the statements?

FUNCTIONAL LANGUAGE
Sounding polite

1 Write the requests more politely.

1 Tell me your address.
2 Lend me your pen.
3 Help me with my homework.
4 Tell me the answers to the exercises on this page.
5 Come for a coffee with me.

2 🔊 R6 Listen and compare your answers. Then act out the conversations with your partner.

◼ LOOKING BACK

- What was your last English lesson like? What was the most interesting thing you learnt?
- What must you do tonight? What else are you going to do?
- Do you have to go to school or work tomorrow? What are you going to do there?

Vocabulary
Help

1 a Complete the jobs and services.

1 ambulance ....
2 charity ....
3 emergency ....
4 police ....
5 help ....
6 fire ....

b Which do you think is the most important? Why?

2 a Work in pairs. How many root words can you think of that take the suffix a) *-ful*? b) *-less*?

b Join another pair. Compare your answers. How many words do you have in total?

Senses

3 a Which verbs of senses 1–5 do we usually use to talk about the things in the box?

clothes and haircuts   food   music   people

1 taste   2 feel   3 look   4 sound   5 smell

b Use an adjective to describe an example of each thing in 3a.

food – Chocolate cake tastes really great.

Health problems

4 a What advice could you give people with these problems?

1 I have a headache.
2 My throat hurts.
3 My tooth hurts.
4 I hurt my arm in an accident.

b 💬 Work in pairs. Put the sentences in order (1 = most serious, 4 = least serious). Does your partner agree with your order?

Grammar
Modal verbs: *can/can't, should/shouldn't*

1 a Write the words in order to make questions.

1 rich more people poor give money people to Should ?
2 young Can find people country in your work ?
3 work shouldn't people fewer Why hours ?

b 💬 Work in groups. Ask and answer the questions.

Modal verbs: *will, may, might*

2 a Change the sentences using the words in the box so that the sentences express your personal opinion.

I don't think   I think   may   might   not

1 In the future we will live on the moon.
2 There will be more homeless people in the world.
3 There will be a cure for all illnesses.
4 Rich countries will cause more harm to the environment.

b 💬 Work in groups. Discuss your opinions.

3 a Work in groups. Write five predictions about the future for each topic.

1 medicine   4 health
2 the environment   5 education
3 work

b Swap your predictions with another group. Put the other group's ideas in order from *most likely to happen* to *least likely to happen*.

Functional language
Advice

1 a Read the pieces of advice. What do you think the problems were?

1 You should go back and ask her to fix it. It looks awful.
2 I'll help you. Why don't you ask a couple of other friends to come over and help too?
3 What about saying you're sorry to your dad? That should help.
4 You shouldn't go somewhere without a recommendation! Ask people, or you could look for a review online.
5 Call an ambulance immediately!

b 🔊R7 Listen and check. What other information did you hear?

2 💬 Work in pairs. Give another piece of advice for each situation in 1a.

■ Looking back

- Which section in this unit did you find a) the most useful? b) the most interesting? Why?
- In this unit, which problem did you find the most serious or difficult? Why?
- Make a prediction about your English learning in the future and compare with your partner.

READING & SPEAKING

1 a Read the online post. How does Tadzio feel about his English exam?

From: Tadzio89	Hello! I'd like some advice. I've got a really important English exam next month. My friends seem quite relaxed about it, but I'm terrified. I'm having nightmares about it! Any ideas?

b Work in pairs. Discuss how you usually feel about tests and exams.

2 Read the replies. Who talks about

1 the month before the exam?   2 the night before the exam?   3 the day of the exam?

From: erikhaakon	Try revising with friends. You can test each other, practise your speaking – and have a bit of fun, too! But don't do this the night before the exam. You'll get too stressed!
From: Easy_going_Alix	Don't panic! You've got lots of time. You should write a study plan for the month before the exam. Give details. Don't just write 'English – all week' – that's scary! Write 'the present perfect, Friday, 6 p.m. to 7.30 p.m.' You'll be amazed how much you can learn in the time!
From: Positive_thinker	Nightmares? That's bad. Start looking at your notes now, and read them regularly. I use highlighter pens to colour the most important information – it helps me to remember it. I always use an orange highlighter pen. I read that orange is the best colour for thinking!
From: Red_rose	Don't do lots of revision in the evening before your exam. You should go to bed early.
From: mjm556	It's really important to stay calm in the exam. If you aren't sure about a question, don't panic! Give your best answer or just guess. And make sure you answer all of the questions. It's always better to write something than to write nothing.

3 a Read the replies again. What do you think are the best ideas?

b Work in pairs. Compare your ideas and choose the three best ideas.

WRITING

4 a Work in pairs. Write an 'exam tips' poster. Include the three headings in **2**. Give at least two pieces of advice for each heading.

b Compare your posters with another pair. Add one more tip to their poster.

5 Work in groups. How many of the tips do you already do? What things are you going to try?

■ QUICK CHECK

Complete the checklist below.

Can you...	Yes, I can.	Yes, more or less.	I need to look again.
1 talk about your past experiences?	☐	☐	☐
2 compare people, places and things?	☐	☐	☐
3 talk about future plans?	☐	☐	☐
4 ask for information on the telephone?	☐	☐	☐
5 give advice?	☐	☐	☐
6 talk about your abilities?	☐	☐	☐
7 describe your feelings?	☐	☐	☐
8 talk about future possibilities?	☐	☐	☐

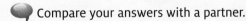 Compare your answers with a partner.

- What else do you know now after studying units 4–6?
- Do you need to look again at any of the sections?
- Do you need any extra help from your teacher?

7 SWITCHED ON

a

b

c

1 💬 Work in pairs. Look at the photos and answer the questions.

- What's the connection between the photos? What's happening in each one?
- When you go to a restaurant do you like to serve yourself or do you prefer a waiter/waitress? Why?
- Do you think the decoration and atmosphere in a restaurant can affect the way you eat? If yes, how?

2 a 🔊 7.1 Listen to an interview about the two restaurants. What is unusual about them?

b Listen again and make notes on what the speakers say about:

1 cameras
2 decisions people make about food
3 lighting and decoration

3 a Listen again. Complete the statements with Inamo restaurant (I) or Wageningen University (W).

1 .... have invented a new system for ordering food.
2 .... have discovered lots of things about how we eat.
3 .... are experimenting with new ideas about design.
4 .... test new food.
5 .... research why people eat what they do.

b 💬 Which of these restaurants would you prefer to go to? If neither, why not?

4 Look at A in the KEY VOCABULARY PANEL ▪️. Work in pairs to complete the task.

5 Read transcript 7.1 on page 165. Underline examples of *make* and *do* and the nouns that follow. Complete B in the KEY VOCABULARY PANEL ▪️.

6 a Complete the gaps in the questions with *make* or *do*.

1 Have you .... any changes in your life recently?
2 Have you .... a lot of work since last week?
3 Did you .... any studying last night?
4 Do you think you are .... progress in your English?
5 What kind of activities do you most enjoy .... in class?

b 💬 Work in pairs. Ask and answer the questions. When your answer is yes, give more details.

7 💬 Share your discoveries about your partner with the class.

▪️ KEY VOCABULARY

Science & research

A Verbs & nouns

● Complete the table with the correct verb or noun.

Verb	Noun
....	a creation
decide	a ....
....	a discovery
experiment	an ....
....	an invention
research	....
test	a ....

● When is the verb and noun the same word? Is the pronunciation the same?

B *Make & do*

● Which five nouns in A can we use with *make* or *do*? Add these to the gaps below.

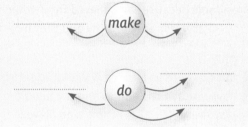

● Complete the gaps with the nouns in the box.

changes	a choice	food
progress	work	your best

make → .... , ... ,
.... , ...
do → .... , ...

NOTICE *MAKE/DO*

Make is often connected with communication.
make a comment/a decision/an excuse/a point
Do is often used with everyday activities.
do the/some cleaning/driving/gardening/shopping/studying

SPEAKING & READING

1 💬 Work in pairs. How often do you do these things?

- do crosswords (or other wordgames)
- learn a new skill
- play computer games
- do sudoku
- spend time with family and friends

I spend time with friends every weekend.

2 a 💬 Which of the activities in **1** do you think is best for keeping your mind alert? Why?

b Read the article and check your answers.

3 Read the article again. Choose the best photo, a or b, to match each paragraph.

4 Complete the gaps in the article with the sentences.

a ~~But can we really do this?~~
b Their research showed that these games had *some* benefits.
c It's a great idea for elderly people like Lottie.
d And more importantly, they will have a lot of fun doing it!
e The games won't help you do any of these things!
f Now, I can't put it down!

Most of us would like to be more intelligent and have better memories, wouldn't we? (1) __a__ *It seems that we can! Scientists now believe we can 'exercise' our brains just like our bodies, to help them be at their best.*

1 Some computer game designers have invented special brain training games. These games have become popular with people of all ages – not just teenagers. Lottie, 88, is a big fan. 'Until a year ago I couldn't even imagine using a games console. (2) _____ I like playing these games, and I love getting the highest score.' Lottie lives in a home for people aged 65 and over. The manager of the home agreed to buy the games for the residents because she believed they would be good for them. '(3) _____ Residents stay healthy and they have fun too. It's perfect!'

2 But do these games really work? Scientists have studied the games and the people who play them. (4) _____ People who played the games every day were slightly better at doing quizzes than people who didn't play the games. However, don't buy a game if you want to have a bigger IQ, pass all your exams or get a better job. (5) _____

3 Scientists have found that there are better (and cheaper) ways that we can keep our minds fit. Some experts recommend learning a new subject. One of the best things you can do doesn't cost anything at all – everyone can afford to do it! Research shows that people who enjoy spending time with family and friends are usually the ones in best mental health in their old age. (6) _____

GRAMMAR

1 a Complete the sentences from the article with the correct verbs.

1 Most of us would like .... more intelligent.
2 I like .... these games.

b Choose the correct option for 1 and 2 in the GRAMMAR PANEL ▪ .

2 Find the verbs below in the article and <u>underline</u> the verb that follows. Add the verbs to A or B in the GRAMMAR PANEL ▪ .

Introduction & paragraph 1: *imagine, love, agree*
Paragraphs 2 & 3: *want, recommend, afford, enjoy*

3 a Read the opinions. Write the correct form of the verbs.

~~do~~ go look play read spend stay

1 *I wouldn't enjoy* (1) ....*doing*.... *these kinds of puzzles because I hate computers! I use one all day at work so I don't want* (2) .... *at a computer in my free time.*

2 *Computer games can be fun, but I wouldn't recommend* (3) .... *them every day . I love* (4) .... *books or* (5) .... *to museums, and I think they're much better for you!*

3 *I'd like* (6) .... *healthy when I get old, and I'll definitely consider* (7) .... *some money on brain training games in a few years.*

b 🔊))) 7.2 Listen and check.

4 💬 Work in pairs. Do you agree or disagree with the opinions? Why?

🔲 THE -*ING* FORM & *TO* + INFINITIVE

We sometimes use an -*ing* form or *to* + infinitive after some verbs.
She really <u>likes doing</u> puzzles.
I <u>want to buy</u> a brain training game.

A We use (1)-*ing* form / *to* + infinitive after these verbs:

like, look forward to, consider, ...
*He **doesn't mind using** a computer at work.*

B We use (2)-*ing* form / *to* + infinitive after these verbs:

would like, decide, ...
*She **decided to buy** a brain training game.*

See page 146 for grammar reference and more practice.

SPEAKING

1 a Read the questionnaire. Choose the answer that is most true for you.

○ **1 What do you enjoy doing to keep your mind alert?**
○ **a** reading **b** taking exercise **c** sleeping

○ **2 Which of these things would you recommend?**
○ **a** owning a pet **b** taking up a new interest
○ **c** seeing more of family and friends

○ **3 Which of these lifestyles would you consider?**
○ **a** working from home **b** working in another country
○ **c** not working any more

○ **4 What are you looking forward to doing next year?**
○ **a** travelling **b** spending more time at home
○ **c** doing more sports

○ **5 What would you like to do in the future?**
○ **a** run a marathon **b** write a book **c** travel the world

○ **6 When do you decide to do things?**
○ **a** at the last minute **b** with a lot of planning
○ **c** after a lot of consideration

b Add one more question of your own.

2 a 💬 Interview other students in your class. Make a note of their answers.

b Write some conclusions from the questionnaire.

● Almost everybody enjoys taking exercise.
● Some people recommend owning a pet.
● Most people would consider...
● Others are looking forward to...
● Nobody would like to...

3 💬 Share your results with the rest of the class. Find three things you have in common as a class.

The perfect city? How science is helping to improve the places we live in.

1 Musical stations

Many underground stations play classical music. Scientists have found that classical music can make people feel calm. There is less crime at stations which play music than at stations which don't play any music.

2 City sheep

Have you got any farm animals in your city? Maybe you should have! Pollution was a big problem in the city of Curitiba in Brazil. The mayor asked the advice of environment and geography experts. First, he created a big pedestrian zone in the city centre, without any cars. Next, he created big urban parks. Some sheep live in the parks and keep the grass short – and they're much better for the planet than lawnmowers!

3 Glass hospitals

Doctors and politicians would like people to spend less time in hospital, as it can be very expensive. Medical research has shown that patients who see some sunlight every day get better more quickly. Some modern hospitals now have glass walls, so that people can use this free 'medicine'.

4 Roads without signs

In some towns, like Bohmte in Germany, there aren't any signs or marks on the roads. Psychologists have discovered that this makes traffic slow down, and people drive more safely.

5 Internet everywhere

Technology is an important part of life in many cities, but sometimes it's hard to read your emails when you're travelling – especially if there are no internet cafés nearby. Taipei was the first city to become 'wireless' in 2006. In a wireless city you can go online anywhere, anytime – when you're in the street or the shopping centre. This helps people do business, as well as have more fun!

6 Robot parking

It can be difficult to park in city centres – there often isn't any space! In Japan, engineers have invented a new type of car park to help with the problem. Special machines put cars in boxes on top of each other.

VOCABULARY: cities

1 **a** Look at the picture of a city. In what ways is the picture similar to your hometown? Which of the things in the box can you see? Use a dictionary to help you.

> bank bench bus stop car park hospital library museum park
> pavement pedestrian zone shopping centre underground station

b Do you have any of these things near where you live?

I live opposite a park.
There isn't a pavement outside my house.

READING & SPEAKING

1 Work in pairs. Read the article. Match paragraphs 1–6 to pictures a–f.

2 a Which of the ideas in the text involve

1 increased use of technology?   2 greener ideas?

b Who are the 'professionals' who have recommended the ideas?

3 Match statements a–f to paragraphs 1–6 in the text.

This idea
a uses a new machine.
b offers free internet access.
c uses an idea from the country to solve a problem in the city.
d makes people feel calm.
e makes roads safer.
f improves care for patients in hospital.

4 🗨 Work in pairs. Discuss the questions.

- Which of the ideas do you think is a) the most interesting? b) the strangest? c) the least practical?
- Are any of the ideas in the text similar to ones in your town/city?
- Would you like to see any of the ideas where you live?
- Do you have any suggestions for other changes?

GRAMMAR

1 a Read A and B in the GRAMMAR PANEL ▪️. Look at the words in **bold** below. Decide if they are countable (C) or uncountable (U).

1 There is less crime at **stations** which play music than at stations which don't play any **music**.
2 Have you got any farm **animals** in your city?
3 **Patients** who see some **sunlight** every day get better more quickly.
4 Some modern **hospitals** now have glass walls.
5 Sometimes it's hard to read your **emails** when you're travelling – especially if there are no internet **cafés** nearby.
6 It can be difficult to park in **city centres** – there often isn't any **space**.

b Underline all the examples of *some*, *any* and *no* in 1a. Complete 1–6 in B in the GRAMMAR PANEL ▪️.

2 a What is your town or city like? Write six sentences using the ideas in the box.

architecture   atmosphere   parks
public transport   restaurants   roads
schools   shops   traffic   weather

There are lots of really good music shops.

b 🗨 Work in pairs. Compare your sentences. Who is the most positive about their town?

3 Write four questions to ask the scientists in the text in READING 1. Use the question form.

Do you think there will be any … in the future?

4 a Work in pairs. Swap questions. Imagine you are a scientist and write your predictions.

Yes, I think there will be some…
No, I don't think there will be any…

b 🗨 Discuss your predictions. Which do you think will *definitely* happen?

▪️ COUNTABLE & UNCOUNTABLE NOUNS, *SOME & ANY*

A Countable & uncountable nouns

Countable nouns have a singular OR plural form:
a station, stations; an animal, animals. We can use *a(n)* with the singular form of countable nouns.

Uncountable nouns only have one form:
traffic (NOT ~~traffics~~), *music* (NOT ~~musics~~) with uncountable nouns. We use a singular verb form after an uncountable noun.
*The traffic **is** terrible today.*
*Sunlight **makes** you feel better.*

B *Some/Any*

1 We use *some* and *any* with
- uncountable nouns e.g. *traffic*
- plural countable nouns e.g. *cars*

2 We usually use (1) *some / any* in positive sentences.
(2) _____ robots will do your housework.

3 We usually use (3) *some / any* in questions.
Do you have (4) _____ *predictions for the future?*

4 We usually use (5) *some / any* with *not*. *Not + any* has the same meaning as *no*.
There isn't (6) _____ *traffic. There's no traffic.*

See page 146 for grammar reference and more practice.

PRONUNCIATION: three- and four-syllable words

1 a Look at the words in the box. Which have

a three syllables?   b four syllables?

environment   hospital   important   musical
pedestrian   politician   psychologist   technology

b 🔊)) 7.3 Listen and check.

2 Listen again and write the words in the correct column.

Three syllables		Four syllables	
Ooo	oOo	oOoo	ooOo

■ PRACTISE QUANTIFIERS
■ TALK ABOUT TECHNOLOGY

SPEAKING

1 a Work in pairs. Look at photos a–f. Name the gadgets.

b 🗨 Do you use any of the gadgets? If yes, how often? What other kinds of technology do you use?

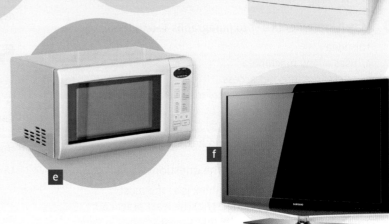

2 🗨 Put gadgets a–f in order of importance for you. Compare with a partner. Are there any pieces of technology you couldn't live without?

LISTENING

1 a 🗨 Work in pairs. Look at the photos of three people who don't use technology every day. Complete the sentences with your ideas.

1 Fontez doesn't use technology because he wants to help
....

2 When she uses technology, Bella feels ....

3 Kerim lives in a place which doesn't have ....

b 🔊 7.4 Listen and check. Correct your ideas.

2 Listen again. Are the sentences true or false? Correct the false sentences.

Fontez
enjoys shopping. *False. He hates shopping.*
1 would like to get a computer.
....
2 doesn't have any technology at home.
....

Bella
3 goes out a lot.
....
4 wants to move to Africa.
....

Kerim
5 doesn't mind living without technology.
....
6 is planning to be a scientist.
....

3 🗨 Compare your answer in pairs and discuss why the people feel like this.

Fontez hates shopping because he thinks it's boring.

4 a How would you feel about not having technology in your life? Write sentences about three things that would be different.

I wouldn't watch any TV!

b 🗨 Compare your answers. Are any of your ideas the same?

GRAMMAR

1 Read the expressions. Are the nouns in **bold** countable (C) or uncountable (U)?

1 How much **technology** do I use? *(U)*
2 lots of energy
3 a little **money**
4 a lot of **information**
5 too many **hours** a day
6 not much **fun**
7 a few **people** feel sick
8 not many **places**
9 lots of **countries**
10 a lot of **gadgets**
11 too much **time**

2 a Which of the underlined expressions mean

1 a large quantity? 2 a small quantity?

b Complete 1–5 in the GRAMMAR PANEL ▪ with the remaining underlined expressions.

> **NOTICE** TOO MUCH/TOO MANY
>
> *Too much* and *too many* always have a negative meaning. They mean 'more than you need'.
>
> *I send a lot of texts.* (This can be good or bad.)
> *I send too many texts.* (This is bad. I should not send this number of texts.)

3 a Choose the correct option to complete the sentences.

1 I don't use *much / a few* electricity at home.
2 I only send a *few / little* texts a week.
3 I play *a lot of / not much* computer games.
4 I spend too *much / many* time online.
5 I don't take *many / a little* photos.

b Which sentences are true for you?

4 a Write questions about technology using *How much* or *How many*. Add one question of your own.

1 emails send every day ?
   How many emails do you send every day?
2 gadgets be in your bedroom ?
3 time spend watching TV every night ?
4 music have on your MP3 player ?

b 💬 Work in pairs. Ask and answer your questions.

> ## ▪ QUANTIFIERS
>
> We use these expressions with countable nouns (*phones, heaters*):
>
> *How many?, a lot of, too many,* (1) ....
> (2) ....
>
> We use these expressions with uncountable nouns (*electricity, health*):
>
> *a lot of, a little,* (3) .... (4) ....
>
> We use these expressions with countable OR uncountable nouns:
>
> *lots of,* (5) ....
>
> *See page 146 for grammar reference and more practice.*

VOCABULARY & SPEAKING: technology

1 Look at the photo and quickly read the advert. Complete the name of the charity.

One L _ _ _ _ _   per C _ _ _ _ _

We believe that every child in the world should have their own laptop. Why? Well, because...

• you can read thousands of books on a laptop.
• children can start learning as soon as they switch on their laptop – anywhere, anytime!
• all children enjoy surfing the internet and having fun.

But not many of the world's children can afford to buy a laptop. That's where you can help. If you buy one laptop, we promise to GIVE another laptop to a child – for free!

Give us a call or send us an email today.

2 💬 Work in pairs. Discuss the questions.

• What does the charity want you to do? Why?
• Do you think there are any pieces of technology which *everyone* should have? What are they?

3 a Match 1–5 to a–e.

1 **give** someone
2 **surf**
3 **switch** something
4 **send** someone
5 **download** something

a from the internet
b an email
c a call
d on OR off
e the internet

b 💬 Work in groups. Talk about the last time you did these things. The rest of the group asks questions with *Who, What, Why* and *Which websites*.

TUNE IN

1 Work in groups. Do you use social networking sites on the internet? How often do you use them?

2 Read the blog post about social networking sites.
1 Is the writer's opinion positive or negative?
2 Why does she think this?

> ⬤ ⬤ ⬤
>
> You know how I feel about social networking sites, right? Well, it seems the scientists agree! I read an interesting article by Professor Greenfield today. She believes the sites are bad, even dangerous, for users. Why? Well, firstly, they encourage us to spend lots of time alone, which is unhealthy. Secondly, they encourage us to do and say childish things. I can't stand reading all those stupid 'status updates'. Things like: 'I'm feeling ☹ today' or 'Did you see last night's show? LOL.' Who cares?! In my opinion, the government should ban all social networking sites. What does everyone else think?

3 a Read the blog posts. Who is a) for social networking sites? b) against them? c) both for and against them?

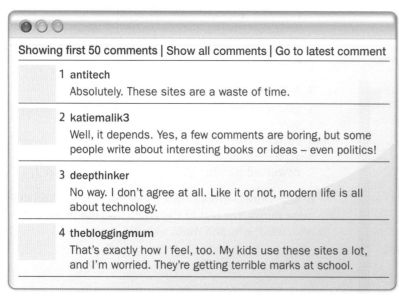

> ⬤ ⬤ ⬤
>
> Showing first 50 comments | Show all comments | Go to latest comment
>
> **1 antitech**
> Absolutely. These sites are a waste of time.
>
> **2 katiemalik3**
> Well, it depends. Yes, a few comments are boring, but some people write about interesting books or ideas – even politics!
>
> **3 deepthinker**
> No way. I don't agree at all. Like it or not, modern life is all about technology.
>
> **4 thebloggingmum**
> That's exactly how I feel, too. My kids use these sites a lot, and I'm worried. They're getting terrible marks at school.

b Which comment do you agree with most?

FOCUS ON LANGUAGE

4 Read the blog post again.
1 Which verbs and expressions does the writer use to talk about opinions?
2 How does the writer ask for other people's opinions?

5 Read the comments in 3a again. Complete the table with more expressions for agreeing and disagreeing.

Agree	*I agree with you.*
	(1)
	(2)
Agree a bit	*Maybe, but...*
	(3)
	(4)
Disagree	*Definitely not.*
	(5)
	(6)

6 Do you agree with the blogger? Write your own comment for the blog post.

> ❝ **Intonation: agreeing and disagreeing** ❞
>
> ◀)) 7.5 Listen and repeat. Then <u>underline</u> the main stress in these expressions.
> 1 *I completely agree with you.*
> 2 *No, I don't agree.*
> 3 *Absolutely not.*
> 4 *I definitely agree with that.*
>
> What kind of words do we stress when we're strongly
> a agreeing with something?
> b disagreeing with something?

OVER TO YOU

7 a ⬤ Read transcript 7.5 on page 166. Take turns to read out the blue sentences.

b Say if you agree or disagree, explaining why.

8 When was the last time you disagreed with someone? What did you disagree about?

TUNE IN

1 🗨 Work in pairs. Look at the image from an article. What do you think the article is about?

> health   the environment
> psychology   technology   transport

2 🔊 7.6 Listen and check.

3 a Listen again and choose the correct options to complete the summary.

1 Geisy *is going to stop eating / has never eaten* meat.
2 He watched an online video of the President of the *Brazilian / Argentinian* Vegetarian Society.
3 Marly thinks that *cars / cows* are worse for the environment than *cars / cows*.
4 They produce dangerous gases, and they're also making the Amazon *rainforest / river* smaller.
5 Geisy's friend is going to *stop eating / eat less* meat.

b 🗨 Work in pairs. What do you think? Should we eat less meat? Discuss your ideas.

Which one of these contributes more to **Global Warming?**

PREPARE FOR TASK

4 a Read the discussion tips. Complete the headings with *listener* and *speaker*.

A good .... should:

1 give an introduction to the topic
2 give reasons for their opinions (*I think… because…*)
3 ask for other people's opinions (*What do you think?*)

A good .... should:

4 ask questions to learn more about a topic (*What about… ?*)
5 express interest (*That's interesting!*)
6 agree or disagree with what the other person says (*Absolutely!*)

b Can you think of any more useful tips?

5 a Look at the expressions from the conversation you've just heard. Match them to 1–6 in 4a.

- Really? Why?
- So that's why…
- I watched a really interesting video…
- What about you?
- I'm not sure I agree…
- That's terrible.

b Can you think of any more expressions like these?

TASK

6 a 🗨 Work in pairs. Choose one of the issues below.

- a science, health, technology or environment issue that you find interesting
OR
- a science issue from this unit (e.g. *Are brain training games good for you?*)

b Make notes about the topic and your opinions. Include useful information and expressions.

7 🗨 Find a new partner. Take turns to discuss your topics. Be a good listener as well as a good speaker.

REPORT BACK

8 Write a short summary of your discussion. Use 3a to help you.

9 🗨 Compare your summaries in a small group. What do people agree and disagree about? Which topic do people disagree about the most?

➡ Go to Review C, Unit 7, p. 102   ➡ Go to Writing bank 4, p. 155   **81**

8 REAL OR FAKE?

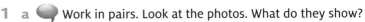

1 a 💬 Work in pairs. Look at the photos. What do they show?

   b Match photos a–c to captions 1–3. Use a dictionary to help you.
   1 a photo montage   2 a fake object   3 a magic trick

2 What is the connection between the photos and the unit title?

3 a 🔊 8.1 Listen to two people talking about the photos. What order do they mention them in?

   b Look at the sentences. Which photo does each one refer to? Listen again and check.

   1 How did they **fake** it then?
   2 The first time I <u>saw</u> it I thought it was **genuine**.
   3 No matter how carefully I <u>look</u>, I really can't <u>see</u> how they do it.
   4 This photo <u>looks</u> **authentic** to me.
   5 It doesn't <u>look</u> very **realistic** to me!
   6 It was taken before the days of **computer-generated** images.
   7 There must be some kind of trick to it!
   8 OK, I see. That's really clever. It had me fooled.
   9 A lot of people believed it was **real**.

True or false?

A Adjectives

● Put the adjectives in the box in the correct category.

> authentic   computer-generated   fake
> genuine   real   realistic

True: ....

False: ....

● Which adjective can you also use as a verb?

● Look at these common collocations with *fake* and *false*. Do you use different words in your language?

fake tan	fake smile
fake fur	false teeth
fake leather	false identity

B Verbs

● Match the verbs in the box to the definitions.

> look   see

1 to notice something using your eyes
2 to understand something
3 to move your eyes towards something so you can see it
4 to seem to be something

4 a Look at the adjectives in **bold** in 3b and complete A in the KEY VOCABULARY PANEL ■.

b 💬 Discuss the question in pairs.

● Have you ever bought something that you thought was real and then you found out it was fake or false?

5 Look at the <u>underlined</u> verbs in 3b and complete B in the KEY VOCABULARY PANEL ■.

6 Read the sayings and answer the questions.

● Which do you think is most appropriate for the photos on page 82? Why?
● Do you have any similar sayings in your language?

7 Do you know of any other fake photos or magic tricks? Tell the class about them.

READING

1 💬 Work in pairs. Look at the pictures. Can you explain what the people are doing? What are the similarities and differences between the pictures?

2 a Quickly read the webpage. Find out the name of the game and how to play it.

   b Read the webpage again. Why is the writer describing the game?

   1 To warn people about a street trick.
   2 To help people play a game better.
   3 To teach people how to make money.

| Home | Hotels | Flights | Restaurants | Holiday Rentals | Holiday Ideas | Write a Review |

Travel tips   [Search]

Travel tip No. 75:

Have you ever seen this game before? You probably have, because the game has been around for about 2,000 years. But you might not know that it is impossible to win this game. Read on and don't lose money on this trick!

The game requires three shells (or bottle caps, plastic cups or match boxes) and a small, soft, round ball. You can play it on almost any flat surface. The person who controls the game (the operator) puts the ball under one of the shells and then quickly moves the shells around. Then the operator asks where the ball is. If the player guesses correctly, he/she wins two times his/her money. If the player doesn't guess correctly, he/she loses the money.

Beware! It is not possible for the player to win the game, if the operator does not want him/her to.

A clever operator can take a ball from under any shell and put it under another shell without the player seeing. This means that you cannot win by watching the movement of the shell or the hands of the operator. The ball will always be under a different shell from the one that you think.

If the operator thinks a player understands the trick or a person just wants to watch, the other people at the table (who are working with the operator) try to move the player away from the table. The shell game (its common name) is quick and simple to set up. It is also quick and easy to put away. So if the police come, the operator simply hides the game in his pockets and walks away.

The shell game is a common game in parts of the world where there are a lot of tourists. Be careful and don't play – you won't win.

a   Budapest 2009

b   *The Conjurer* by Hieronymus Bosch painted in the 1500s

3 Read the webpage again. Are the statements true (T) or false (F)?

   1 The game is modern.
   2 It is played in a place which must be flat.
   3 The ball always stays under the same shell.
   4 It is possible to win if you watch the ball.
   5 The operator likes people to watch.
   6 The game is easy to move to another place.

4 💬 Work in groups. Discuss the questions.

   ● Have you played any games like this?
   ● Are these types of game popular in your country?
   ● Why do you think games like this are often not legal?

GRAMMAR (1)

1 a Match the two parts of the sentences.

1 If the player guesses correctly
2 If the player doesn't guess correctly
3 If the police come

a the operator hides the game in his pockets.
b he/she wins two times his/her money.
c he/she loses the money.

b Check your answers in the article in READING 2.

2 a Look at the sentences in 1a again and answer the questions.

1 Which group of phrases, 1–3 or a–c, describes
   a) a situation? b) the result of the situation?
2 Is the result always the same in each situation?
3 Underline all the verbs. What tense are they?
4 Find two more sentences in the text in READING 2 which include *if*. What is the position of *if* in each sentence?

b Complete 1 and 2 in the GRAMMAR PANEL ▪.

3 Add *if* to the sentences.

1 The weather's bad, we usually go to a shopping centre.
2 We have visitors, we always take them on a tour of the old town.
3 I usually go to the gym three times a week I have time.
4 I love going to the cinema with friends there's a good film on.

4 Complete the sentences so they are true for you.

1 If I have enough time, I ....
2 I often .... if the weather is nice.
3 If my friends are away, I usually ....
4 I don't usually .... I have a lot of work or have to study for an exam.

▪ *IF* + PRESENT SIMPLE (1)

Sentences with *if* have two parts. The *if* part introduces a (1) *result / situation*. The second part explains the (2) *result / situation*.

We use the **present simple** in **both parts of the sentence** when the result of a situation is <u>always true.</u>

Situation	Result
If the player guesses correctly	she wins two times her money.

The part of the sentence with *if* can come first or second.
If the police come, the operator hides the game.
The operator hides the game if the police come.

See page 147 for grammar reference and more practice.

LISTENING

1 a 8.2 Listen to two tourists talking about the shell game. What do they want to do?

b Listen again. How do they think the game operator will respond to their requests?

2 Listen again and complete the extracts.

1 Be really .... If he sees you, he'll pack up and go somewhere else.
2 If you ask him, he'll probably be .... with it.
3 Do you think he'll let me video him if I don't include his .... ?
4 If you film him without asking permission, he'll get really .... !
5 If he's ...., he'll let the next player win. That way you won't learn the .... of his trick.

GRAMMAR (2)

1 a Look at the sentences in LISTENING 2a and answer the questions.

1 Are the speakers talking about a) a result that is always true? b) the probable result of a specific situation?
2 Do they know the result of the situation yet?

b Underline all the verbs in LISTENING 2a and complete 1 and 2 in the GRAMMAR PANEL ▪.

2 Choose the correct form of the verbs to complete the sentences. Then practise the conversations in pairs.

A If *it's / it'll be* a good photo, I *post / I'll post* it on my blog.
B If *he sees / he'll see* it, *he's / he'll be* angry.
A *He isn't / He won't be* angry if *I ask / I'll ask* him first.

A If *it stops / it'll stop* raining tomorrow, *we probably go / we'll probably go* for a picnic.
B If *I finish / I'll finish* my work on time, *I come / I'll come* with you.

3 Complete the sentences so they are true for you.

1 If the weather's nice at the weekend, ...
2 If I don't have any work to do tonight, ...
3 I'll probably .... this evening, if I have time.

▪ *IF* + PRESENT SIMPLE (2)

We use *if* + present simple in the first part of the sentence, and (1) .... in the second part to talk about a <u>probable future result</u>.

Situation	Result
If he sees you	he (2) .... pack up and go.

See page 147 for grammar reference and more practice.

LISTENING

1 💬 Work in pairs. Look at the photo. Where are the people? What are they doing? What are their relationships to each other?

2 🔊 8.3 Listen to the advertisement for a radio show about the people in the photo. Choose the best title.

1 Two sisters who didn't know each other
2 The baby that got heavier
3 The mother who knew the truth
4 The strange letter from my father

3 Listen again. Choose the best options to complete the information about the show.

> ***This American Life*** is about the true story of Marti Miller and Sue McDonald – two girls born in (1)*the same / a different* hospital in (2)*1915 / 1951*. Mary Miller realises that Marti (3)*is / is not* her baby, but her husband does not want to (4)*return / tell* anyone. Mary doesn't tell the girls until they are (5)*34 / 43* years old. Mary writes (6)*an email / a letter* to Sue McDonald to say that Sue is really her (7)*mother / daughter*. Tune in on (8)*Sunday / Monday* at (9)*1 / 10* p.m. to find out what happens.

4 a 💬 Work in groups. Discuss what you think happened to

1 Sue McDonald?
2 Marti Miller?
3 the relationship between Sue and Marti?

b Turn to page 160 to check your answers.

GRAMMAR

1 a Read phrases a–d from the story. Number them 1–4:

1 = I'm sure it's true   2 = I'm sure it's not true
3 = I think it's true   4 = I don't think it's true

a It **might not** be her baby. ....
b It **can't** be her baby. ....
c People **may** think the doctor isn't a good one. ....
d Her baby **must** be with the other family. ....

b Complete 1–8 in the GRAMMAR PANEL .

2 Read sentences 1–4. Match them to the best explanation and second part of the sentence.

1 She must be a doctor,
2 She can't be a doctor,
3 She may not be a doctor,
4 She might be a doctor,

  a because she never works at weekends.
  b because she doesn't know anything about medicine.
  c because I heard someone ask her for medical advice.
  d because her name is Dr Robson and she works in a hospital.

3 Complete the sentences so that they express your opinion.

1 Mary Miller .... be really afraid of her husband.
2 Sue and Marti .... be sad because they didn't know their real mothers.
3 Sue and Marti .... be angry with Mary Miller because she knew the truth.
4 Mary .... feel sorry, because she decided to tell the women.
5 Mary Miller's husband .... be a good father.

4 💬 Work in groups. Discuss your answers in **3** and give reasons for your opinions. Do you have similar ideas?

■ MODAL VERBS: *MUST, CAN'T, MAY, MIGHT*

We can use *must/may/might/can't* + verb to make deductions.

If we are sure that something is true we use (1)................ .

She (2)................ be French. She lives in Paris and speaks French and her parents are French.

If we are sure that something is not true we use (3)................ .

She (4)................ be French. Her parents are German and she doesn't speak French.

If we are not sure, but think that something is possible we use (5)................ or *might*.

She (6)................ be French. She speaks French.

If we think something is not true, but are not certain we use (7)................ or *may not*.

She (8)................ / .... not be French. She lives in Canada.

See page 147 for grammar reference and more practice.

READING

1 a 🗨 Work in pairs. Look at photos a–d. Do you recognise the actor? If so, what do you know about him?

b Identify the different roles in the photos. How do you know?

1 an American Indian   3 a doctor's patient
2 a boxer   4 a psychiatrist

2 Read the first paragraph of a film review. Explain what is happening in the photos.

Leonard Zelig: *The Human Chameleon*

I think Woody Allen's film *Zelig* might be the first *mockumentary* ever filmed. 'What's that?' you ask. Well, Allen uses *real* documentary material, but mixes it with *fictional* material. The whole thing is filmed in black and white which makes it more believable. Allen plays Leonard Zelig in the film. This man's problem is that he has absolutely no identity of his own, so he has developed the ability to change himself, physically and mentally, into the image of whoever he's with.

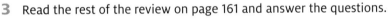

3 Read the rest of the review on page 161 and answer the questions.

1 Why is the film so technically clever?
2 Who else does Zelig become in the film?
3 What is the reviewer's final opinion of the film?

4 🗨 Work in groups. Do you know anyone like Zelig in real life or other fictional material? If so, tell the group how this person changes his/her identity. Why do you think he/she does this?

SPEAKING

1 Make notes about how different you think you are in these situations.

- at work / at school
- with family
- on Facebook / Twitter or other social networking sites
- with strangers
- with close friends

2 🗨 Compare your notes with a partner. Do you think your identity changes a lot in these situations? Which do you think is your 'true' identity? Why?

When I meet people online I'm more confident, but I can be very shy with strangers when I meet them face to face.

NOTICE *BLACK AND WHITE*
We always say 'black and white', never '~~white and black~~'. What do you say in your language? Do you know how to say it in any other languages?

Look at these other expressions with 'and'. Are they in the same order in your language?
bread and butter, salt and pepper, knife and fork, husband and wife

READING

1 💬 Work in pairs. Read the definition of urban legends. Choose the correct options to complete characteristics 1–6.

2 Look at the pairs of photos. Which urban legends do you think they might be about?

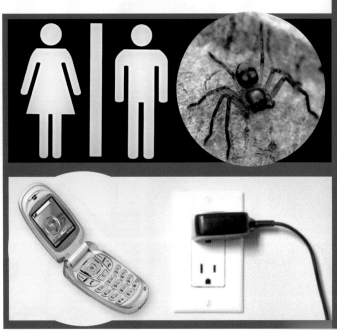

URBAN LEGENDS are popular stories. They are usually about funny, scary or strange events which people say are true. Typically, the storyteller says that the events really happened to someone, but not to *them*. They say, e.g. 'I heard this from a friend of a friend', to make it seems as if the story is true. Sometimes there is a warning in the story ('Be careful, or this could happen to you!'). People tell the stories face to face, or often by email, so that the stories pass quickly from person to person. A story often changes each time someone tells it, so there are different versions of the same urban legend in many different cultures and languages.

Characteristics of urban legends

1   The storyteller says they are *true* / *false*.
2   The events *always* / *never* happened to the teller.
3   The story is about someone the teller *knows* / *doesn't know*.
4   There is *always* / *sometimes* a message in the story.
5   The stories pass *quickly* / *slowly* from person to person.
6   The story stays the *same* / *changes* over time.

3 a Work in pairs. Student A, read email a. Student B, read email b. Check your ideas in 2. Then choose the best subject line for your story.

> Always keep your mobile phone connected
> You can get sick in a hospital
> Mobile phones can shock you
> Watch out for dangerous spiders
> A new use for your mobile phone
> Take care in public bathrooms
> This restaurant has bad food

b 💬 Tell your partner about your story. Then answer the questions.

1   How did the writer find out about the story?
2   Why did the people in the story have to go to hospital?
3   What does the story tell you to do or not to do?
4   Which characteristics from the definition in READING 1 does each email have?

4 Do you know any other urban legends? Why do you think people tell urban legends? How do they become popular?

a Subject:

I heard this from my brother's friend. You should never answer a mobile phone while the phone is charging!!
A few days ago, a teenager was recharging his mobile phone at home. Just then a call came and he answered it with the phone still connected to the socket. After a few seconds electricity went through the mobile phone and the force of the electric shock threw the teenager to the ground. His parents ran into the room and found him lying on the ground. He was weak and his fingers were burned. They took him to hospital, where he is now recovering.
Mobile phones are an essential modern invention. However, they are also dangerous.

NEVER use a mobile phone while it is plugged in to the electric socket!

SEND THIS TO THE PEOPLE THAT YOU CARE ABOUT.

VOCABULARY:
common collocations with *say* & *tell*

1 **a** Work in pairs. Which words in the box go with a) *say*? b) *tell*? Clue: We use *say* with the actual words that we say and *tell* with a noun, e.g. *tell the time*.

> goodbye   hello   a joke   lies
> sorry   stories   the truth

b Complete the sentences with words from the box.

1 He told a great _____ . Everyone laughed, even my grandmother!
2 My dad always used to tell us great _____ at bedtime.
3 I always try to tell the _____ , even if it gets me into trouble sometimes.
4 A: You know it's wrong to tell _____ , don't you?
   B: Yes, Dad, I'm sorry. I won't do it again.
5 I always hate saying _____ at the end of a holiday.
6 It can be really difficult to say _____ , even when you know you've done something wrong.
7 A: Say _____ to Kate from me when you next see her.
   B: I will do!

2 **a** Ask and answer the questions in pairs.

1 Did your parents tell you bedtime stories? What kind of stories did they tell?
2 Can you think of a situation where it's a good thing to tell a lie?
3 Have you ever got into trouble for telling the truth?
4 In your country, do people always say hello when they walk into a shop or a lift?
5 Which do you find most difficult to say, sorry or goodbye? Why?

b Compare your answers with the rest of the class. Which question created most discussion?

PRONUNCIATION: /əu/

1 8.4 Listen to this sentence. Notice the pronunciation of the *o* in *told*. Then listen again and repeat.

/əu/

He told me an incredible story.

2 **a** Look at the questions. Underline the words with the sound /əu/.

1 When did you last get a new mobile phone?
2 Do you know any good jokes?
3 How many languages can you say 'hello' in?
4 Does it ever get very cold in your home town?

b 8.5 Listen and check. Then listen again and repeat.

3 Work in small groups. Discuss the questions in 2a.

SPEAKING

1 **a** Work in pairs. Look at the pictures. What connection do they have to the lesson title?

b Decide what order the pictures go in. Then practise telling the story. Start with: *A friend of mine once...*

2 **a** Tell the story as a class. Each student tells one line of the story for the next student to continue until the story ends.

b What do you think is the moral (lesson) of this story?

New   Reply   Reply all   Forward | Delete   Junk   Sweep ·   Mark as ·   Move to ·

b Subject:

My colleague told me about something that happened to a friend of hers at the hospital where she works. Three women arrived at hospital on different days, all very sick, with poison in their blood. These women did not know each other, but they had all visited the same restaurant before they became sick. The health department checked the restaurant, but found nothing wrong with the food or water. Then someone became sick who did not eat in the restaurant, but used the bathroom.

A clever scientist inspected the bathroom and found a small spider. He took it to the lab and discovered it was the South American Blush Spider (*arachnius gluteus*). This spider's poison is very strong and they live in cold, dark, wet places.

So please, before you use a public bathroom, take a look for other visitors. It could save your life! And please pass this on to your loved ones.

TUNE IN

1 **a** Work in groups. Look at the photo. Who are the people and what are they talking about?

b 🔊 8.6 Listen and check.

2 Read the sentences from the conversation. Which are warnings and which are promises?

1 If you don't work harder, you'll fail this course.
2 Your grades are very low. Be careful!
3 If you give me your essay by tomorrow, I'll give it back to you by Monday.

3 🔊 8.7 Listen to six people. Which are warnings (W) and which are promises (P)?

1 .... 2 .... 3 ....

4 .... 5 .... 6 ....

FOCUS ON LANGUAGE

4 Listen again and complete the phrases.

1 Be ....! You mustn't play here. It's dangerous.
2 If you don't .... more carefully, you'll have an ....
3 If you sit quietly, ... play with you later.
4 I'll drive next time if you .... me to.
5 .... out for that hole in the road!
6 .... that. And don't .... or I'll take you home.

5 Decide which phrases in **4** best fit the photos. Compare with a partner.

6 Complete this table of warnings and promises.

don't   I'll   be   out   I'm

Warnings	Promises
• .... careful!	• If .... not busy, ...
• Watch .... (for)...!	come and see you.
• .... do that!	
• If you don't..., you'll...	
• If you..., you won't...	

Look at the warnings. Practise saying them a) gently, b) with urgency.

Be careful! Watch out for the glass!

🔊 8.8 Listen to two ways of saying the warnings. Which sounds more urgent, a) or b)? Why?

Listen again and repeat the warnings using the same intonation.

OVER TO YOU

7 **a** 💬 Work in pairs. Think of a promise or warning for each situation. Write what the person says.

b Compare your ideas with another pair.

8 Think of three promises or warnings you have made or someone has made to you. Tell your partner about them.

TUNE IN

1 Work in pairs. Look at the photo. Do you think the man is real? Why/Why not? Do you know who he is?

2 Read this question sent to an online teenage forum. What kind of advice does Dario need?

Dario

I need your advice. I look at photos of men in fashion magazines and in the media and I feel awful. I try to go to the gym, but I'll never look like Cristiano Ronaldo or anyone like that. I just don't have the time! What do you suggest? Can anybody out there help? Dario

3 Read two replies (1 and 2). What's the difference between the advice they give? Who do you think gives the best advice? Why?

YOUR ANSWERS **Topic:** Looking attractive

Open

Sort by: ▶ Newest ▶ Most Popular ▶ Fewest Answers

Donatella

Hi Dario,
If you want to look like a footballer, just put lots of gel in your hair and wear make up ;-) Just look in the mirror and see what you would like to improve. It's easy to change things. You might be surprised! Men can now buy a hundred creams for their skin, for example. If you start now, you'll never look old.

Answer #1

Sian

Hi Dario,
You don't need to look like those models or stars! Don't try to look like a model because they're fake. It's all done in Photoshop these days. See this picture of Cristiano? It's a wax model! If you don't have time to do sport, consider walking to college and getting fit that way.
Why don't you just be yourself? Someone will find you attractive if you don't worry about it all the time, honestly!

Answer #2

PREPARE FOR TASK

4 Read the replies again. <u>Underline</u>

1 phrases used to give advice.
2 sentences including *if*.

5 Correct these sentences using the structures in 4.

1 Don't try be someone you are not.
2 If you'll want to look good, just take care of your appearance.
3 Consider to go to the gym.
4 Why you don't get fit?
5 You don't need look like a filmstar.

TASK

6 a Work in pairs. Look at the problems below which appear on a website for teenagers. Choose one and think of some advice to give the person.

- I can't concentrate on my work/studies.
- I don't have any energy.
- I don't do anything in my free time.
- I always fail my exams.

b Write a short blog post giving your advice. Follow the same format as Donatella or Sian's posts.

REPORT BACK

7 Swap your blog posts with others in the class. Whose advice do you think is the best? Why?

➜ Go to Review C, Unit 8, p. 103

9 MAKING ENDS MEET

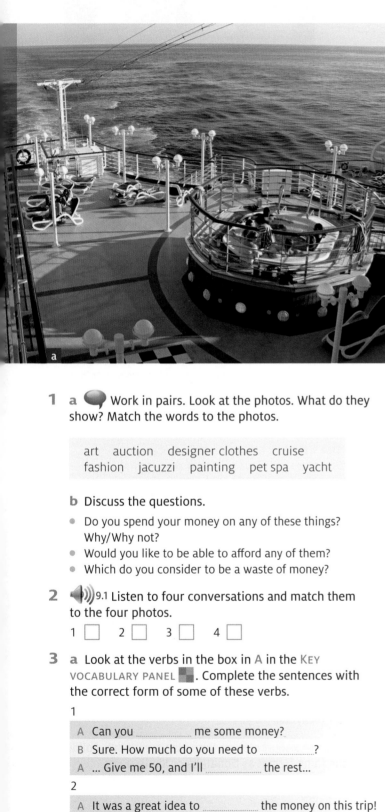

1 a 🗨 Work in pairs. Look at the photos. What do they show? Match the words to the photos.

art   auction   designer clothes   cruise
fashion   jacuzzi   painting   pet spa   yacht

b Discuss the questions.

- Do you spend your money on any of these things? Why/Why not?
- Would you like to be able to afford any of them?
- Which do you consider to be a waste of money?

2 🔊 9.1 Listen to four conversations and match them to the four photos.

1 ☐   2 ☐   3 ☐   4 ☐

3 a Look at the verbs in the box in **A** in the KEY VOCABULARY PANEL ▨. Complete the sentences with the correct form of some of these verbs.

1

A Can you _____ me some money?
B Sure. How much do you need to _____?
A ... Give me 50, and I'll _____ the rest...

2

A It was a great idea to _____ the money on this trip!
B ... well, we _____ a lot of money this year.
A And, of course, we _____ all that money, too...

3

A It's too much money to _____...
   I don't want to _____ our money.

4

A How much does this handbag _____?
B $400.
A Oh, I can't really _____ it.

b Listen again and check your answers.

92

KEY VOCABULARY

Money

A Money verbs

afford   borrow   buy   cost   earn   invest
lend   pay for   save   spend   waste   win

- Complete the sentences with the verbs in the box. Use a dictionary to help you.

1 You .... money from work.
2 You .... money in a prize or lottery.
3 You .... money in shops and on things.
4 You .... money in a business.
5 You .... money if you don't spend it well.
6 You .... money when you keep it in the bank and don't use it.
7 If you can .... to .... something, you have enough money to .... it.
8 If something .... a lot, it's expensive.
9 You .... money <u>to</u> someone.
10 You .... money <u>from</u> someone.

> **NOTICE**   *LEND/BORROW*
>
> *Lend* is when <u>you give</u> something to somebody (for a period of time). *Borrow* is when <u>someone gives you</u> something that you need (for a period of time).

B Money nouns

- Answer the questions with the words in the box. More than one answer is possible and some words answer more than one question. Use a dictionary to help you.

bank account   bills   cash   credit card
loan   mortgage   rent   salary

1 Which do you keep in your wallet? ....
2 Which can you get from a bank? ....
3 Which do you have to pay regularly? ....
4 Which is usually paid into your bank account?
....

4 Look at A in the KEY VOCABULARY PANEL ▓ again. Work in pairs to complete the task.

5 a 🔊))9.2 Look at the photos again. Listen to four people responding to the photos. Which speakers agree with this way of spending money? Which disagree?

b Listen again. Who makes these points?

1 It's good to think about the future. ☐
2 It's OK to spend money if you have it. ☐
3 Something can be more expensive than you first think. ☐
4 There might be a problem later. ☐

6 Work in pairs. Read transcript 9.2 on page 166 and complete B in the KEY VOCABULARY PANEL ▓.

7 Complete the sentences to show your opinion with words from A or B in the KEY VOCABULARY PANEL ▓. More than one word is possible.

1 It is better to pay by .... than with a ....
2 You should never .... or .... money.
3 The best way to .... money is to buy a house.
4 To .... money is better than .... it.

a   b

READING

1 💬 Look at the photos. Answer the questions with your opinion.

- Where does he live?
- What does he have in his home?
- What sort of lifestyle does he have?

2 Read the article about the man in the photos. Answer the questions.

1 What is a freeconomist?
2 Tick the things that Mark has.

    a   a place to live   d   a car   g   a computer
    b   energy   e   a well-paid job   h   a bank account
    c   food   f   a bathroom

3 Mark the statements that are true (T) or false (F). Correct the false statements.

1 Mark paid for his caravan.
    F He found one that nobody wanted.
2 He receives money to work on the farm.
3 He has electricity in his caravan.
4 He makes a lot of phone calls.
5 He buys toothpaste.
6 He gets food in four different ways.
7 He prefers living without money.
8 He thinks his way of life is bad for the planet.

Mark Boyle is a 30-year-old freeconomist. A freeconomist is somebody who doesn't use money. But how is this possible? And how did Mark make the change to living without money?

The first thing he needed was somewhere to live. Luckily, he found a caravan that nobody wanted. Although Mark doesn't work for money, he volunteers on a farm three days a week in exchange for a place to put his caravan. As he can't any pay bills for his home, he had to find a way to get energy: he burns wood for heating, he uses olive oil cans for cooking, and he has a solar panel to collect energy from the sun to make electricity.

His caravan has lights, a laptop and a mobile phone (though he can only receive calls, he can't make them). Mark washes in a river (without soap) and uses natural things like fish bones and seeds as toothpaste.

He grows his own food on the farm where he lives, or finds wild food such as mushrooms and berries. He also gets waste food from restaurants or shops and exchanges food with other people. He owns a bike and cycles everywhere he needs to go. His clothes come from a free website.

Mark says that he is a happier person now that he lives this way, and he wants to continue living without money. 'It does have challenges, but I don't have the stress of bank accounts, bills, traffic jams and long hours in a job I don't enjoy.'

Freeconomists like Mark say their way of life can help save the planet from climate change and pollution. As Mark explains, 'There's so much waste. If we all grew our own food, we would eat everything. If we all made our own tables and chairs, we wouldn't throw them away. If we had to clean our own drinking water, we wouldn't waste it.'

LISTENING

1 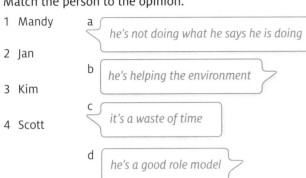9.3 Listen to four people talking about Mark Boyle. Which people agree with what he is doing?

Mandy ☐   Jan ☐   Kim ☐   Scott ☐

2 Match the person to the opinion.

1 Mandy

2 Jan

3 Kim

4 Scott

a *he's not doing what he says he is doing*

b *he's helping the environment*

c *it's a waste of time*

d *he's a good role model*

GRAMMAR

1 a Match the two parts of the sentences.

1 If we all grew our own food,

2 If we all made our own tables and chairs,

3 If we had to clean our own drinking water,

a we wouldn't waste it.

b we would eat everything.

c we wouldn't throw them away.

b Look at the article again and check your answers.

2 a Look at the first half of the sentences in 1 and answer the questions.

1 Is Mark Boyle talking about a situation that
a) already exists or is real? b) he is imagining?

2 Underline the verbs. What tense are they in?

b Look at the second half of the sentences.

1 What verb form is used?

2 Are the sentences describing a) an imaginary situation? b) the imagined result?

3 Choose the correct option to complete 1–4 in the GRAMMAR PANEL ■.

4 a Choose the correct verb to complete the questions and answers.

Q If ⁽¹⁾*you lived / you'd live* in a caravan, ⁽²⁾*did / would* you stay in the same place?

A No, ⁽³⁾*I travelled / I'd travel* all over the world.

Q ⁽⁴⁾*Did / Would* you be lonely if ⁽⁵⁾*you lived / you'd live* on your own?

A ⁽⁶⁾Yes, but *I got / I'd get* a dog. Then I ⁽⁷⁾*didn't / wouldn't* feel alone.

b Work in pairs. Ask and answer the questions in 4a.

5 a Complete the sentences so they are true for you.

1 If I had more time _____.

2 If I spoke English perfectly _____.

3 If I _____ I'd be really happy!

b Work in pairs. Compare your answers.

IF + PAST SIMPLE

We use sentences with *if* + past simple to talk about ⁽¹⁾*a real / an imaginary* situation. *If* sentences have two parts. We use the first part, *if* + past simple, to ⁽²⁾*introduce the situation / explain the result*.
*If I **lived** in a caravan…*

We use the second part of the sentence to ⁽³⁾*introduce the situation / explain the result*. We use *would* + infinitive. This shows that we are talking about ⁽⁴⁾*a real / an imaginary* situation.
*If I lived in a caravan, I **wouldn't** pay rent. I **would** save money.*

Notice the contracted form of *would: I **would** buy a house → **I'd** buy a house.*

The part of the sentence with *if* can come first or second.
I would buy a house if I won the lottery.

See page 148 for grammar reference and more practice.

NOTICE *IF I WERE…*
We use *If I were you…* to give advice.
If I were you, I'd organise an environment day.

PRONUNCIATION: *would*

1 a 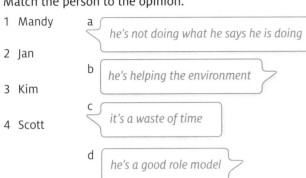9.4 Listen and write the sentences you hear.

b Look at transcript 9.4 on page 166. Underline the contracted forms in 1a. Listen again. Notice the pronunciation of *would* and its contracted forms.

2 Work in pairs. Practise saying the sentences.

SPEAKING

1 Work in groups. Discuss the questions.

- What do you think of Mark Boyle's life?
- Could you live your life this way?
- Do you know anyone whose lifestyle is unconventional?

READING

1 💬 Work in groups. Discuss the questions.

- How popular is the lottery in your country?
- What would you do if you won a lot of money?
- Would you share your money with other people? Who?

2 Look at the photo. Who do you think the people are? What has happened to them? Read the article and check your ideas.

In 1986, a 28-year-old man called William Murphy found a wallet on the street in Montreal, Quebec. The wallet contained $18 and six lottery tickets. It belonged to Jean-Guy Lavigueur, a French-Canadian. William returned the wallet immediately by posting it to Jean-Guy, but he kept the lottery tickets. Later that day he checked the lottery tickets and discovered that one of the tickets was worth over $7 million! This was **such** a big surprise that at first he didn't know what to do. He finally decided to return the tickets.

Jean-Guy had four children but his wife was dead. Jean-Guy's son opened the door to William. William was an English speaker who didn't speak French. However, the Lavigueur family only spoke French. The family were **such** suspicious people that when Lavigueur's son didn't understand William, he told him to go away.

The next day William returned to the Lavigueur home with a friend who spoke French. Jean-Guy Lavigueur was **so** surprised at the news of his big win that he invited William for a drink. When he found out the whole story he was **so** grateful to William that he offered him a share of the prize. The prize money was shared between Jean-Guy, his daughter Sylvie (19), his sons Michel (14) and Yve (18), and his brother-in-law, Jean-Marie Daudelin, who had helped him raise the family since his wife died. The only child who didn't receive any money was Louise, who did not give money to buy the tickets. Both Jean-Guy Lavigueur and William Murphy were unemployed at the time, and overnight they became rich men.

3 💬 Work in pairs. Read the article again. Choose the best way to complete the sentences.

1 *William Murphy / Jean-Guy Lavigueur* found *Jean-Guy Lavigueur's / William Murphy's* wallet.
2 William returned the wallet *immediately / the next day*.
3 *William / Jean-Guy* checked the lottery tickets.
4 Jean-Guy's son told William to go away because he *only spoke English / didn't understand him*.
5 Jean-Guy offered William *a drink / money / both a drink and some money*.
6 *Six / Seven* people shared the prize money.
7 Both Jean-Guy and William were *rich / didn't have a job* before they won the lottery.

4 💬 Work in groups. Discuss the questions.

- Do you think William made the right decision?
- Do you think Jean-Guy made the right decision?
- Would you do the same or something different?
- Do you know any other lottery stories?

GRAMMAR

1 a 💬 Work in pairs. Look at the words in **bold** in the article. When do we use *so*, *such* and *such a(n)*?

b Complete 1–3 in the GRAMMAR PANEL ▪▪.

2 a Complete the sentences with *so*, *such* and *such a(n)*.

1 I was _____ tired that I didn't go to the party.
2 It was _____ boring class that I nearly fell asleep.
3 She's _____ tall!
4 It was _____ amazing film that I went to see it again.
5 They're _____ good children.
6 It was _____ hot yesterday that we had to stay inside.

b Look at the sentences in 2a again. Which are exclamations and which are sentences showing a result? Complete 4–9 in the GRAMMAR PANEL ▪▪.

3 a Complete the sentences with your own opinions.

a English is such a(n) _____ subject.
b Today I feel so _____ that I'm going to _____ after class.
c Last weekend was so _____.

b 💬 Work in pairs. Compare and explain your answers.

▪▪ SO & SUCH

We use *so* and *such* to talk about extremes.

FORM

We use	before...
(1) _____	an adjective
(2) _____	an adjective + a singular noun
(3) _____	an adjective + a plural or uncountable noun

USE

1 We use *so* and *such* (*a/an*) in exclamations.
   She's (4) _____ rich!
   That's (5) _____ nice surprise!
   It was (6) _____ interesting news!

2 We also use *so* and *such* (*a/an*) with *that* to show the result of something extreme. It is possible to omit *that* from these sentences:
   She was (7) _____ tired (that) she went home.
   It was (8) _____ lovely day (that) they went for a picnic.
   It was (9) _____ awful food (that) we couldn't eat it.

See page 148 for grammar reference and more practice.

LISTENING & SPEAKING

1 💬 Work in pairs. What do you think happened to the Lavigueur family?

2 a 🔊 9.5 Listen to the discussion about what happened. Complete the first column with *yes* or *no*.

	Alive?	Details
Jean-Guy	(1) _____	He was *illiterate / educated*. He found it *easy / difficult* to manage the media.
Yve	(2) _____	He wrote a book and *worked on / acted in* a TV series.
Sylvie	(3) _____	She started a *hairdressing / television* business. She is a very *public / private* person.
Louise	(4) _____	She *wanted some / didn't want any* money.
Michel	(5) _____	*He killed himself. / Criminals killed him.*

b Listen again and circle the correct answers in the second column.

3 💬 Work in groups to discuss these questions. Give reasons for your answers.

- Are you surprised by what happened to the Lavigueur family?
- Which family member's story do you find the most tragic?
- Do you think money can bring happiness to people?

READING & VOCABULARY: money (2)

1   Read this definition of a get-rich-quick scheme. Do you think it's possible? Why/Why not?

> A *get-rich-quick scheme* is a plan that makes it possible for you to make a lot of money in a short time.

2   Read the *get-rich-quick* adverts. Rank them in order of how much money you need to participate.

Who wants to be a millionaire?

You do, of course! And we'll show you how. This Saturday at the Millstone Hotel we'll have our millionaire experts here to tell you their secrets of how to make your first million. All this for a $10 entry fee. **Everybody** wants to be a millionaire – and why can't it **a**   be you? Sign up today.

Are you looking for extra income?

I made $500 dollars a week by working only two hours a day. It's easy because it's all on commission. Just sell our great vitamin supplements and in no time at all you'll be making money. You don't have to invest **anything** so you have **nothing** to lose. You too can earn $500 if you sell 20 bottles.

Call 333-6754 today!
b

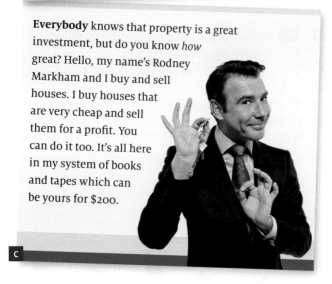

Everybody knows that property is a great investment, but do you know *how* great? Hello, my name's Rodney Markham and I buy and sell houses. I buy houses that are very cheap and sell them for a profit. You can do it too. It's all here in my system of books and tapes which can be yours for $200.

c

Do you know **anybody** who needs some extra cash? Yes! Did you know that you can receive money for doing online surveys? Yes! That's right! You don't have to go **anywhere**. You can earn money by giving your opinions – from your own home! Simply sign up for a list of websites where you will get money for doing surveys.
d   It's easy! For $20 you could be making easy, fast money.

3   Find money words in the adverts which mean

   1   money you pay for professional services.
   2   money you make every time you sell a product.
   3   money you make by selling something for a higher price than you paid for it.
   4   money someone gets from working or investing.

4   Read the adverts again. Which advert(s) do the sentences describe?

   1   You can make money in your house.
   2   Someone will teach you how to do something.
   3   You need to sell something to make money.
   4   You can become very, very rich.
   5   You pay before you can make money.

> **NOTICE**   *FEE/COMMISSION*
>
> **fee** can also refer to the money that you can charge.
> *My fee is $100 per hour.*
> **commission** is also charged by banks.
> *When you change money, the bank takes a commission.*

5   💬 Work in groups. Discuss the questions.

   ●   Which type of people would be interested in these different schemes?
   ●   Which advert sounds the most interesting to you? Why?
   ●   Which advert is the least interesting?
   ●   Do you think it's a good idea to encourage people to make money in this way? Give reasons.

GRAMMAR

1 **a** Look at the sentences. Do you agree with them? Why/Why not?

1 **Anyone** can be a millionaire.
2 If you really want **something**, you need to work hard to get it.
3 **Nobody** wants to be a millionaire more than I do!
4 A millionaire is **someone** who has too much money and not enough time to spend it!
5 **Nothing** is more important in life than money.
6 I don't know **anybody** who's got rich quick.

b 💬 Compare your answers with a partner.

2 **a** Look at the words in **bold** in 1a and answer the questions.

1 Which refer to a) people? b) things?
2 Do they refer to a) a specific person or thing? b) people or things in general?

b Choose the correct options to complete 1–5 in the GRAMMAR PANEL ■.

3 Complete the sentences using *-body/-one* or *-thing*.

1 A dreamer is some........... who thinks about getting rich, but doesn't do any........... about it.
2 No........... works harder than Jim. He deserves to do well.
3 I heard some........... on the news about the high stress levels of millionaires.
4 I'm looking for some........... to help me with my new project – any........... will do!
5 A: Would you like some........... to eat?
   B: No, no........... thanks.
6 Has any........... ever given you a large sum of money?

4 **a** Choose the correct words to complete the sentences.

1 I don't know *anything / nothing* about cars. I don't even know how to drive!
2 I live next to *anyone / someone* who plays the trumpet!
3 *Nobody / Somebody* cooks better than my mother!
4 There's *nothing / something* better than a long hot bath to help you relax.

b Work in pairs. Are the sentences true for you? If not, can you change them to make them true?

SOME-/ANY-/NO- + -ONE/-BODY/-THING

We use *some-*, *any-* and *no-* with *-one/-body* and *-thing* to talk about [1]*specific people and objects / people and objects in general*.

	some-	any-	no-
a [2]*person / thing*	someone	anyone	no one
	somebody	anybody	nobody
a [3]*person / thing*	something	anything	nothing

USE

Some-
We usually use *someone*, *somebody* or *something*
1 with [4]*affirmative / negative* verbs:
   If you really want something...

2 in offers and requests:
   Would you like something to eat?

Any-
We often use *anyone*, *anybody* or *anything*
1 in questions and sentences with *not*:
   Did you do anything last night?
   I don't know anyone.

2 in affirmative sentences. Here *any* = <u>all</u> people/things with <u>no exception</u>:
   Anyone can be a millionaire.

No-
We use *no one*, *nobody* and *nothing* with affirmative verbs, but they have a [5]*positive / negative* meaning.
Nobody wants to go to the party.

NOTE: The verb is always singular.
*Nothing **is** more important than money.*

See page 148 for grammar reference and more practice.

SPEAKING

1 Work in groups. Read the situations. Choose three to talk about and make notes about them.

Talk about a time
● you lost something.
● you wasted money on something.
● you met somebody interesting.
● you couldn't find anybody to talk to.
● nothing was going right.

2 💬 Take turns to talk about each situation in your group. The group makes notes on your talk.

3 💬 What interesting situations did you hear? Tell the class.

TUNE IN

1 Work in pairs. Look at the photos. Where are the people? What problems do you think they might have with money?

2 🔊 9.6 Listen and check your answers.

3 Why are the following things important in each conversation?
1 a PIN   3 a 50 dollar note
2 a card number   4 a sign

4 Listen again and answer the questions.
1 In which of the situations is the problem a) solved, b) not solved?
2 How is the problem solved in each case?
3 Why is it not solved in the others?

FOCUS ON LANGUAGE

5 a 🔊 9.7 Listen to the requests and responses from the conversations and complete the gaps.

1
A .... your PIN, please?
B Sure...

2
A Now .... your full name?
B Sure, it's Darren John Elliot.

3
A .... anything smaller?
B No, sorry, I don't.

4
A .... the bill please?
B Of course, just a moment.

b 💬 Practise the requests and responses in pairs.

6 Look at the statements. Who says them? <u>Underline</u> the apologies in each sentence. Circle two excuses.

1 It's not our fault... sometimes the connection's a little slow...
2 I'm sorry to hear that, sir.
3 I'm sorry, but I'm afraid you're wrong...
4 Sorry, I didn't notice.

> ❝ **Intonation: saying sorry** ❞
>
> 🔊 9.8 Listen to the four apologies in 6. In which do the people sound a) genuinely sorry? b) not sorry?
>
> What is the difference in intonation?
>
> Practise saying the sentences in a sympathetic and non-sympathetic way.

OVER TO YOU

7 a 💬 Work in pairs. Choose one of the above situations or another involving money problems (e.g. reporting a lost credit card).

b Student A, you are the person with the problem. Make notes on how to explain the problem and request help from B.

Student B, you are the person trying to help. Make notes on how to apologise for the problem and try to find a solution for A.

8 💬 Practise the conversation. Was it possible to solve the problem?

TUNE IN

1 Look at the photo. What do you think they are discussing?

2 **a**))) 9.9 Listen to the discussion between the man and a financial advisor. What is the problem that he has, 1, 2 or 3?

1 spending his money
2 managing his money
3 saving his money

b))) 9.10 Listen and complete the table with the numbers you hear.

3 **a** Work in pairs. Complete 'Total income' and 'Total expenses'. How much money does Steve have left at the end of the month?

b How could Steve save money? What would you do if you were Steve? Write five ideas.

4 **a**))) 9.11 Listen to the advice. Did you make similar suggestions?

b Listen again and complete the extracts.

1 As you .... , you spend more than you earn...
2 So, what we .... is look at...
3 First of .... , you say you buy...
4 Then, the .... thing...
5 It .... you could also .... on...
6 Ok – the next .... is the gym.
7 The .... area .... you can save money is on...

Name: Steve Murray	
Income per month	**£**
'take home' pay	....
any other income	....
Total income	....

Expenses per month	**£**
accommodation	....
transport	....
bills (telephone, gas, electricity)	....
food	....
entertainment and eating out	....
subscriptions (gym, cable TV, internet)	....
other	....
Total expenses	....

Income minus expenses	....

PREPARE FOR TASK

5 Turn to page 161 and read about Melanie Fulton. Complete her 'Total income' and 'Total expenses'. How much money does she have left at the end of the month?

6 💬 Work in pairs. What would you do if you were Melanie? Compare with a partner.

TASK

7 Work in pairs. Prepare a budget for Melanie and think about where she can save money. Write your thoughts and advice and prepare what you are going to say to her.

8 💬 Change partners. Take turns to role play your conversation with Melanie. Explain your thoughts and advice to your partner.

REPORT BACK

9 Tell the class about the recommendations. Make a list of the five most important things Melanie could do to save money. Who had the best recommendations?

VOCABULARY
Science & research

1 a Choose five words from section A of the vocabulary box on page 73. Write five sentences using each word.

b 💬 Work in pairs. Read your sentences to your partner, omitting the verb/noun. Your partner guesses the missing word.

2 💬 Work in pairs. Discuss the questions.
- Did/Do you enjoy studying Science at school? Why/Why not?
- What interesting scientific research have you read/heard about recently?

Cities

3 Make a list of things you find in cities. Does your city have all these things?

4 Which city in your region/country has the best quality of life? Why?

Technology

5 a Complete the words.

1 I usually s____ f the int____ at weekends.
2 I s____t three em____s yesterday.
3 I prefer down____g music fr____ the internet to buying music at the shops.
4 I always swi____ the lights o____ when I leave a room.

b Make the sentences true for you. Compare in groups. Are your answers similar?

GRAMMAR
-ing form & to + infinitive

1 a Complete the sentences with the correct form of the words in the box.

move   live   read   learn   run

1 I would like ____ in a big city one day.
2 She considered ____ a new skill to keep her mind alert.
3 Shazia couldn't afford ____ to a bigger house because she had lost her job.
4 We all agreed ____ the marathon, so now we're training hard!
5 I can really recommend ____ a good book to help you relax.

b Check your answers with a partner.

Countable & uncountable nouns, some & any

2 a Are the nouns in the sentences countable (C) or uncountable (U)?

1 In the (1)future, (2)technology will be even more important than it is today.
2 Every single (3)person needs to do more to help the (4)environment.
3 I think (5)scientists can find an (6)answer for every (7)problem.

b 💬 Work in pairs. What do you think about the sentences in a?

3 a Complete the sentences with *some* or *any*.

1 There aren't ____ parks near my house.
2 There are ____ really good restaurants and cafés on my street.
3 My flat has ____ outside space, but only a very small terrace.
4 ____ people think it's a good idea to keep farm animals in city parks.
5 Are there ____ new exhibitions on?

b 💬 Work in pairs. Are the sentences true for where you live?

Quantifiers

4 a Choose the correct words.

1 I don't do *much / many* exercise.
2 I have played *lots of / a little* brain training games.
3 I don't eat *a lot of / too many* healthy food.
4 I spend *not many / too much* time in bed.
5 I only drink *a little / a few* cups of coffee a week.

b Which sentences best describe you? Are there any habits you would like to change?

FUNCTIONAL LANGUAGE
Agreeing and disagreeing

1 🔊 R8 Listen and complete the sentences with the words in the box.

believe   depends   absolutely
agree   terrible

1
PROF WILD   All students should study Computer Science at school.
TOM   I completely ____ .

2
PROF WILD   I ____ that Computer Science is more important than History.
TOM   Oh, ____ !

3
PROF WILD   Computers can teach students.
TOM   No way! That's a ____ idea.
ANA   Well, it ____ ...

2 💬 Work in pairs. Discuss Professor Wild's ideas in 1. Use expressions for agreeing and disagreeing.

■ LOOKING BACK

- Think of three things you learned to say about science or technology.
- What type of technology do you use in your home? Would you like to buy more gadgets?

VOCABULARY
True or false

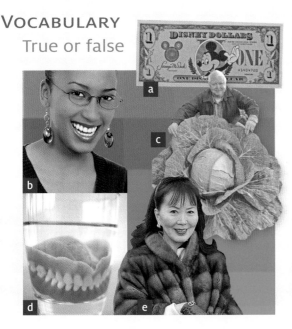

1 **a** Look at the pictures. What can you see? Are they real or fake? How do you know?

b Think of at least two synonyms for the words *true* and *false*. Then write a sentence describing each of the pictures in 1a using the synonyms.

2 Look at the verbs *look* and *see* in the instructions in 1a. What is the difference between the two verbs?

Collocations with *say* and *tell*

3 Write the words and expressions in the box in the correct word map.

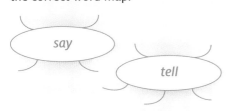

> excuse me   a great story   sorry
> the time   goodbye   a terrible lie
> a very funny joke   hello   the whole truth

4 **a** Complete the questions with *say* or *tell*.

1 Excuse me, can you .... me the time, please?
2 Who was the last person you .... goodbye to today?
3 Have you .... sorry to anyone today?
4 Do you know anyone who .... really terrible jokes?
5 Do you think it's always important to .... the whole truth?

b Work in pairs. Ask and answer the questions.

GRAMMAR
If + present simple

1 **a** Complete the sentences using the correct form of the verbs.

1 If you .... *(put)* a diamond in acid, it dissolves.
2 If a mosquito .... *(bite)* you, it's a female.
3 A cockroach can live for weeks if you .... *(cut)* its head off.
4 If you .... *(have)* a ten-minute conversation you will probably tell a lie.

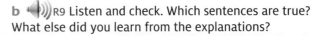

b R9 Listen and check. Which sentences are true? What else did you learn from the explanations?

Modal verbs: *must, can't, may, might*

2 Read sentences 1–4. Match them to the best explanation a–d.

1 That can't be his sister.
2 That must be my aunt.
3 That may be Jack's mother.
4 Jen might not come.

a She said she was tired and had to do homework.
b She's much thinner than him!
c I don't know her, but she looks like him.
d That's her car. She drives a blue Peugeot.

3 **a** Work in pairs. Do you think the photo shows a) jewellery? b) cans? c) money? Discuss your answers and your reasons.

b Turn to page 161 to check your answer.

FUNCTIONAL LANGUAGE
Warnings and promises

1 **a** Match the phrases to find two warnings and a promise.

1 If you don't give me back my book,
2 If you help me with my homework,
3 Don't do that!

a I'll make you dinner.
b It's dangerous.
c I'll tell mum.

b R10 Listen and check.

2 Work in groups. Think of a warning and a promise you could make in each situation.

1 Your sister called you and she is taking the bus home, but she thinks she's going to be late for dinner.
2 A student in your class tells you that he can't complete the class project with you because he's going to a party.

■ LOOKING BACK

● What was the most interesting story in this unit? Why?
● What promises could you make to a) your teacher? b) your best friend?
● Which areas of learning English have become easier for you?

Vocabulary

Money

1 Choose the correct words to complete the adverts.

1

> This is a great *investment / invest* opportunity. You *pay / invest in* just $25 to receive a list of email addresses and you can *sell / buy* our product directly to those people.

2

> Are you trying to *save / waste* money? Our new bank account makes it easy. Every month we automatically take 5% out of your *income / expenses* and put it into this special account. So you can't *waste / earn* it on things you don't need.

3

> Do you need a *lend / loan*? Everyone needs to *borrow / lend* money at some time. We *lend / borrow* you the money and let you *pay / spend* it back when you can *afford / cost* it.

2 💬 Work in pairs. Discuss the adverts in 1. Which ones sound like a good idea and which sound like a bad idea? Why?

Grammar

If + past simple

1 a Complete the sentences using the correct form of the verbs.

1 If I _____ (win) a lot of money, I _____ (buy) an expensive car.

2 I _____ (not stop) working if I _____ (find) a lot of money.

3 If I _____ (be) president, I _____ (not change) anything.

4 I _____ (live) in another country if I _____ (can).

b 🔊 R11 Listen and check.

2 💬 Work in pairs. Change the sentences in 1a so they are true about you and compare your answers.

So & such

3 Match the two parts of the sentences.

1 She was so happy that
2 He was such a rich man that
3 They won so much money that
4 He earned so little money that

a they decided to stop working.
b she couldn't stop smiling.
c he had to find another job.
d he could afford to give a lot of his money away.

4 💬 Work in pairs. Write two exclamations about each of the pictures using *so* and *such*.

Some-/any-/no- + -one/-body/-thing

5 a Complete the sentences so that they are true about you.

1 _____ I know won first prize.

2 _____ in my family can speak French.

3 I'm (not) doing _____ this weekend.

4 _____ I work with is running the marathon on Sunday.

5 I (don't) cook _____ we eat at home.

b 💬 Work in pairs. Compare sentences. Ask your partner more questions about two of the sentences.

Functional language

Money transactions

1 a Complete the conversations using the words in the box.

bill   change   key   pay   PIN   smaller   you

1 A How would you like to _____ the _____?
   B Card, please. There _____ go.

2 A Please can you _____ in your _____?
   B Sure.

3 A Do you have anything _____?
   B No, I don't have any _____, sorry.

b 🔊 R12 Listen and check.

2 💬 Work in pairs. Act out the conversations in 1a.

🔲 Looking back

- What do you hope for in your English learning?
- Think of five useful words or expressions you have learned. Why do you think they are useful?
- Think of five things you would do if you could.

READING

1 **a** Read the article about different learning styles and complete it with the headings below.

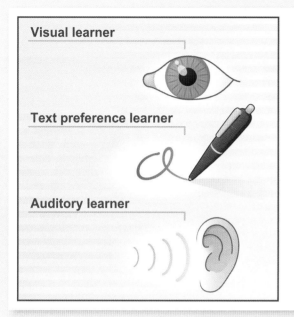

Visual learner

Text preference learner

Auditory learner

What kind of learner are you?

1 ....

a You sometimes ask a friend or relative to test your vocabulary by asking you questions. ☐

b You often practise new language by saying it out loud. ☐

2 ....

c If you've got a dictionary, you prefer to look up new words and write a translation. ☐

d You use example sentences in your vocabulary notebook. ☐

3 ....

e You use drawings to help you to remember vocabulary sets. ☐

f You write new words in a list or chart and tick (✓) or cross (✗) them when you can remember them perfectly. ☐

b 💬 Which techniques do you use? What kind of learner are you? Compare your answers with a partner.

LISTENING

2 **a** 🔊 R13 Listen to Aliki and Carlos talking about the list. Which of a–f in **1a** do they already do? What kind of learner are they?

Aliki   Carlos

b Listen again and answer the questions. Do you do any of the things?

1 Who revises words from his/her vocabulary notebook every week?
2 Who regularly studies with friends?
3 Who records him/herself speaking?

SPEAKING & VOCABULARY

3 💬 Think of three more ways to revise vocabulary. Share your answers with the class.

4 **a** 💬 Work in pairs. Look back at units 7–9. Choose one set of new vocabulary that you want to practise.

b Choose two of the ways to revise vocabulary in 1 – or your own ideas. Discuss the pros and cons of these two ways. Which way would you like to try in the future?

🔲 QUICK CHECK

Complete the checklist below.

Can you...	Yes, I can.	Yes, more or less.	I need to look again.
1 agree and disagree with someone politely?	☐	☐	☐
2 give your opinions on an issue?	☐	☐	☐
3 give someone a warning or make a promise?	☐	☐	☐
4 write a thank-you note?	☐	☐	☐
5 give advice?	☐	☐	☐
6 say what you would do if you won the lottery?	☐	☐	☐
7 talk about your hopes and wishes?	☐	☐	☐
8 talk about spending and saving money?	☐	☐	☐

💬 Compare your answers with a partner.

● What else do you know now after studying units 7–9?

10 A GLOBAL MARKET?

a

b

1 💬 Work in pairs. Look at the photos and discuss the questions.

- How many different adverts can you see?
- What products do you think the adverts are selling?

2 a Complete A in the KEY VOCABULARY PANEL ▪.

b 💬 Work in pairs. What adverts can you see in and around your town? Use the words in A to describe them to a partner.

3 a 🔊 10.1 Listen to three people talking about adverts. Is their attitude a) positive? b) negative? c) neutral?

b Listen again and make a note of

1 the product
2 the type of advert (e.g. flyer)
3 what they like or dislike about the adverts

4 a Listen again and complete the extracts.

1 I hate the way they show the .... adverts over and over on ....
2 .... adverts in particular annoy me.
3 I don't like the way they're selling a '...............'.
4 I hate it when I get ads on my ....
5 I don't mind that we see posters and .... every day.
6 The last thing I want is more .... in my pocket!
7 What I liked was the fact that the advert was on his ....

b Which speaker has a similar opinion to you? Why?

5 💬 Think of a) a type of advert or advertising that really annoys you, b) an interesting or original advertising campaign. Tell your partner about them.

6 Complete B in the KEY VOCABULARY PANEL ▪.

KEY VOCABULARY

Advertising

A Types of advertising

- Look at the words and their definitions. Find an example of each one in the photos.

advert	a poster, short TV-film, or radio programme which is designed to persuade us to buy something
billboard	a large board in a public place used for showing adverts
brand	the name of a product or group of products that are made by the same company
campaign	a series of adverts
flyer	an advert that is printed on paper and given to people in the street or through their door
logo	a symbol that represents an organisation or company
slogan	a short phrase that is easy to remember and is used to advertise something

NOTICE *ADVERTISING, ADVERTISEMENT, ADVERT*
Use *advertising* to talk about the activity. Use *advertisement* to talk about a specific example. We often shorten *advertisement* to *advert* or *ad*.
I really like this ad.
Have you seen the new Coke advert?

B Expressing your opinion

- Look at the expressions and answer the questions.
  - I hate the way...
  - ...in particular annoy me
  - I don't like the way...
  - I hate it when...
  - I don't mind that...
  - The last thing I want is more...
  - What I liked was the fact that...

1 Which can you use to show a) a positive reaction? b) a negative reaction? c) a neutral reaction?

2 Which do you use with a) a clause (subject and verb)? b) a noun?

7 **a** Look at the slogans below. Do you know what brand or product they are advertising?

b Can you think of any other slogans? What are they selling? Which is your favourite? Why?

SPEAKING

1 💬 What is the connection between the photos on the right and the title of the lesson?

> **merchandising** *(noun)* selling clothes, books, toys and other items that are associated with a popular sports team, TV programme, film, etc.

2 💬 Work in pairs. Discuss the questions.

- Do you (or does anyone you know) ever wear a football shirt?
- If so, what kind? Is it a local team or a national team? Is it a home shirt or an away shirt?
- Do you like football shirts?
- If not, why not?
- If yes, do you have a favourite? What do you like about it?
- What information does a football shirt normally have on it?
- In what way is a football shirt also an advert?

LISTENING

1 🔊 10.2 Listen to a sports journalist talking about football shirts. Which topic does she NOT talk about?

a business sponsorship
b fashion and identity
c fake football shirts
d her favourite T-shirt design
e football as a symbol of globalisation

2 Work in pairs. Try to remember other things the journalist said about each topic. Make notes. Then listen again and check.

3 Match extracts 1–6 to topics a–e in 1.

1 everyone wants the latest shirt
2 there is a big market for imitation shirts
3 the shirt advertises two things at the same time
4 most football shirts are manufactured in the developing world
5 the shirt says something about you
6 it's also an example of exploitation

4 a 💬 Work in pairs. Do you agree with the points the journalist is making in these extracts? Why/Why not?

b What do you think football shirts symbolise? What do they say about the people who wear them?

> **NOTICE** *LATEST*
> We say *latest* to mean the most recent or the newest (it suggests that it is good).
> *Everyone wants the latest shirt.*

GRAMMAR

1 Look at the sentences. What is important in these sentences, a) the action? b) the people who do the action?

- Huge profits are made from the shirt sales.
- Football is followed all over the world.
- Football shirts are manufactured in the developing world.

2 a Complete the sentences with the people who are responsible.

1 The _____ make huge profits from the sales.
2 _____ follow football all over the world.
3 Football shirts are manufactured by _____ .

b Compare the two sets of sentences and complete 1–6 in the GRAMMAR PANEL ■ .

3 Turn to page 167 and <u>underline</u> all the examples of the passive in transcript 10.2. Which verbs have irregular past participles?

4 Look at the images. What process are they showing? Match a verb from the box to each step.

buy   make   sell   transport   wear

5 Complete the description using the passive form of the verbs in 4.

This is a typical football shirt. It (1) _____ in China. In fact, most football shirts (2) _____ in China today. The shirts (3) _____ to other countries in ships. Then they (4) _____ in the shops. They (5) _____ by football fans and they (6) _____ by people all over the world.

6 Think of an object and how it is manufactured. Write three or four sentences describing the process. Do not name the object. Can the class guess what it is?

First it's written. Then it's sold to a production company. Actors and locations are found and a lot of money is spent making it. Finally, it's shown to the public.

PASSIVE (1): PRESENT SIMPLE

We often use **passive** verb forms to focus on an action:

FORM

is/are + past participle:

Football (1) _____ *played all over the world.*
Football shirts (2) _____ *seen everywhere.*

The subject of the passive sentence is the object of the active sentence.

(3) _____ *is played all over the world.*
People play (4) _____ *all over the world.*

USE

We use (5) _____ to say who does the action in a passive sentence.

The clubs are sponsored (6) _____ *companies who want their logos on the shirts.*

See page 149 for grammar reference and more practice.

SPEAKING

1 💬 Work in groups. Discuss the questions.

- What other products do you associate with merchandising?
- What items are most commonly merchandised?
- Have you ever bought anything because of the brand? Was it for yourself, or was it a present?

■ PRACTISE THE PAST SIMPLE PASSIVE
■ TALK ABOUT CLOTHES

SPEAKING

1 💬 Discuss in pairs. When you go shopping for clothes

- do you tend to go to the same places?
- do you buy similar labels/styles/ colours?
- what's most important for you when you're buying clothes: the price, the quality, the design, the material, where they're made?

2 💬 Work in pairs. Look at the photos of the American clothing company Carhartt. Discuss the questions.

- What, if anything, do you know about the brand?
- What kind of clothes does it sell?
- What price range do you think the clothes are in – low-cost, mid-price or luxury?
- What kind of people do you think shop at Carhartt? Would you like to shop there?

READING

1 Read the newspaper article about Carhartt. Check your answers from **SPEAKING 2**. Who a) wears Carhartt clothes now? b) wore them in the past?

2 Look at these adjectives. Which do you associate with workwear and which with streetwear?

> cool   durable   fashionable   high technology
> resistant   stylish   top quality   tough   trendy

3 Read the article again. In which paragraph (a–e) does the writer refer to

1 new clothes for new markets?
2 how the company started?
3 the way Carhartt is run?
4 the journalist's opinion?
5 a link with the music world?

4 💬 Work in pairs. Discuss the questions.

- What do you think is the writer's attitude to Carhartt? Find words in the article to support your answer.
- According to the author, what makes Carhartt different from other clothing companies?
- Which is more important, the clothes themselves or the people behind the brand? How do you know?

A brand transformed

a Carhartt was originally founded to make work clothing for railroad workers. In the 1890s, they became famous for their tough work overalls which they still sell today. They went on to manufacture durable, high technology materials resistant to flames, wind and water. Today Carhartt is commonly found on construction sites, farms, and ranches in the USA.

b In the 1990s, Carhartt displayed its workwear for the first time at fashion shows. They became popular in countries like Japan, where trendy jeans and jackets were sold by the million. The brand became even more cool when rap groups and hip-hop artists wore their clothes on music videos, CD covers and on stage.

c Carhartt clothes were even featured in the pages of *Vogue* and *Harper's Bazaar* when they launched their women's range in 1997. Into the new century, the company continued to vary their styles of fashionable clothing, introducing caps, baggy jeans and their stylish T-shirts and hoodies to appeal to skateboarders and urban tribes.

d The company has always had a refreshingly different image from other American clothing firms. From the start, Carhartt's clothes were made in local factories in Kentucky and their employees were paid decent salaries. In this globalised world, they are still independently owned.

e Carhartt has now become one of the best-known clothing companies in the world, catering for a young, middle-class audience who can pay the high price tags for their fashion range. However, they still produce the workwear that originally brought them their reputation for top quality. It's great that these two lines continue, it's what makes their clothes different from the competition.

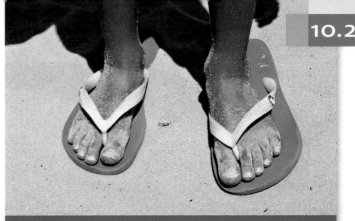

GRAMMAR

1 a <u>Underline</u> the verbs in the sentences. Are they in the past or the present?

1 They are still independently owned.
2 Carhartt was originally founded to make work clothing.
3 The company was started in the USA. It wasn't founded in the UK.

b Complete 1–6 in the the GRAMMAR PANEL ▧ with the correct form of the verb in brackets.

2 a Read the article about the history of flip-flops. <u>Underline</u> the correct options.

b 🔊)) 10.3 Listen and check. Discuss the questions.

● Do you like flip-flops? If not, why not?
● If yes, how many pairs have you got?
● Where and when do you wear them?
● Is there anywhere where you can't wear them?

▧ **PASSIVE (2): PAST SIMPLE**

FORM

was/were + past participle

(+) *The clothes* (1)............................ *(make) in local factories.*
The company (2)............................ *(give) the award of Retailer of the Year.*

(–) *The first shop* (3)............................ *(open) until 2003.*
Shops (4)............................ *(open) outside the USA until 1998.*

(?) *When* (5)............ *the company* .... *(create)?*
Where (6)............ *the clothes* .... *(make)?*

See page 149 for grammar reference and more practice.

PRONUNCIATION: *was/were*
strong & weak forms

1 a 🔊)) 10.4 Listen to the sentences. Notice the difference in pronunciation between the strong, stressed forms /wɒz/ /wɜː/ and the weak, unstressed forms /wəz/ /wə/ .

1 Was /wəz/ it made in Japan? Yes, it was /wɒz/ .
2 It was /wəz/ made in Japan. It was /wɒz/ n't made in China.
3 Were /wə/ they made in Spain? Yes, they were /wɜː/ .
4 They were /wə/ made in Spain. They were /wɜː/ n't made in Portugal.

b Listen again and repeat.

2 Look at the sentences. Choose the correct options.

We usually stress *was* and *were* in *questions/short answers* and *negative/positive* statements.

3 🔊)) 10.5 💬 Work in pairs. Listen to three sentences. Write them down. Are they true for you? Compare your answers with a partner.

From beach wear to high fashion

Apparently, the flip-flop as we know it today (1)*was/is* invented in New Zealand. Cheap and easy to make, the design (2)*was/is* based on Japanese sandals known as zori. For that reason, they (3)*were/are* first called jandals or Japanese sandals. However, the most famous examples of these rubber sandals today come from Brazil. The company Havaianas (4)*is/was* formed there in the 1960s, but the brand has only become famous abroad in recent years. Now, a large percentage of the world's flip-flops (5)*are/were* made by this Brazilian company. In fact they have recently become an expensive fashion item and new Havaianas designs (6)*are/were* introduced all the time. This is ironic, considering that for millions of people in the world, flip-flops are the only shoes they can afford to buy.

SPEAKING & VOCABULARY:
describing clothes

1 a Look at the adjectives in the box. Which can you use to describe the clothes in picture a on page 108? Use a dictionary to help you.

> baggy   bright   colourful   long-sleeved
> patterned   plain   short-sleeved   striped   tight

b What kind of T-shirts do you usually wear? Do you have a favourite? If yes, what does it look like?

2 a 💬 Work in pairs. Think of a favourite item of clothing. Describe it to your partner in as much detail as possible. Can he/she guess what it is?

It's made of wool, it's orange and green. It was given to me by my mother when I was a kid... I think it was made in Scotland...

b Do you and your partner have a similar taste in clothes?

LISTENING

1 💬 Look at the photos and answer the questions.

1 Where were they taken?
2 What are the people doing in each photo?
3 What do the photos have in common?
4 Which is your favourite? Why?

2 🔊 10.6 Listen to three people talking about the photos. Check the answers to the questions in 1.

3 **a** Listen again and complete the extracts with the missing adjectives.

> 1
> ...a coffee stand, with its .... logo , its .... smell and its .... taste!

> 2
> I bought an extra-large latte. The .... thing for keeping my hands nice and ....!

> 3
> A contrast in style and architecture, the .... and the ancient side by side...

> 4
> Why anyone wants to eat .... pizza at the pyramids when there are .... dates and .... falafel for sale outside for a fraction of the price, I really don't know!

> 5
> The interesting thing was the contrast: the .... colours of the .... dress, the mother holding the lamb, and the inevitable, ... fast-food label.

b 💬 How do the three people feel about the international fast-food brands in the photos? Do you agree with them?

VOCABULARY: adjectives

1 **a** Listen again. Look at the adjectives. Which two were NOT used?

> ancient ~~beautiful~~ delicious disgusting familiar fresh great international local modern mouth-watering nice processed warm wonderful

b Decide if the adjectives are positive, negative or neutral. *Positive: beautiful ...*

2 💬 Work in pairs. Which adjectives in 1 can you use to describe a) places? b) food? c) both? Think of something you have eaten recently to match each adjective.

SPEAKING

1 **a** Look at the comments. Do you think they refer to a) international fast-food chains? b) traditional, local food?

1 They're cheaper.
2 You always know what you're going to get.
3 The food is prepared at the restaurant.
4 All the ingredients are fresh.
5 The service is quick and friendly.

b Write two more comments about a) and b). Read them to the class. Can they guess which category they are describing?

2 💬 Work in pairs. Discuss the questions.

● Are there international fast-food chains where you live?
● Which is the most popular? What kind of food is served there? What kind of people eat there?
● Do you ever eat there? Why/Why not?

SPEAKING & READING

1 🗨 Work in pairs. Look at the map and discuss these questions.

- What does it show? What information do you find most interesting? Why?
- Are there any Starbucks coffee shops in your town? If yes, do you ever go to them?

2 🗨 Look again more carefully and answer the questions.

1 Which continents provide the ingredients for the Starbucks products?
2 Which countries have the highest number of Starbucks outlets?
3 Are there any parts of the world where there aren't any outlets?
4 What does the map tell you about the relationship between richer and poorer countries?
5 Do you know anything else about this chain?

3 Look again at the map and find words that mean

1 the place that something comes from
2 across the world
3 a synonym for shop or outlet
4 a group of businesses that belong to the same company

4 **a** Use the correct form of the words in 3 to complete the text below.

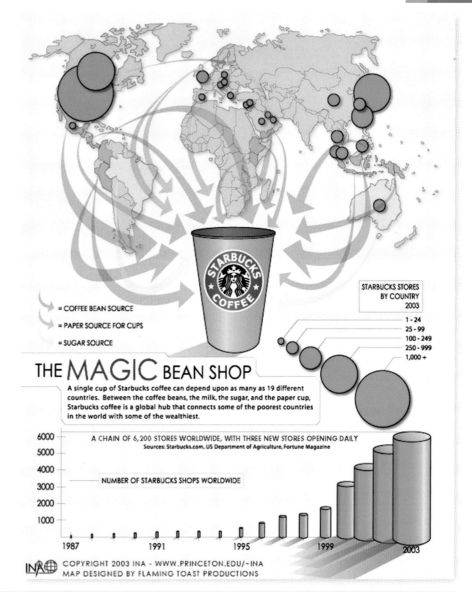

= COFFEE BEAN SOURCE

= PAPER SOURCE FOR CUPS

= SUGAR SOURCE

STARBUCKS STORES BY COUNTRY 2003

1 - 24
25 - 99
100 - 249
250 - 999
1,000 +

THE MAGIC BEAN SHOP

A single cup of Starbucks coffee can depend upon as many as 19 different countries. Between the coffee beans, the milk, the sugar, and the paper cup, Starbucks coffee is a global hub that connects some of the poorest countries in the world with some of the wealthiest.

A CHAIN OF 6,200 STORES WORLDWIDE, WITH THREE NEW STORES OPENING DAILY

Sources: Starbucks.com, US Department of Agriculture, Fortune Magazine

NUMBER OF STARBUCKS SHOPS WORLDWIDE

6000 5000 4000 3000 2000 1000

1987 1991 1995 1999 2003

COPYRIGHT 2003 INA - WWW.PRINCETON.EDU/~INA
MAP DESIGNED BY FLAMING TOAST PRODUCTIONS

Mr Bigg's may not be a (1) _____ franchise, but in its home country of Nigeria it is the biggest local fast-food (2) _____. It has more than 170 (3) _____ in 46 Nigerian towns and cities. All the food comes from local (4) _____. It sells international favourites like burgers and fries, but it's the local food (for example, rice and tomato or bean pudding) which is most popular.

Mr Bigg's – Nigeria's favourite fast-food store

b 🗨 Work in pairs. Would you like to eat at Mr Biggs? Why/Why not? Are there any similar food chains in your country? If yes, what kind of food do they serve?

TUNE IN

1 Look at the food in the photos. What kind of food do you think it is? Can you get this in your town?

2 🔊 10.7 Listen to two people discussing one of the photos. Which photo is it?

3 **a** Listen again and complete the description.

Jollof rice is ⁽¹⁾.............. cooked with ⁽²⁾.............. and ⁽³⁾.............. It's a traditional Western ⁽⁴⁾.............. dish. It's served with moin moin, a ⁽⁵⁾.............. paste, made with steamed ⁽⁶⁾.............. .... and vegetables. It tastes great with ⁽⁷⁾.............. chicken.

b 💬 Discuss in pairs. Do you have a similar dish in your country?

FOCUS ON LANGUAGE

4 🔊 10.8 Listen to two people discussing the second dish. What is the main ingredient?

5 **a** Listen again and complete the conversation with the words and phrases in the box.

> basically   fried   kind of   looks
> served   tastes   typical

A What's that?

B Laver bread. It's a ⁽¹⁾.............. Welsh fisherman's dish.

A Laver bread? It doesn't look like bread to me.

B No, ⁽²⁾.............. it's boiled seaweed.

A It ⁽³⁾.............. disgusting!

B I know, but it ⁽⁴⁾.............. great – believe me. It's usually ⁽⁵⁾.............. with bacon fat and ⁽⁶⁾.............. with cockles.

A Cockles?

B Yes, a ⁽⁷⁾.............. shellfish. Look, they're eating them at the table over there.

b 💬 Would you like to try laver bread?

6 Think of three local dishes. Write short definitions of them using the words and phrases in 5.

❝ Intonation: echoing ❞

🔊 10.9 Listen to the exchanges below. Does the voice go up or down on the underlined words?

1 A What's that?
   B <u>Jollof rice</u>.
   A <u>Jollof rice</u>?

2 A What's that?
   B <u>Laver bread</u>. It's a typical Welsh fisherman's dish.
   A <u>Laver bread</u>? It doesn't look like bread to me!

Why does the voice go up?

Listen again and repeat. Then repeat with a partner, paying special attention to the intonation.

OVER TO YOU

7 You are in a restaurant in your town which serves traditional local food. Think of three dishes that are sure to be on the menu. Write them on a piece of paper.

8 **a** 💬 Work in pairs. Student A, you are in the restaurant with a visitor from another country. Show the menu (from 7) to student B.

Student B, you are a visitor from another country. You don't understand the menu. Ask your friend to help.

b Swap roles and repeat the situation.

9 💬 Which dish was most difficult to explain? Why? Try to explain the dish to the class.

We ♡ street food

a I love *arrosticini*. It's a real taste of home. These miniature cubes of local lamb's meat are grilled on tiny barbecues at the side of the windy mountain roads where my grandma used to live. They sell them all year round on Sunday afternoons. They're delicious with a slice of freshly baked village bread!

b This sweet, sweet tea is boiled in milk and water. It is served extremely hot. You really have to watch out not to burn your fingers – or your tongue! But it's a great pick-me-up at any time – especially first thing on a cold winter's morning.

c This is THE fried fish shop in town. At midday, all through the week, there's a huge crowd of people waiting outside. All the fish is fresh from the market and it's fried there before your eyes. Then it's given to you in a big paper cone so you can eat it as you walk down the street. It makes me lick my lips just thinking about it.

TUNE IN

1 💬 Look at the pictures of street food and drink. Which would you prefer to try? Why?

2 Match the pictures to their descriptions.

3 Read the texts again. Which text(s) explain(s)
1 how the food is cooked or made?
2 where and when it is usually sold?
3 when it is most popular?
4 when the writer thinks it's at its best?
5 the writer's feelings about the food?

PREPARE FOR TASK

4 **a** Look at the texts again. Find
1 four words that describe how the food or drink is prepared.
g _ _ _ _ _ _   b _ _ _ _ _
b _ _ _ _   f _ _ _ _
2 four adjectives used to describe the food.
l _ _ _ _   h _ _
d _ _ _ _ _ _ _ _   f _ _ _ _

b Think of two more words for each category.

5 Find these phrases in the text and explain what they mean.
1 a real taste of home
2 a great pick-me-up
3 this is THE fried fish shop
4 before your eyes
5 It makes me lick my lips just thinking about it.

TASK

6 💬 Discuss the questions with a partner.
- What kind of food is sold on the street in your town? Are there any local specialities? If yes, where's the best place to buy them?
- Would you recommend any of them to a visitor to your town?

7 You are going to write a short description of a particular kind of food in your town or area. Make notes about the information you want to include.
- The ingredients and preparation: ....
- What you like about it: ....
- Where you can buy it: ....
- The best time to eat it: ....
- Anything else: ....

8 Write a short description of no more than 80 words.

REPORT BACK

9 Read each others' descriptions and answer the questions.
- Were you surprised by any of the foods or places described? If yes, why?
- Which description do you think is the most informative? Which is the most appetising?

➡ Go to Review D, Unit 10, p. 136

11 NICE TO MEET YOU

1 💬 Work in pairs. Look at the people in the photos and discuss the questions.

- Where are they? What are they doing?
- What's the relationship between the people?
- Do you think they get on well? Why/Why not?

2 **a** What do you think are the best ways to meet new people and make friends? Make a list.

b Compare your list with A in the Key vocabulary panel ■.

■ KEY VOCABULARY

Meeting people

A Making friends

in a bar   at the coffee machine
at the gym   at school   at university
at work   chatting online   doing sport
going out   through friends

B Adjectives to describe personality

calm   creative   easy-going   friendly
funny   generous   kind   lively
outgoing   quiet   sensible   sensitive
serious   shy   sociable   sporty

NOTICE QUESTIONS WITH *LIKE*
What is he like? asks for a general description of
a person's personality.
What does he like? asks for the person's preferences.
What does he look like? asks for a description of
the person's physical appearance.

3 ◀))) 11.1 Listen to two people talking about how they met
their best friend. Tick the expressions they use from A in
the KEY VOCABULARY PANEL ■.

4 a 💬 Work in pairs. Think of two or three of your
closest friends. How did you meet?

b 💬 Share your story with the class. Which was the
most common way of making friends in your class?

5 Look at the adjectives in B in the KEY VOCABULARY
PANEL ■. Which do you think are positive? Are any of
them negative? Use a dictionary to help you.

6 a Think of one of your best friends. Which adjectives
describe him/her? Which ones don't?

b 💬 Tell a partner about your friend.
● what he/she does
● how you met
● what he/she is like
● what you like to do together
● what you appreciate most about them

7 a Complete this sentence: *A good friend is...*

b 💬 Share your sentence with the rest of the class.

Unexpected romances: How we met

Ten years ago, Karissa Moreno, who is now 39, was living in San Francisco after she came back from Guatemala. She was working as a waitress, but she said her plan was to go to graduate school.

At work there was a new kitchen assistant. His name was Carlos Martin, from Argentina (he's now 37). He said he didn't speak any English at that time, but Karissa spoke good Spanish and the two became friends. Soon after they met, Carlos said that he was interested in a romantic relationship. Karissa said that she was sorry, but that she wasn't interested because there were too many differences between them.

Carlos was a meat eater; Karissa was a vegetarian. He smoked; she hated smoking. She was a graduate; Carlos didn't finish high school. He had two daughters from his first marriage in Argentina and Karissa didn't want children.

But, at the same time, Karissa said, 'His green eyes were gorgeous!' It took a long time, but they both finally knew that they were in love.

Karissa said she would never get married, but in 2005 Carlos and Karissa decided to get married.

SPEAKING & READING

1 💬 Work in pairs. Discuss the questions.

- Look at the photo. What do you think is the relationship between the two people?
- What attracts a person to another person?
- What are the things you like/don't like in other people?

2 a Read the article about the couple. Where are they from? Where did they meet?

b Read the article again. Complete the table.

	Karissa	Carlos
Nationality		
First language		
Food preference		
Smoker?		
Profession		
Education		
Marriages		
Children		

3 Are the sentences true or false? Check your answers in the article.

1 Karissa spent some time in Guatemala.
2 She planned to be a waitress for many years.
3 Carlos and Karissa worked in the same restaurant.
4 Carlos went to high school in Argentina.
5 Carlos has brown eyes.
6 Karissa always wanted to get married.

4 💬 Work in groups. Do you think it is true that opposites attract? Do you have any friends who are very different from you?

GRAMMAR

1 a Find how these statements are expressed in the article and underline them.

1 'My plan is to go to graduate school.'
2 'I don't speak any English at the moment.'
3 'I am interested in a romantic relationship.'
4 'I'm sorry, but I'm not interested because there are too many differences between us.'
5 'I will never get married.'

b Complete 1–4 in the GRAMMAR PANEL ▉.

2 Read what Karissa and Carlos said in an interview. Complete the sentences.

Carlos is so funny and easy-going.   **Karissa**

Carlos   *And she's so intelligent... and an intelligent woman needs an intelligent man.*

1 Karissa said that Carlos ....
2 Carlos said that Karissa .... and that ....

3 **a** Rewrite the quotes as reported speech.

1 Jane: 'I always look at a person's smile. It needs to be warm and friendly.'

2 Rob: 'It's the eyes that are important for me. I really like big, brown eyes.'

3 Kristen: 'I don't look at physical things. I'm more interested in personality and conversation.'

4 Dave: 'Everyone is different. I can't really say what attracts me to someone.'

b Work in pairs. Compare your answers. What question are the four speakers answering? Do you agree with any of them? Which and why?

4 Dani met Sam on a singles website. In reality Sam was very different to his profile description. Read his profile and complete sentences 1–5 with Dani's reactions. Use your imagination.

Sam's profile	Dani's reaction
I have short dark hair.	1 *He said that he had dark hair, but he didn't have any hair!*
I am 1.90 m tall.	2 ....
I am slim and sporty.	3 ....
I live alone.	4 ....
I work for a bank.	5 ....

▪ REPORTED SPEECH: *SAY*

USE

We use *say (that)* to report what someone said.

FORM

The verb tense changes when we report what people said.

Direct speech	Reported speech
Present simple	(1) .... simple
'I like people.'	He said that he liked people.
Present continuous	(2) past ....
'I'm watching TV.'	She said that she was watching TV.
will + verb	(3) .... + verb
'We'll help you.'	They said that they would help me.
can + verb	(4) .... + verb
'She can go home.'	I said that she could go home.

NOTE: other changes:

today → that day

tomorrow → the next day

See page 150 for grammar reference and more practice.

PRONUNCIATION:

stress to change meaning

1 **a** 🔊 11.2 Listen to the sentences being said in two different ways. Underline the main stress in each one.

1 *She said that she was tired.*

2 *She said that she was tired.*

b Which sounds like the speaker doesn't believe what the person said?

2 **a** Read the situations. Say the sentence in **bold** with suitable stress.

1 Kerry didn't go to work, but Jake saw her at the cinema that night. She said, 'I've got a sore throat.' Jake didn't believe her.

Jake: **She said that she had a sore throat.**

2 Grant was off work and called Rosa from hospital. He said, 'I'm having an operation tomorrow.' Rosa was really worried.

Rosa: **He said that he was having an operation the next day.**

b 🔊 11.3 Listen and check.

3 Read the sentences with suitable stress.

1 Bill said his mother was very ill, but I saw her today and she was fine.

2 You said you would help me, but then you went out!

3 Marcos said he lived in Paris for five years, but he doesn't speak a word of French.

LISTENING

1 🔊 11.4 Listen to the radio phone in. How are the caller and his girlfriend different?

2 **a** Listen again. Who said the statements: the presenter, John, Simon, or Dr Mintbury?

1 'I have John Ferguson on the line from Birmingham.'

2 'My girlfriend is very different from me.'

3 'People usually choose a partner similar to them.'

4 'Opposites don't attract.'

5 'People with similar personalities are the happiest.'

6 'Even if you are different in some things, you can still have a great relationship.'

b Write the statements in 2a in reported speech.

3 💬 Work in pairs. Choose a reported speech sentence from 2a and read it to your partner. Your partner reads the statement that matches.

READING & LISTENING

1 Look at the photos. Discuss the questions.

- Are the people friends, family members or couples?
- What are the reasons why these people argue?

2 💬 Work in groups. What do you do if your friend or someone in your family does something you don't like or don't agree with?

- forget about it and say nothing
- don't talk to them for a while so they know you are hurt or angry
- talk to them about it and say why you are hurt or angry
- something else

3 Read the tips about arguing. Put the headings in the correct place in the text.

Be fair

Plan the right time to talk

Listen carefully

Understand your own weaknesses

> **NOTICE**   EXCUSE
> An excuse is a false explanation.
> *I didn't want to go to the party so I made an excuse and stayed at home.*

Arguing and Relationships

We all know it's hard to argue with the people we love. But sometimes we need to do it and here are four basic tips that might help you make an argument into a conversation.

1 ....

Make sure that what you want to talk about is really important and that it's not just an excuse to argue.

Don't start an argument just before you are going to go out or go to bed. Arguing in front of other people, especially children, is a very bad idea.

Last week my partner told me he wanted to talk about something and that we needed to make time to talk. I wanted to talk right then, but he was right to wait until we both had time.

2 ....

Use the pronoun *I*. Don't blame someone else. When I got home late last week I told my partner that I sometimes made mistakes and that I knew I wasn't perfect. This makes the other person less angry.

3 ....

You do not always know what other people think – remember this and pay attention to what people say. My partner told me that I was often late for dinner and that I often didn't call. I told him that I wasn't aware of this. I realise now that this was because I didn't listen.

4 💬 Work in pairs. Read the tips again. Are sentences 1–8 good or bad things to say in an argument? Why/Why not?

1 'I know it's time for bed, but I need to talk about something with you.'
2 'Now that we're alone I'd like to talk to you.'
3 'I'm sorry that I have to work late every night. I know it's a problem.'
4 'You're always at work when I need you here!'
5 'You never listen to me.'
6 'I think what you're saying is that you need me to help more. Is that right?'
7 'Let's not talk about last year – I want to find an answer to our problem now.'
8 'You're such a loser!'

5 a 🔊 11.5 Listen to the people arguing. How did the argument begin?

b Listen again. Name three things they do wrong, according to the tips.

6 💬 Work in pairs. Read transcript 11.5 on page 167. Change their words and make the argument into a conversation.

4 _____

Do not hit below the belt – that means don't say things that you know will hurt the other person. I told my partner that he was lazy during an argument last week. This just made him more angry and hurt.

Don't use bad words or shout, and try not to use extreme words like *ever* and *never*.

Stay on topic and don't talk about the past and things that are not part of this argument.

Good luck – remember it's not about winning!

GRAMMAR

1 Look at the sentences. Did the writer or her partner say them?

1 We need to make time to talk.
2 I know I sometimes make mistakes.
3 You're often late for dinner and you don't call to tell me.
4 You're lazy.

2 a Read the article again. Find where the sentences in 1 are reported and answer the questions.

1 What verb is used to report what was said?
2 What words follow directly after the verb?
3 Who are they referring to? The person who's speaking or the person who's listening?

b Complete the GRAMMAR PANEL ▪ using the words in the box.

after   him   name   talking

3 a Replace the words in **bold** with an object pronoun.

1 She told **her father** that she was angry.
2 He told **his sister** that he wouldn't be late this time.
3 He told **his family** that he was very sorry.
4 She told **me and John** that it wouldn't happen again.

b Write out the exact words that were said. Have you said these words recently? Who were you talking to? Use *tell* to report the conversations to your partner.

> **REPORTED SPEECH:** *TELL*
>
> When we use *tell* to report speech we always include information about who the person is (1)_____ to. We can use a (2)_____, a noun or an object pronoun.
>
> *John, her father,* (3)_____ .
>
> *She told her father that she was very angry.*
>
> This information always comes (4)_____ the verb *tell*.
>
> **Tell + person or thing + (that) + reported speech.**
>
> *He told   her   that   he was very sorry.*
>
> *See page 150 for grammar reference and more practice.*

SPEAKING

1 Think of a conversation that you have had today or recently.

● Who were you talking to? – a friend, colleague, family member
● What did you talk about? – news, gossip, work issues, relationships
● Was it interesting? Why/Why not?

2 💬 Work in pairs. Tell your partner about the conversation.
My friend told me that...   The woman explained...

3 🔊 11.6 Listen and complete the summary of the conversation.
Luke told (1)_____ that he (2)_____ . Mali said that (3)_____ .
Luke told (4)_____ that (5)_____ .

4 💬 Work in pairs. What would you say if you were Luke and Mali? Continue their argument. Then report another pair's argument.

READING

1 Divide into two groups, A and B. Group A, make notes on the advantages of being single. Group B, make notes on the disadvantages.

2 **a** Look at the photos. Group A, read Text A. Group B, read Text B. Which of the men in the photos is Costas and which is Jake? How do you know?

b Read the texts again. Did the texts include any of your notes from 1?

a

b

YOUR ANSWERS **Topic:** Staying single?

Open

Sort by: ▶ Newest ▶ Most Popular ▶ Fewest Answers

Text A 'I love being single!' says Jake.

The best thing about being **single** is the freedom – you can do what you want, when you want to do it. You don't have to go shopping when you want to watch TV and you don't have to remember birthdays and anniversaries.

This might sound really **selfish**, but being single means that I don't have to spend money on anyone else. You can be completely selfish and you don't have to feel guilty about it.

Meeting new people is possible again. You can **flirt** without feeling guilty and you can go on dates with someone you **fancy** whenever you want.

Finally, it's less stressful. Trying to stay together with someone is too much work. Two people together always argue and when you're single you don't have this problem.

Don't get me wrong, I still hope to find the right partner for me, but it doesn't matter if I don't. I like being single and I'm happy to stay single.
Answer #1

Text B Costas says, 'Being single is awful.'

I've been single for about five months and I hate it. Here's why.

First of all, I **miss** having someone around who I can tell all my problems and stories to. And I miss hugging another person. Everything is so much more fun with a partner – I like being **attached**.

Secondly, I no longer get the chance to go to nice places like restaurants, quiet bars or cinemas. If I go there by myself I just feel **lonely** and sad, so I always go to noisy bars or clubs.

Thirdly, I find I **resent** my friends' partners for stealing my friends away from me. I want them to be with me instead of going out with their partners. I guess I just don't want to be alone! When I was with my partner I didn't need to meet new people and now I don't know how to do it! I don't know where to start and I don't want people to feel sorry for me.
Answer #2

---

3 💬 Work in pairs, one student from A and one from B. Discuss the advantages and disadvantages of being single. Can you add more advantages and disadvantages?

4 Look at the texts again and match the words in **bold** to definitions 1–8.

1 with no partner
2 with a partner/spouse
3 feeling alone
4 to feel sad because someone or something is not there
5 to show someone that you find her or him attractive by the way you talk and look
6 to like someone in a romantic way
7 not considering other people
8 to have bad feelings about

VOCABULARY: relationships

1 Work in pairs. Read the list of events. In which order do these usually happen in a relationship? Use your dictionary to help you.

- **break up with** someone
- **fall in love with** someone
- **fancy** someone
- **go on a date with** someone
- **go out with** someone
- **live together**
- **get married**
- **meet** someone

2 **a** 💬 Work in pairs. Look at the photo. Describe what is happening. Are any of the events in 1 happening?

b Compare your ideas with another pair. Do you agree? Why/Why not?

LISTENING & SPEAKING

1 **a** 🔊 11.7 Listen to two people talking about a relationship. How did they meet their boyfriend/girlfriend?

b Listen again. Number the events in the order in which they happened.

	Kendra	Alex
They met		
He/she fancied him/her		
They went out		
They fell in love		
They lived together		
They got married		
They broke up		

2 Listen again. Are the sentences true or false?

1 Kendra found her partner attractive when she first saw him.
2 He introduced himself to her first.
3 He asked her to go out with him.
4 They started living together after about a year.
5 They are still together.
6 Alex met Petra at work.
7 She had a boyfriend when they met.
8 She broke up with her boyfriend two months after they met.
9 Alex and Petra got married six years ago.

> ### NOTICE *EVEN*
> We use *even* to express that something is surprising because it is extreme or unlikely.
> *I'll do anything for you. I'll even wash the dishes.*
> How do you express this idea in your language?

3 **a** 💬 Work in pairs. Tell the story of Kendra or Alex in your own words. Add one more 'false' event to the story.

b Read the story to the class. Who has the most interesting 'false' event in their story? Who has the funniest?

4 💬 Work in pairs. Do you know any interesting stories about how two people met and fell in love? Tell your partner.

TUNE IN

1 Is your telephone an important part of your life? Why? What do you use it for?

2 **a** 🔊 11.8 Listen to five messages. Which ones are about work?

b Listen again and complete the notes about the messages.

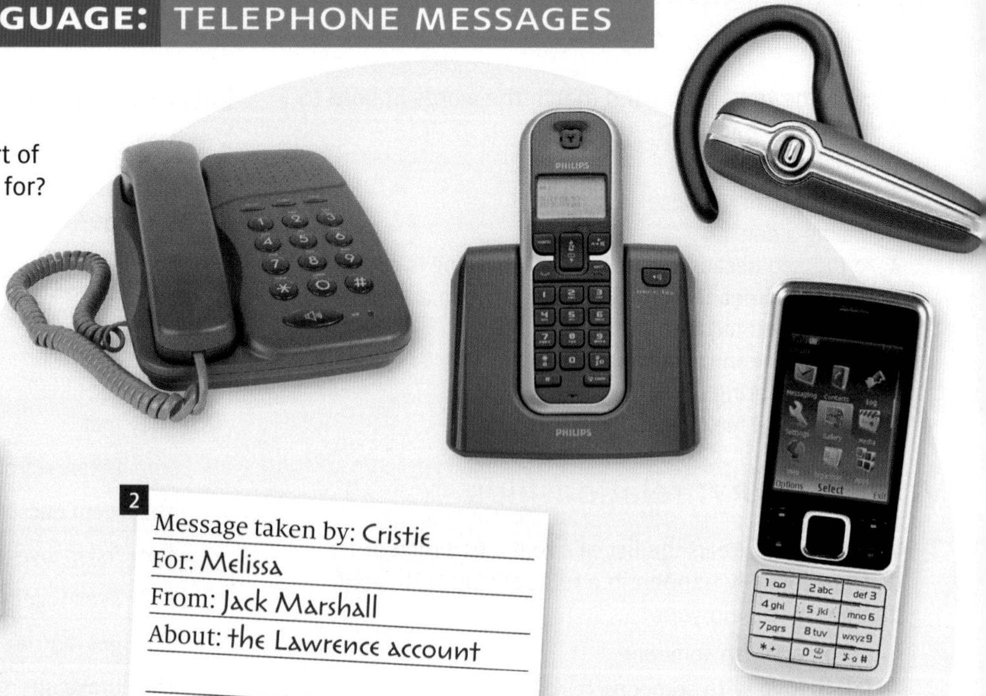

1

> Jody
>
> Drink after .... ?

2

> Message taken by: Cristie
> For: Melissa
> From: Jack Marshall
> About: the Lawrence account
> _____
> _____
>
> Please call back   immediately ☐
>   later ☐
>   tomorrow ☐

3

> Amanda called.
> Have you .... the
> report?
> Call her back.

4

> **Dr Bridges**
> Message from: Constance Jarman
> Number: ....
> Notes:
>   Appointment on .... ?

5

> GAV
> DAVE CALLED.
> HE'LL PICK YOU UP AT ....

FOCUS ON LANGUAGE

3 Listen and complete the phrases.

1 I was .... calling to see if...
2 Give me .... back.
3 How can I .... you?
4 Can I .... a message?
5 Could you .... her to .... me back
6 .... me back when you ....
7 I'll .... him.

4 Put the phrases in 3 in the correct place in the table.

Taking a message	Leaving a message
• Do you want to leave a message?	• I'm calling about...
• Would you like to... ?	• I was (just) .... to...
• .... help you?	
• Can I give him/her a message?	
• I'll .... him/her/them.	

❝ Intonation: sounding helpful ❞

🔊 11.9 Listen to two sentences and say which one sounds more helpful, a or b.
Practise with your partner and make sure you sound helpful.

5 💬 Work in pairs. Read this note. Act out the conversation between the person who telephoned and the person who took the message.

> Message taken by: (your name)
> _____
> Message from: Kelly Morgan
> For: Kevin Stanford
> About: the meeting this afternoon at 3 p.m.
>   Please call back before 11 a.m.

OVER TO YOU

6 💬 Work in groups of three. Student A, prepare and write/record a message for Student B.

Leave your telephone message.
• A calls B.
• B is not in. A leaves a message with C.
• C tells the message to B.

TUNE IN

1 🔊 11.10 Listen to Rosie talking to Lee about what's happening in her life. Choose the photo that shows Rosie.

a

b

c

2 Listen again. Match the person/people to what they are doing now.

1 at university	a Rosie and Pete
2 enjoying classes	b Pete
3 living in London	c Rosie's mum and dad
4 seeing each other at weekends	d Rosie's brother
5 working in a bank	e Rosie
6 getting married next year	
7 running a shoe shop	

3 🔊 11.11 Listen to Lee telling someone what Rosie said. What three things did he get wrong? Correct the mistakes.

PREPARE FOR TASK

4 🔊 11.12 Listen and complete the notes.

> 1 new ....
>
> 2 new .... (20 years old)
>
> 3 football – .... a week
>
> 4 gym .... times a week
>
> 5 needs to find new place
>
> to ....

5 a Work in pairs. Prepare to tell your partner what he said by completing the summary.

1
> He said he .... a new .... in a hairdressing salon and he said he had a new ....

2
> He said she .... and that she .... a ....

3
> He told me he .... football .... a week and that he .... to the gym .... times a week so he said he .... in good shape.

4
> He told me that he .... to find somewhere else to .... because his landlord .... to sell the house.

b 💬 Take turns to tell your partner what he said.

TASK

6 Prepare an update. Talk about you, your family and friends and the things that are happening in your life at the moment.

7 💬 Work in pairs. Take turns to give your update to your partner and make notes on your partner's update.

REPORT BACK

8 💬 What were the most interesting things that you heard about your classmates? Report back to the class on the most interesting things.

➡ Go to Review D, Unit 11, p. 137   ➡ Go to Writing bank 6, p. 157   **125**

12 ENTERTAIN ME

1 💬 Look at the photos. Discuss the questions.

- Where are the people and what are they doing?
- What do the two photos have in common? What is the main difference?

2 Work in pairs. Look at **A** in the KEY VOCABULARY PANEL ▪. Which type or types of entertainment

1 cannot be seen/heard live?
2 are sometimes broadcast live on TV or the internet?
3 are best seen/heard in person?

3 **a** Look at **B** in the KEY VOCABULARY PANEL ▪. Match the types of entertainment in **A** to the places in **B** where you can see/hear them. More than one answer is possible.

a concert – at the stadium, at a concert hall, at home, on TV, on your computer, in a bar, on the street, on the beach

b Look at the prepositions used in each phrase. Answer the questions in **B** in the KEY VOCABULARY PANEL ▪.

4 **a** 🔊 12.1 Listen to two conversations about something people have seen recently. Answer the questions.

1 What was it? Was it live or recorded?
2 Did they enjoy it? Why/Why not?

b

KEY VOCABULARY

Entertainment

A Types of entertainment

an album   a concert   a film/movie
a football match   the news   a play
a podcast   a radio interview
a TV show

B Places

in a bar   on the beach   on the bus
in your car   at the cinema
on your computer   at a concert hall
at home   on your phone
at the stadium   on the street
at the theatre   on TV

- Which preposition is used with technology?

- Which preposition is used with places that are specifically built for entertainment purposes?

- Which prepositions do you use in your language for each expression?

> **NOTICE** *LIVE*
>
> **live** /laɪv/ *(adj/adv)* **1** performed in front of you **2** shown or played on TV, the internet, the radio at the same time as it happens
> *I love live concerts.*
> *I saw the band live at the stadium.*
> *The match was shown live on local TV.*

- How do you translate *live* in your language in the three examples above?

b Listen again. Complete the gaps in the extracts.

1 I found this great **clip** on YouTube last ....
2 It's great, isn't it, really funny! My .... sent me the **link**.
3 The **venue**'s ...., but it was full, and the **atmosphere** was ....

5 Look at the words in **bold** in 4b. Match them to the definitions.

1 an electronic address
2 a place where you can see live entertainment
3 a short film
4 the mood or feeling in a place

6 💬 Work in pairs. Tell your partner about something you have seen/heard recently that you really enjoyed.

SPEAKING & VOCABULARY: music

1 Work in pairs. Look at the photos. What is each one showing? Match the words to the photos.

busker
someone who performs music in a public place, usually on the street, for money

collector's market
where people buy and sell second-hand items such as records, books, stamps, etc.

gig
informal word for a live concert

merchandise table
at a concert, the place where the band sell their T-shirts, posters, CDs, etc.

MP3 downloads
audio files that you can copy from your computer

online music store
a website that sells music

records
we listened to these before CDs and MP3 files

single track
just one song or piece of music

2 💬 Work in pairs. Discuss the questions. Use the words in **1** in your answers.

- When was the last time you bought some music? Or anything related to music? Where did you buy it from?
- Was it for you or was it a present? How much did you pay for it?
- How much do you think you should pay for music? Or should it be free?

READING

1 Read a blog post from a music lover and match it with one of the photos.

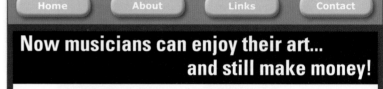

> | Home | About | Links | Contact |

Now musicians can enjoy their art... and still make money!

Fewer CDs are being sold both in shops and online, music is available free on the internet and the big bands on tour are making more money from merchandising than from tickets. Musicians are no longer in the music business, they are in the T-shirt business! OK, that may be a bit extreme. But with less money coming in from selling music the conventional way, artists need to find new ways to make a living from their art. But how?

Well, one of the best ways I know is by letting fans decide how much they want to pay. Lots of bands already do this quite successfully online (Radiohead were one of the first bands to do it with their album *In Rainbows* – fans paid anything or nothing for it). When you do it at the merchandise table at a live gig, the result is even better. To those fans that really like the band and ask about the price of a CD, your answer should be: 'How much would you like to pay?'. The answers might be something like these: 'I only have $4,' 'I'd like to give you $10,' 'You guys were great, here's $20,' 'I have no money.'

You should sell your CD at those different prices to all of those fans and give one free to the guy with no money. They will never forget the experience and they will tell their friends that you are the coolest band on earth for doing that.

2 Read the blog post again. Complete the summary. Do you think this idea can work?

> Musicians don't make as much money selling their (1)................. as they used to. One option to make (2)................. is to let the fans decide (3)................. they should pay for (4)................. at live concerts.

3 a Read three blog posts. Who is

1 in total agreement?
2 in total disagreement?
3 not completely sure?

Andres

Musicians shouldn't give their music away for free. It devalues music. True music fans will always be ready to pay for the music they love.

Juanita

It's an interesting idea. I'm certainly in favour of giving money directly to the artists. But would this idea still work the third or fourth time? Would people just start saying they didn't have any money on them?

Tomas

You really should try this out. We did. It really worked. We sold twice as much merchandise and at much higher prices than usual. Thanks, your idea rocks!

---

b What do you think about the idea now?

GRAMMAR

1 Work in pairs. Look at the extracts from the blog post. <u>Underline</u> the modal verbs.

1 Now musicians <u>can</u> enjoy their art... and still make money!
2 OK, that may be a bit extreme.
3 Your answer should be: 'How much would you like to pay?'
4 The answer might be something like these.
5 They will never forget the experience
6 Musicians shouldn't give their music away for free.
7 Would this idea still work the third or fourth time?

2 a Are the following rules true for modal verbs?

1 Use *do*, *does* and *did* to form questions and negatives.
2 Add *-s* to the third person singular.
3 Always use an infinitive after a modal verb.

b Check your answers in the GRAMMAR PANEL ▇ and complete 1–3 with examples from the blog post.

3 Look again at the modal verbs in 1. Use them to complete 4–9 in the GRAMMAR PANEL ▇ .

4 a Use modal verbs to complete the sentences. Choose the modal verb that is closest to your opinion.

1 CDs .... soon become a thing of the past.
2 Musicians .... find new ways of making money.
3 You .... download free music from the internet.
4 I .... like to be a professional musician.
5 I .... learn to play a/another musical instrument one day.

b 💬 Compare your answers with a partner.

MODAL VERBS REVIEW

FORM

We use modal verbs with the infinitive without *to*.
(1) ....

We use modal verbs without *do/does/did* to make questions.
(2) ....

and negatives
(3) ....

We do not add *-s* to the third person singular.
He can play the guitar well, NOT *He cans play the guitar well*.

USE

Modal verbs add information to the verb.
Different modals add different information.

Modal verb	Use
(4)	to talk about the future
(5) .... (6)	to say something is possible, but you aren't sure
(7)	to talk about ability, possibility and permission in the present
(8)	to make recommendations
(9)	to talk about imaginary situations

See page 151 for grammar reference and more practice.

SPEAKING

1 a Work in groups. Write two more questions about entertainment.

1 What's your idea of a perfect night's entertainment?
2 What music would you like for a romantic dinner?

b 💬 Ask your class the questions. Make notes of their answers. What did you find out?

I used to believe...
the childhood beliefs site

LISTENING & SPEAKING

1 💬 Look at the photos from a website called www.iusedtobelieve.com. What kind of information do you think appears on this website?

2 🔊 12.2 Listen to four messages left on the website. What forms of entertainment are they talking about?

> radio   TV   cinema   computer games

3 Listen again. Complete the extracts from the website.

1
> When we went to see a movie ... I used to believe that the credits at the end were a list of .... that were watching, and I used to look for ....

2
> ...when I was little, I listened to a lot of .... When I was looking for channels I used to think that AM and FM meant 'American Music' and '.. .'

3
> I used to think that the high scores on the screens of games were the highest scores ever recorded ....

4
> Our .... used to think that when you turned it ...., it used to .... your place like a bookmark in a book.

My grandmother thought that electricity escaped from the holes in the sockets during the night if you didn't put a plug in them!

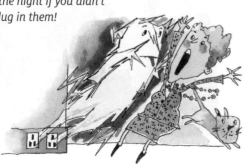

GRAMMAR

1 a Work in pairs. Look at the short conversation. Are they talking about a) a specific moment in the past? b) a past habit or situation?

> A Did you use to watch a lot of TV when you were a kid?
>
> B We didn't use to have a TV. But I used to spend a lot of time listening to the radio.

b Complete 1–5 in the GRAMMAR PANEL ▪▫.

> **NOTICE** *USED TO*
> We don't use *used to* in the present tense. We have to use an adverb (*usually*, *often*) instead.
> *I don't usually watch James Bond films,*
> NOT *I don't ~~use to watch~~...*

2 a Make as many true sentences as possible using the prompts.

> *I didn't use to..., but now I...*
> *I didn't use to like rap music, but now I love it.*

b 💬 Compare your answers with a partner.

3 Put the words in the correct order to form questions.

1 What   did   to   use   watch   TV programmes   you   ?
2 the cinema   How often   use to   go to   did you   ?
3 use to   video games   play   What type of   did you   ?
4 you   with your friends   use to   What   did   do   ?

4 💬 Work in pairs. Answer the questions so that they are true for you when you were younger. Compare the situation in the past with what you do now.

1 *I used to love watching James Bond films with my family, but now I don't like them. I usually watch TV online...*

◼ USED TO

USE

We use *used to* + infinitive to talk about
(1) .... habits, routines, actions
and beliefs.

*We **used to watch** a lot of TV together as a family.*
*I **used to think** that every time an ad came on TV
it was live.*

FORM

(+) (2) .... + infinitive:
   I used to love TV ads.

(–) (3) .... + infinitive:
   We didn't use to have a TV.

(?) Did you (4) .... + infinitive:
   Did you use to watch a lot of TV?

Notice that in the negative and in questions
we use (5) .... and NOT ~~used to~~.

*See page 151 for grammar reference and more
practice.*

PRONUNCIATION: *used to*

1 a 12.3 Read and listen to the
conversation. Notice the pronunciation of *s* in
use(d) to. Is it /s/ or /z/?

   A We didn't u<u>s</u>e to have a TV when I was a kid.

   B What did you u<u>s</u>e to do in the evenings?

   A We u<u>s</u>ed to play cards, or listen to the radio.

   b Listen again and repeat.

2 💬 Work in pairs. Think of three things you
did when you were younger that you don't do
now. Student A, tell your partner. Student B,
ask a follow-up question.

SPEAKING & LISTENING

1 💬 Look at the photos. Answer the questions.
   1 What changes do they show in the way we watch TV?
   2 How many of these changes have already happened?
   3 Which do you think will never take place?

2 🔊 12.4 Listen to Professor Jane Gruber discussing TV. How many
of the changes you discussed in 1 does she mention? Does she talk
about any others?

3 Listen again. Choose the best answer, a, b or c, for each question.
   1 What point does Gruber make about TV viewing habits today?
      a Children watch less TV than in the past.
      b Nobody finishes watching a TV programme now.
      c People can choose what to watch and when to watch it.
   2 What has changed in the way we watch TV?
      a We don't watch TV together as a family as much.
      b People do other activities together.
      c We only watch video clips now.
   3 Is this the end for conventional TV?
      a No, we watch more, but at different times and using different
        media.
      b Yes, online TV is now more popular than conventional TV.
      c No, watching conventional TV is still people's favourite hobby.

4 a Look at the extracts from the listening. Explain the words in **bold**.
   1 if you want to watch an episode of a favourite series, you can find it
     on many **online media sites**.
   2 now we can **download our own entertainment**...
   3 Now there is no **prime time**. **Prime time** is all the time.

   b 💬 Do you agree with what Professor Gruber says?
   Why/Why not?

THE WEEKLY

MOSCOW

RT **ANDREY KORTUNOV**
POLITICAL ANALYST, THE NEW EURASIA FOUNDATION

SPEAKING & VOCABULARY: the internet

1 💬 Look at the photos. What are they showing? Which clip would you prefer to watch? Why?

2 **a** Look at the comments. Which photo do they refer to?

> That **post** was really popular – I got 400 **hits** in one day on my blog!

> If you want to know more about this band, visit their **website**! It's great! You can **download** their new album. Free!!
> **Click** here.

> Have you got any funny photos to send us?
> **Upload** them here.

> More than 10,000 **viewers** have seen this news clip today. Add your name to the list!

b Match the words in **bold** with definitions 1–7.

1 the number of times people connect to an online site.
2 to copy information from the internet onto your computer
3 to copy information from your computer onto a page on the internet
4 an entry that you place on a blog
5 people who watch something
6 a page or group of pages on the internet
7 press a button on your mouse to go to a new page

3 Do you use any of the words in your language?

4 💬 Work in groups. Discuss the questions.
● How often do you watch video clips on the internet? What type of videos do you usually watch? How long are they?
● Do you have a favourite video-sharing website? If yes, what do you like about it?

READING

1 💬 Work in pairs. Look at the title of an article about online video clips and the 'audience attention span' chart. What do you think the article is going to say about video clips?

2 Read the article. Choose the best answer to the question in 1.
1 Many video clips on YouTube are only one minute long.
2 Most people who watch YouTube stop watching after one minute.
3 According to a survey, one-minute video clips are the most popular type on YouTube.

3 Read the article again. Are the sentences true or false? If false, explain why.

1 YouTube watchers are similar to television viewers.
2 TubeMogul is a website that shows video clips.
3 Most viewers stop watching after ten seconds.
4 Fewer than 10% of people watch clips for longer than five minutes.

4 💬 Work in groups. Discuss the questions.

- Does any of the information in the article surprise you? If yes, what and why?
- Do you think the internet has an influence on people's ability to concentrate?
- Do you think we have developed any new skills as the result of the internet?

A MINUTE OF YOUR TIME...

by Peter Kafka

Everyone knows that YouTube is one of the most popular websites in the world. Yet nobody actually watches that much video on it. Confused? Don't be. There's a simple explanation: people who watch video clips on the internet watch a lot of videos. But none of the clips are very long. Just like TV viewers, they're always looking for the latest thing. In fact, it is unlikely that most viewers will get to the end of longer video clips.

It's common sense, really. TubeMogul, a company that studies people's viewing habits, shows exactly how long the average web video watcher stays with any particular clip. Answer: Less than one minute!

Ten seconds into an average clip – which is nothing – and more than 10% of viewers have started watching something else, TubeMogul says! And by 60 seconds,

more than half of viewers have closed the window. Anything more than five minutes is exceptional: more than 91% of viewers have gone by then.

Are you finding it hard to believe that our attention spans are so short? Let me invite you to put it to the test. Click <u>play</u> on the 6-minute, 48-second clip below: Stevie Wonder singing 'Superstition'. If anyone gets all the way to the end, I'll send them a link to a free album download!

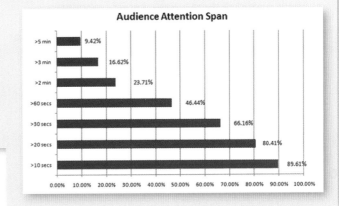

Audience Attention Span

>5 min	9.42%
>3 min	16.62%
>2 min	23.71%
>60 secs	46.44%
>30 secs	66.16%
>20 secs	80.41%
>10 secs	89.61%

0.00% 10.00% 20.00% 30.00% 40.00% 50.00% 60.00% 70.00% 80.00% 90.00% 100.00%

LISTENING & SPEAKING

1 Work in pairs. Look at the photos from an online slideshow. What do you think the slideshow is about?

2 **a** 🔊 12.5 Listen and check.

b Listen again. How many slides are there in total? What does each slide show?

3 **a** Work in groups. You are going to design a slideshow for your English class. Follow the instructions below.

1 Decide what you want to present to the class.
2 Think of the six photos that make up the slideshow.
3 Decide on the order and what you want to say.
4 Practise presenting your slideshow.

b 💬 Take turns to present your slideshows. Listen to the other groups and make a note on each photo.

4 Which slideshow was the most original? Which was the most amusing? Why?

TUNE IN

1 💬 Look at the photo. Where is she? Who is she texting? What do you think she might be saying?

2 Reorder the words to find out what she wrote.

> park in at concert. playing band great. them you'd love. again playing next they're week. go to you have just!

3 💬 When was the last time you recommended an event to a friend? What was it? Did your friend go?

4 🔊 12.6 Listen to extracts from three phone conversations. Answer the questions.

1 What kind of event is the speaker recommending?
2 Why are they recommending them?
3 Is the other person interested?

FOCUS ON LANGUAGE

5 a Complete the recommendations using the words and phrases.

> have   kind of thing   love   must   should

1 We were in the park yesterday, and they've got this great photo exhibition on. You'd absolutely .... it.
2 You really .... go. It's just the .... you like.
3 You .... to see it. It'll make you laugh.
4 Siva and his band are playing. You .... go!

b Listen again and check.

6 a Match the recommendations in 5a with the responses.

a I'm not sure. It's not really my kind of thing.
b I had no idea! I'm so sorry I missed it.
c Really? I'll have to take a look.
d Sounds interesting. When is it on until?

b Read transcript 12.6 on page 167 to check your answers. Underline other language that is useful for making recommendations or responding.

7 💬 Work in pairs. Use transcript 12.6 and act out the three phone conversations. Remember to use appropriate intonation for the responses.

❝ Intonation: sounding interesting ❞

🔊 12.7 Listen to the exclamations. Notice how the speaker's voice changes on the main stress. What effect does this create?

Sounds _interesting_.
Really?
I had _no_ idea!

Listen again and repeat, paying special attention to the intonation.

OVER TO YOU

8 Think of an event, a TV programme, a YouTube clip, or any other kind of entertainment that you can recommend to your class. Think of a good reason for recommending it and make some notes.

9 💬 Move around the class and recommend your idea to as many students as possible. Remember to respond appropriately to the other students' ideas.

TUNE IN

1 💬 Look at the photos. Do you recognise the TV series? Do you watch any of them? Which TV series are most popular among your friends? Why?

2 Match the series with the summaries.
   1 An animated comedy series that is based on the lives of the Griffin family.
   2 A TV medical drama that focuses on the life and work of an unconventional medical genius and his team of doctors.
   3 A TV drama that describes the lives of plane crash survivors on a mysterious tropical island.
   4 A crime series which follows a team of crime scene investigators as they use physical evidence to solve mysteries and murders.

3 a Think of another TV series. Write a one-sentence description – but don't say the name.

   b Read your description to the class. Can they guess which TV series it is?

4 Read the description of a local TV show. Would you like to watch it? Why/Why not? Is there anything similar on TV in your country?

PREPARE FOR TASK

5 Read the description again. Match the information in the box to the paragraphs where it appears.

   main characters   one-sentence summary
   storyline   personal recommendation
   reason for success   setting

   Paragraph 1: ....
   Paragraph 2: ....
   Paragraph 3: ....
   Paragraph 4: ....

6 Think of a TV series which is broadcast in your country. Complete the sentences with information about the series.
   1 The show is set...
   2 The main characters are...
   3 It talks about...
   4 The reason for its success is...
   5 I'd recommend this programme to...

| Article | Discussion |

Pobol y Cwm (People of the Valley)

Pobol y Cwm (People of the Valley) is a Welsh language TV soap opera which has been produced by the BBC since 1974. The show is set in the fictional village of Cwmderi and talks about complex social themes such as death, bullying and mental health in a sensitive and sympathetic way.

The characters are all people who live in the village. Marian, a sweet, old lady, knows everything about everybody. Meic and Anita are the owners of the pub, which is at the heart of village life. They share in everybody's problems, even though they have plenty of their own, including a fire which burns down the pub. They have to close down and start again in a new building.

The lives of the people of Cwmderi are full of personal tragedies and difficult choices, which are followed by thousands of fans five nights a week. The key to its success is the fact that life in Cwmderi reflects the problems and choices that people face in the world outside, and it is easy for the audience to feel sympathy for them.

With English subtitles and a great website with information and downloads, I'd recommend this programme to anyone who wants to know a little more about Wales and its language.

TASK

7 Write a short description of the series. Use the paragraph structure in 5 and the sentences you wrote in 6 to help you.

REPORT BACK

8 💬 Tell the other students in the class about your TV series. How many follow it regularly? Which series is most popular?

➜ Go to Review D, Unit 12, p. 138

VOCABULARY
Advertising

1 **a** Write the letters in the correct order to make words.

1 ogol ....
2 ravtde ....
3 aosnlg ....
4 anbdr ....
5 yfrle ....
6 doblabril ....

b 💬 Work in pairs. Take turns to describe three words from a. Can you guess which words your partner is describing?

Adjectives

2 Look at the adjectives in the box. Which are often used to describe a) food? b) buildings/places? c) clothes?

> ancient beautiful colourful delicious
> disgusting fresh modern mouth-watering
> patterned processed tight

3 Think of a noun to combine with each adjective in 2. Use a different noun each time.

an ancient temple

GRAMMAR
Passive

1 **a** Complete the football quiz questions with the correct form of the verbs.

> **1** Football is a global sport but it ....
> *(not play)* much in...
>   **a)** Africa   **b)** Central America **c)** North America.
>
> **2** The 1966 World Cup .... *(win)* by...
>   **a)** Brazil   **b)** England   **c)** France.
>
> **3** Over...
>   **a)** 125 million **b)** a billion   **c)** 275 million
>   people .... *(involve)* in football – 4%
>   of the world's population.
>
> **4** The rules of football .... *(invent)* by
>   the...
>   **a)** Brazilians **b)** English   **c)** Italians.

b Do the quiz and check the answers on page 161.

2 💬 Work in groups. Write four quiz questions about a topic using the passive form. Test your class.

3 **a** Complete the text about jeans using the best form of the verb *to be* (present or past, positive or negative).

> **1** They .... originally created for workers and sailors, but now they .... worn by everybody.
>
> **2** In the 1950s, they .... sometimes banned because they were a symbol of youth rebellion.
>
> **3** But now millions of pairs .... worn by people of all ages all over the world.
>
> **4** Like flip-flops, they .... originally created to be a fashion item.

b 💬 Work in pairs. Do you know any facts about other clothes? Tell your partner. Use the passive form.

FUNCTIONAL LANGUAGE
Describing a local dish

Açaí na tigela

1 **a** Match the questions to the answers.

1 What are the ingredients?
2 What kind of dish is it?
3 Where is it eaten?
4 How is it served?

a In the street, from stalls or shops.
b Açaí berries from a palm tree.
c Usually with muesli and fresh fruit.
d It's a kind of cold dessert.

b 🔊 R14 Listen and check. What other information did you find out about the dish?

2 💬 Work in pairs. Would you like to try the dish in 1? Why/Why not? Compare your answers with your partner.

▪ LOOKING BACK

- Describe an advertisement you have seen or heard in the last week. Did you like it? Why/Why not?
- Describe the clothes you are wearing to a partner. Where were they were made? Where were they were bought?
- Which topic in this unit did you like best?

VOCABULARY
Adjectives to describe personality

1 Complete the adjectives.

1 Calm, g _____ r _____ older woman is looking to meet an intelligent, s _____ n _____ man.

2 Energetic student wants to meet c _____ a _____ friends for art projects.

3 S _____ , quiet young man would like to meet a k _____ woman, who is f _____ n _____ and o _____ .

2 Match photos a–c to the descriptions of the people they would like to meet in **1**.

3 **a** Name someone you know who is

1 sociable   2 sporty   3 fashionable   4 artistic

b 💬 Work in pairs. Tell your partner where you met the people in **3a**.

Relationships

4 **a** Complete the conversation with a suitable word or expression.

CHAS	Hi Mel! Where's Steve?
MEL	He's not coming. We ⁽¹⁾_____ .
CHAS	Oh, I'm sorry to hear that.
MEL	It's OK. I'm enjoying being ⁽²⁾_____ . I'm ⁽³⁾_____ a date with someone tonight though.
CHAS	Wow! That was fast!
MEL	Yes, I've ⁽⁴⁾_____ him for a long time and now I don't feel ⁽⁵⁾_____ about it!
CHAS	Well, have fun!

b 🔊R15 Listen and check. Who was Steve?

5 💬 Work in pairs. Act out the conversation in **4a**.

GRAMMAR
Reported speech: *say*

1 🔊R16 Listen and write what the people said. Use reported speech.

1 Rob said *he couldn't go out with Candy* _____

2 Gwen said _____

3 Marie said _____

4 Harry said _____

Reported speech: *tell*

2 Report what happened in the conversation.

MEG	I'm going out tomorrow.
SANJAY	I'm not doing anything – I can come with you.
MEG	That's a good idea. You need to meet some new people.

Meg told Sanjay that _____

FUNCTIONAL LANGUAGE
Telephone messages

1 **a** Put the conversation in the correct order.

☐ A Ms Lam is not available at the moment. Can I take a message?

☐ B Thank you. Goodbye.

1 A Good afternoon, Tech World.

☐ B Yes, can you tell her that Laura Walters called to say that the meeting is on Friday, not on Monday.

☐ A I'll tell her as soon as she arrives.

☐ B Hello, could I speak to Kay Lam, please?

b 🔊R17 Listen and check. Write the message for Kay Lam.

2 💬 Work in pairs. Act out conversations with different messages.

■ LOOKING BACK

- In this unit, which are the most useful words you learned for describing someone's personality?
- What is your favourite expression to talk about relationships?
- How often do you give messages and describe what people told you?

UNIT 12

VOCABULARY
Entertainment

1 Work in pairs. Look at the nouns in the box. Which nouns are a) types of entertainment? b) venues for entertainment?

> album   cinema   concert hall   film
> football match   live concert   play
> podcast   stadium   theatre   TV show

2 💬 Work in pairs. When did you last see some live entertainment? What was it? Where was it? Did you enjoy it?

3 a Complete the sentences using a preposition from the box, or nothing.

> at   in   on

1 I usually listen to music .... the bus.
2 I don't watch sport .... TV, I prefer to watch it .... live.
3 I like to watch people playing music .... the street.
4 I don't buy much music anymore, you can download it all .... home.
5 When I'm .... my car, I don't like listening to music.

b 💬 Work in pairs. Are the sentences true for you? Discuss with a partner.

Buying music

4 a Put the words in the box in the correct columns.

> buskers   fans   MP3 downloads
> music store   merchandise table
> musicians   online   records   single track

People	Types of music	Ways of buying music

b 💬 Work in pairs. Choose a word from 4a and describe it. Can your partner guess? Take turns to describe words.

GRAMMAR
Modal verbs review

1 Complete the text using suitable modal verbs.

My music blog

It was my friend Ricky who told me, 'you know so much about music, you really (1).............. start a blog about it'. He was right, I started the blog and now I have lots of friends who follow it. It's great because I (2).............. write about any group or music that I like and people (3).............. leave comments. It's very interactive. I (4).............. also see how many people log on to my blog everyday. What do I write about? Well, I give advice about what music to listen to, you know, 'you (5).............. listen to this!' or if I want to insist, 'you (6).............. listen to this right now!'. Now people are asking me, '(7).............. you start a second one?'

Used to

2 a Correct the mistakes in the sentences.

1 I use to go to the cinema once a month, but now I just rent a DVD.
2 I didn't used to like classical music, but now I do.
3 I don't use to give money to buskers.
4 I used to downloading music without paying, but now I think it's not fair on the artists.

b Are any of the sentences true for you? Change the ones that aren't.

FUNCTIONAL LANGUAGE
Making recommendations

1 Write the words in the correct order to make sentences.

1 try should You to see it .
2 it love You'd !
3 must You go !
4 really You live to a should match go .

2 🔊 R18 Listen to four conversations. What types of entertainment are the people talking about? What do the people say about them? Are the people enthusiastic or not?

◼ LOOKING BACK

- Think of two things you used to do in the past that you don't do now.
- Think of four different types of entertainment and four different situations in which you could enjoy them.
- Which activities in this unit were a) the most interesting? b) the most useful? Why?

138

SPEAKING & READING

1 💬 Work in pairs. Look at the photos and answer the questions.

1 What are the people doing?
2 How can these activities help you to improve your English?

2 Quickly read the webpage. Match two of 1–3 to the photos in **1**. What other idea does the webpage mention?

a   b

⟹⟹ English online ⟸⟸

Computers are used for many things – work, fun, chatting – and, of course, studying! Many of you have told us that you regularly use computers to improve your English. Here are some of your ideas.

1 Rika from Germany suggests

I love reading, and I also think it's the most useful way to improve your vocabulary and grammar when you're learning a language. Unfortunately, not many English books or newspapers are sold where I live – and they're usually really expensive! But you can find some great American and British news websites online for free. So I can practise my English, and read some interesting articles, too. Perfect!

2 Yani from Albania suggests

Why not download music in English? There are some great websites with song lyrics, so you can read the words, too. I've learnt lots of new vocabulary that way, and it's great fun – learning shouldn't always feel 'boring'! But watch out – sometimes the grammar in song lyrics is a bit strange! If I'm not sure about anything, I ask my English teacher for help. You can't learn everything online!

3 Sabita from India suggests

I love watching American films on my laptop. I usually prefer to watch films with subtitles, so I can listen and read at the same time. When I was growing up, I used to love musicals, like Mary Poppins. Now I can watch them again! Sometimes I even try watching them without the subtitles. It's good to try something a bit more difficult, now and then. For me, listening is the hardest skill, so I need to practise it lots.

3 Read the webpage again. Do you think the writers would agree or disagree with these statements?

1 'Reading lots of texts is the best way to improve your English.'
   Rika would **agree/disagree**.

2 'Learning can be fun.'
   Yani would **agree/disagree**.

3 'You don't need to go to English classes if you can use the internet.'
   Yani would **agree/disagree**.

4 'Learning should always be easy.'
   Sabita would **agree/disagree**.

5 'Listening is more difficult than reading, writing or speaking.'
   Sabita would **agree/disagree**.

4 a Which of the opinions in **3** do you agree with?

b 💬 Work in pairs. Say why you agree or disagree with the statements.

■ QUICK CHECK

Complete the checklist below.

Can you...	Yes, I can.	Yes, more or less.	I need to look again.
1 talk about actions without saying who did them?	☐	☐	☐
2 describing what people are wearing?	☐	☐	☐
3 describe a dish?	☐	☐	☐
4 describe what people are like?	☐	☐	☐
5 report what people say?	☐	☐	☐
6 leave a telephone message?	☐	☐	☐
7 talk about what you used to do in the past?	☐	☐	☐
8 make recommendations?	☐	☐	☐

💬 Compare your answers with a partner.

● What else do you know now after studying units 10–12?

1.1 PRESENT SIMPLE & PRESENT CONTINUOUS

Present simple

+	I/You/We/They	understand	French.
	He/She/It	understand**s**	
–	I/You/We/They	don't	understand	Japanese.
	He/She/It	do**es**n't		

Use the present simple to talk about
1 general truths or situations *I live in São Paulo. Roberto works as a teacher.*
2 regular habits / routines *School starts at 6 a.m. every day. I usually get up at 8 a.m.*
Use time expressions like *usually, sometimes, never, always* and *often*.

Present continuous

| + | I'm
You're/We're/They're
He's/She's/It's | reading. |
| – | I'm not
You/We/They aren't
He/She/It isn't | reading. |

Use the present continuous to talk about actions that are happening at the moment. *We're reading our English book right now.*
Use time expressions like *at the moment, today* and *right now*.

Stative verbs

Stative verbs describe feelings, thoughts and sensations. We do not usually use these verbs in a continuous form. *I like this class.* NOT ~~I'm liking~~ this class.
Stative verbs include *be, like, love, hate, need, belong, know, want, believe, understand*.

▶ 1.1

1.2 QUESTIONS

Questions with the verb *to be*

The verb *to be* comes before the subject in both yes/no questions and *Wh-* questions. *Are you Canadian? Was he happy with his course? Where is your English school? Where were you yesterday?*

Yes/no questions with other verbs

The subject comes between the auxiliary verb and the main verb. In the present simple and past simple use *do, does* and *did* as the auxiliary verb.

Present simple

| Do | I/you/we/they | speak | French very well? |
| Does | he/she/it | understand | Japanese? |

Past simple

| Did | I/you/we/they/he/she/it | understand | German? |

Wh- questions with other verbs

In *Wh-* questions the question word comes at the beginning of the question followed by the auxiliary, the subject and the main verb.

Wh- ?	Auxiliary verb	Subject	Main verb	
What	are	you	studying	at the moment?
What	did	they	do	last night?
Where	does	he	go	to school?

▶ 1.2

1.1

a Read the sentences. Tick the ones that are correct and correct the ones that are not.

1 I usually play football on Sundays.
2 We are often watching TV in the evening.
3 I'm not understanding the words of English songs.
4 I'm learning French at the moment.
5 We eat dinner right now.
6 I'm not really liking sports.

b Are any of these sentences true for you?

c Complete the conversation with the present simple or present continuous.

MARSHA Where _____ you _____? *(go)*
TIM I _____ *(go)* to my yoga class. I always _____ *(do)* yoga on Mondays.
MARSHA What time _____ the class _____? *(start)*
TIM It _____ *(start)* at 6 p.m. and _____ *(finish)* at 7.30. _____ you _____ *(want)* to come?
MARSHA No, thanks. I _____ *(do)* my homework. I _____ *(not like)* to do homework late at night.
TIM Ok, I'll see you later.

1.2

a Write the words in the correct order to form questions.

1 musical instrument you play Do a ?
2 sport do do How often you ?
3 have you favourite a Do TV show ?
4 exam you for Are an studying at the moment ?
5 last What you night did do ?

b Answer the questions. Use full sentences.

c Write the questions for the answers.

1 _____
I live in New York City.
2 _____
No, I'm single.
3 _____
I'm working on a film about a person with an unusual hobby.
4 _____
My last film was about a person who lives in Thailand.
5 _____
I go to the cinema about twice a week.

2.1 PAST SIMPLE

+	verb + -ed *	I/You/He/She/It/We/They	watched	the film.
–	didn't + infinitive	I/You/He/She/It/We/They	didn't watch	the film.
?	did + subject + infinitive	Did	I/you/he/she it/we/they	watch the film?

* Some verbs have an irregular form: *make → made, do → did, have → had, fly → flew, sleep → slept, take → took, eat → ate.*

Use the past simple to talk about completed past actions and past situations.

The Tate Modern opened in 2000.
I lived in a small flat in Barcelona five years ago.

Past simple time expressions

Use time expressions like

in 2007, last week, last night, last year, ago, yesterday, on Tuesday, in January, an hour ago, when, at 8.30.

▶ 2.1

2.2 PAST CONTINUOUS

+	I/He/She/It You/We/They	was were	eating.
–	I/He/She/It You/We/They	was not (wasn't) were not (weren't)	eating.
?	Was Were	I/he/she/it you/we/they	eating?

Use the past continuous to talk about an action in progress at a certain time in the past.

I was walking home at 5.30 this afternoon.
My friends were waiting outside the restaurant.

▶ 2.2

2.3 PAST SIMPLE & PAST CONTINUOUS

Use the past continuous to show that one action was in progress when another, shorter action took place.

I was putting the tent up when I heard a strange noise.

We often use *while* + past continuous.

I took a photo of the zebra while it was eating.

Use two past simple verbs to show that one action followed the other.

I heard a strange noise and looked up to see what it was.

We often use *and, then* and *so* to link the two actions.

I finished putting up the tent then I went to park the car.

NOTE: We do not usually use stative verbs in the continuous form.

I loved animals when I was a child. NOT *I ~~was loving~~ animals when I was a child.*

(See also 1.1.)

▶ 2.3

2.1

a Read the text about Bear Grylls. Look at the verbs in italics. Find and correct five mistakes.

> Bear Grylls *learned* to swim and climb when he *were* very young. When he *finished* school he *spended* some time hiking in the Himalayas before he *joined* the Army. In 2000 he *rode* around the UK on a jet ski. Three years later he *cross* the Atlantic. In 2008 he *went* on an expedition to climb the highest peak in Antarctica but he *didn't completed* his mission because he *breaked* his shoulder. But this *didn't stop* him and two years later he was back again, trying to break yet another record!

b What else can you remember about Bear Grylls from the lesson? Write three sentences about his adventures. Then check your answers on page 17.

2.2

a Look at the picture. It shows a party that took place at João's flat last night. What were the people doing? Write six sentences using the verbs in the box.

choose   dance   eat   play   read   watch

b Write three more sentences explaining what they weren't doing.

2.3

a Complete the text using the past simple or the past continuous form of the verbs in brackets.

It was a beautiful day. The sun [1] .... (shine) and the sky was blue. We [2] .... (cycle) along a quiet road in the countryside when we [3] .... (heard) some dogs. But they were very far away so we [4] .... (not/think) any more about it and [5] .... (continue) on our ride. We [6] .... (just/come) round a corner in the road when suddenly an enormous white dog [7] .... (jump) out in front of us. Three other dogs [8] .... (follow) him. They were wild dogs and we were scared. We [9] .... (throw) sticks and rocks at them. Eventually they [10] .... (ran) away.

3.1 RELATIVE CLAUSES

Use relative clauses when you want to give more information about a person or thing.

— *Who's that?*
— *Oh, he's the guy **who painted our house.***

Relative pronouns

Relative pronoun	Refers to
who	person
which	thing
that	people and things

Main clauses and relative clauses

When we use relative clauses the sentence has two parts.

Main clause	Relative clause
This is the person	**who** lives next door to me.
Have you seen the film	**that** won the Oscar this year?

▶ 3.1

3.2 ARTICLES: *A/AN*, *THE*, NO ARTICLE

A, *an* (indefinite article)

Use *a* and *an* to talk about single objects without referring to a specific object.

*Do you have **a** pencil?* (I'm interested in one pencil, but I don't mind which pencil it is)

We use *a/an* with singular countable nouns. We use *a* before a consonant and *an* before a vowel sound.

*I think I need **a** new phone.*
*Can I have **an** apple?*

NOTE: not all words that are written with a vowel start with a vowel sound.

university /ˌjuːnɪˈvɜːsɪtɪ/ *He went to a university in the States.*
European /ˌjʊərəˈpɪən/ *I've got a European passport.*
euro /ˈjuːrəʊ/ *Can you give me a euro?*

The (definite article)

Use *the* to refer to a specific person or thing.

*Can I have **the** pencil I gave you?* (= a specific pencil)

We also use *the* when there is only one in the context.

***The** boss isn't very happy today.* (there's only one boss)

We use *the* before

• uncountable nouns *I love **the** coffee your mother makes.*
• singular countable nouns ***The** computer I use at work is really slow.*
• plural countable nouns *They put **the** logos on the front page.*

No article

Don't use an article before singular or plural nouns when we are referring to people or things in general.

I like old buildings.
I visited temples in Thailand.

▶ 3.2

3.1

a Read the sentences. Cross out any unnecessary words.

1   Kim introduced me to the man who he is going to be our teacher next year.
2   I love that coffee shop that you took me to it last week.
3   Can you tell me some more about that film which you saw it last night?
4   Your brother is probably the funniest person that I've ever met him.

b Use *who* or *which* to join the two sentences. Remember to drop any unnecessary pronouns.

1   This is the photo. I took it last year on holiday.
2   These are the people. We met them at the hotel.
3   This is the hotel. It was in the centre of town.
4   This was my favourite bar. We visited it every night!

c Match the photo to one of the sentences in b. Think of one or two holiday photos that you have taken. Write sentences with *who* or *which* to describe the photos.

3.2

a Choose the correct article to complete the conversation.

A   My favourite sign is [1]*the/a* sign for [2]*the/a* fire escape. Have you seen it?

B   Which one?

A   The sign they put up on [3]*the / -* side of [4]*a/the* building for example. You know, there's [5]*a/the* little man and he's running as fast as he can away from [6]*the/ -* fire.

B   I love [7]*an/the* old-fashioned sign for roadworks. You know [8]*a/the* little man with his spade, he's digging [9]*a/an* hole or something, but it looks more like he's opening [10]*a/an* umbrella.

A   I know [11]*the/-* sign you mean.

b Complete the description of this sign using *a/an, the* or no article *(-)*.

A   This sign shows [1]............... children crossing [2]............... road. I like [3]............... way they are walking so slowly and seriously. [4]............... children I know don't look like that!

B   I don't think it's two children. It's [5]............... girl and her mother. But I don't know what they're carrying! They don't look like [6]............... schoolbags to me!

A   No it looks more like [7]............... handbag.

4.1 PRESENT PERFECT

Form the present perfect with *have/has* (*'ve/has*) + past participle.
Regular past participles end in *-ed*. Many verbs have irregular past participles.

+	I/You/We/They He/She/It	have has	eaten.
−	I/You/We/They He/She/It	haven't hasn't	eaten.
?	Have Has	I/you/we/they he/she/It	eaten?

Use the present perfect to talk about past experiences in a general way
without saying exactly when those experiences took place.

I've tried it before. (at some time in the past, but it isn't important when)

Time expressions

We often use *ever* with question forms and *never* with negative forms.

*Have you **ever** been to New York? I've **never** visited the National Museum.*

▶ 4.1

4.2 PRESENT PERFECT & PAST SIMPLE

Use both the present perfect and the past simple to talk about actions in the
past. Use the present perfect when you are more interested in the action than
the time it happened.

They've found him.

Use the past simple to talk about when and where an action or event
happened. We often use time expressions like *yesterday, ago, last.*

They found him in Oxford two months ago.

Present perfect + *for/since*

Use the present perfect with *for* to talk about a period of time that continues
into the present.

I've lived here for six years.

Use the present perfect with *since* to talk about when an action or situation
started. The action or situation continues into the present.

I've lived here since 2005.

▶ 4.2

4.3 COMPARATIVES & SUPERLATIVES

Use comparative and superlative forms of adjectives to compare two or more
things or people.

We normally use comparatives to compare two things, or two groups of
things. Form a comparative adjective with adjective + *-er* or *more* + adjective.
We use *than* to link the two parts of the comparison.

Moscow is bigger than Paris. Kids are more creative than adults.

Use superlatives to talk about a person or thing that has more of a certain
quality than others of their type. Form a superlative adjective with adjective
+ *-est* or *most* + adjective. We often use *the* or a possessive adjective with
superlative adjectives.

Sara is my oldest friend. Nico's the most patient teacher I know.

SPELLING: With a small group of one-syllable adjectives you need to
double the final consonant and then add *-er* or *-est*. These adjectives end
in a consonant-vowel-consonant combination and include:

hot → hotter → hottest, big → bigger → biggest,
fat → fatter → fattest, red → redder → reddest,
thin → thinner → thinnest, sad → sadder → saddest

▶ 4.3

4.1

a Complete the conversations using the present perfect
form of the verb in brackets and short answers.

1 A (1) _____ (you/ever/do) any belly-dancing?

 B No, I (2) _____ , but I'd love to. And you?

 A Yes, I (3) _____ , I (4) _____ (just/start)
 classes at the gym. You should try. You'd love it!

2 A I (5) _____ (always/want) to try kite-surfing.

 B Really? I (6) _____ (not try), but my brother
 (7) _____ (do) it. He's really good at it.

 A (8) _____ (he/try) paragliding as well?

 B No, he (9) _____ , he's too scared!

b Re-write the conversations for people you know,
using new activities.

4.2

a Read the sentences. Tick the ones that are correct
and correct the ones that are not.

1 We didn't play tennis since May.

2 They've lived in Tokyo for two years.

3 That's a nice dress. How long did you have it?

4 I've forgotten the name of the film.

5 I didn't finish the homework yesterday.

b Complete the sentences with *for* or *since*.

1 They've been married _____ 15 years.

2 Peter has worked at the bookstore _____ 2007.

3 He's been in a meeting _____ 11 o'clock.

4 I've had my car _____ 18 months.

c Underline the time expressions in the sentences in
b. Write sentences that are true for you using the
present perfect.

4.3

a Look at the table about three Australian cities.
Complete the sentences with the comparative or
superlative form of the adjectives in brackets. Add
than and *the* where necessary.

	Sydney	Melbourne	Perth
Population	4 million	3.5 million	1.5 million
Average temperature January	26°	27.2°	31°
Average annual rainfall	1200 mm	650 mm	790 mm
Average house price	$250,000	$225,000	$495,000

1 The population of Melbourne is _____ than
 the population of Perth, but Sydney has _____
 population. (*big*)

2 Melbourne is _____ Sydney, but Perth is
 _____ . (*hot*)

3 Melbourne is _____ city, but Perth is _____
 Sydney. (*dry*)

4 Houses in Perth are _____ , and houses in
 Sydney are _____ than in Melbourne. (*expensive*)

b Write four sentences comparing three cities in your
country.

5.1 PRESENT CONTINUOUS & *GOING TO*

Present continuous

Use the present continuous to talk about things that are happening now. (See 1.1.)

We can also use the present continuous to talk about the future. Use the present continuous to talk about fixed plans for the future, often with a time or place.

I'm meeting Joan for dinner this weekend. (= I've arranged this)

Going to

Use *going to* with the verb *to be* and the infinitive.

+	I'm You/We/They're He/She/It's	going to	start a new course.
–	I'm not You/We/They aren't He/She/It isn't	going to	start a new course.
?	Am I Are you/we/they Is he/she/it	going to	start a new course?

We can also use *going to* to talk about plans for the future. We don't need to give a specific time.

We're going to buy a house (one day). (= a general plan)

In some cases, we can use both forms without changing the meaning.

I'm cooking dinner this evening. I'm going to cook dinner this evening.

In other cases, there is a clear difference in meaning.

We're going to get married (one day). (= a general plan)

We're getting married next March. (= it is arranged)

NOTE: We normally don't repeat *to go*.

They're going to the cinema. NOT *They're going to go to the cinema.*

▶ 5.1

5.2 *MUST(N'T)* & *(DON'T) HAVE TO* FOR OBLIGATION

Must & have/has to

Must is a modal auxiliary verb. It follows these rules of form:

1 use *must* + infinitive without *to*
2 use *must* to form questions and negatives.

Must you do that right now? I mustn't be late.

3 you don't need an *-s* for the third person singular.

He must report to the director's office immediately.

Use *must* and *have/has to* to talk about rules and obligations.

I must/have to be at the office by nine. I must/have to work this evening.

NOTE: *must* is not often used in question forms. *Do I have to?* is more common. *Do I have to call her?* NOT *Must I call her?*

Mustn't & don't/doesn't have to

Use *mustn't* to say that it is important NOT to do something, or that something is against the rules.

You mustn't eat or drink near the computers. (= do not do this)

Use *don't/doesn't have to* to say that it is not necessary or obligatory to do something, you are free to choose.

You don't have to bring your own laptop. (= this is not necessary but you can do it if you want to)

▶ 5.2

5.1

a Look at the calendar for three flatmates. Write sentences about their future plans. Use the present continuous.

	Pablo	**Krista**	**John**
Monday		(1) 8 p.m. – dinner with mum & dad	
Tuesday			(2) 2 p.m. – Spanish exam
Wednesday	(3) 10 a.m. – dentist		
Thursday		(4) 1 p.m. – shopping w/Dana	
Friday			(5) 7.30 p.m. cinema
Saturday	(6) 9 a.m. – football semi finals		
Sunday			

b Complete the sentences with *going to* and a verb of your choice.

1 Hey, it's your birthday on Saturday! What are you going to do?
   I ....
2 Marco, you know smoking is really bad for you.
   Yes, I know, I .... I promise!
3 Are you going on holiday this year?
   No, I don't have enough money. I ....
4 Is Krassy coming to see the film with us tonight?
   No, I think he ....

c Think of three things you are going to do next weekend. Write three full sentences.

5.2

a Complete the sentences using *must*, *have to*, *don't have to* and *mustn't*. Sometimes more than one answer is possible.

must (x2)   mustn't   have to   don't have to (x2)

1 You really .... study harder if you want to pass the exam.
2 This isn't a direct train to Brussels. You .... change at the next station.
3 My brother's band are playing at the park tonight. The concert's free. You .... pay.
4 I really .... remember to call mum this evening. I forgot yesterday!
5 We can't have the meeting on Friday. Friday's a bank holiday so we .... go to work.
6 I'm really sorry, but you do know that you .... smoke in the office, don't you?

b Look at the sentences again. Who do you think each person is speaking to? Where are they?

6.1 MODAL VERBS: *CAN/CAN'T, SHOULD/SHOULDN'T*

Can, should, will, may and *might* are modal auxiliary verbs. Use modal auxiliary verbs to add information about the speaker's attitude to the main verb.

I don't swim. (This tells us a fact.)
I can't swim. (This adds information about the person's ability.)

All modal verbs follow these rules of form (see also 5.2):

1 use the modal + infinitive without ~~to~~
2 use the modal to form questions and negatives
   Can you speak Chinese? I might not come tonight.
3 you don't need an *s* for the third person singular
   He should see a doctor. She can't see you right now.

+	I/ You/He/She/It/We/They	can	paint.
–	I/You/He/She/It/We/They	can't	paint.
?	Can	I/you/he/she/it/we/they	paint?

Can/Can't

Meaning	Example
to have the ability	*I can play the piano.*
not to have the ability	*She can't speak French.*
something is possible or allowed	*I can go to the party tomorrow.*
something is not possible or not allowed	*We can't stay very long because I need to get home early.*

Should/Shouldn't

Meaning	Example
something is a good idea	*You should do more exercise.*
something is a bad idea	*You shouldn't eat so many sweets.*

▶ 6.1

6.2 PREDICTIONS: *WILL, MAY, MIGHT*

sure – yes	*She will be there tomorrow.*
perhaps – yes	*She might be there tomorrow.* *She may be there tomorrow.*
perhaps – no	*She might not be there tomorrow.* *She may not be there tomorrow.*
sure – no	*She won't be there tomorrow.*

Use *will*, *might* and *may* to make predictions about the future.
Use *will* to say that we are **sure** something will happen.
Use *might* or *may* to say that we **think** something is **possible** but we're not sure.

She'll give you some ideas. (I'm sure this is true.)
She might/may give you some ideas. (This is a possibility, but I'm not 100% sure.)

When we want to ask other people what their opinion is about the future we usually use *will*.

Will his father help him? What will he do?

▶ 6.2

6.1

a Look at the signs and complete sentences 1–6.

1 You _____ smoke here.
2 You _____ smoke.
3 You _____ eat here.
4 You _____ eat more fruit.
5 You _____ do more exercise.
6 You _____ run here.

b Complete the conversations with the best modal verb, *can, can't, should* or *shouldn't*.

JANIE Mum, (1) _____ I go to Solmaz's party on Saturday?
MUM No, you (2) _____. You're too young.

DOCTOR Hmm. You (3) _____ try to eat less, because you need to lose some weight.
PATIENT OK. (4) _____ I still eat cakes?
DOCTOR Well, you (5) _____ eat a cake now and again, but you (6) _____ eat one every day.

6.2

a Choose the most suitable explanation (a–c) for sentences 1–3.

1 If it doesn't rain this weekend, we're going to go camping.
   a We won't go camping.
   b We might not go camping.
   c We will go camping.

2 Tariq is not going to the meeting.
   a He won't be at the meeting.
   b He may not be at the meeting.
   c He'll be at the meeting.

3 Rachel and Xiaofan are going to win the contest.
   a They might not win the contest.
   b They may win the contest.
   c They'll win the contest.

b Complete the text using *will, won't, might* or *might not*.

Dario and Lina are six years old. They (1) _____ leave school for at least another ten years. What (2) _____ the world be like when they do? (3) _____ their university courses be online? What languages (4) _____ they need to know? They (5) _____ want to study. They (6) _____ want to do something else instead. But what? What jobs (7) _____ be on offer? The same ones as today? Who knows! We (8) _____ just have to wait and see.

c Write three sentences describing any changes that you think might take place in the next ten years.

7.1 THE -ING FORM & TO + INFINITIVE

We sometimes use two verbs together. The second verb can be a verb + -ing or the infinitive with to.

I love playing chess.   **Would** you like **to play** chess?

-ing form

Many verbs that express emotions like *enjoy, hate, mind* and *look forward to* are followed by the -ing form.

I don't mind travelling by train.   I enjoy watching films.

Other verbs that are followed by -ing include *recommend, consider.*

to + infinitive

Many verbs that describe plans or intentions like *decide* and *would like* are followed by the infinitive + *to*.

He decided to go on his own. I'd really like to go out this evening.

Other verbs that are followed by infinitive + *to* include *afford, agree, want.*

NOTE: *Like* and *love* are followed by both the -ing form and the infinitive + *to*.

I like watching/to watch TV on my own.   I love swimming/to swim in the ocean.

▶ 7.1

7.2 COUNTABLE & UNCOUNTABLE NOUNS, SOME & ANY

Countable nouns can be counted. *a house, three houses*

Use *a* or *an* with the singular form of countable nouns. *a cup, an apple*

Uncountable nouns can't be counted. *money, air*

Use a third person singular verb form after an uncountable noun.

Freedom is important.   Safety comes first.

Some/Any

Some and *any* are used with uncountable nouns and plural countable nouns. We often use *some* in affirmative sentences and *any* in negative sentences and questions.

*I've got **some** money. I haven't got **any** money. Have you got **any** money?*

We often use *some* in questions when we are making a request or an offer.

Could I have some water, please? (request)
Would you like some coffee? (offer)

We can use *any* in affirmative sentences when we want to say that it doesn't matter which, how much, when, etc.

Call me any time you like. (= it doesn't matter when you call me)

▶ 7.2

7.3 QUANTIFIERS

We use quantifiers like *much, many, lots, a little, a few* to talk about quantity in general terms. Some quantifiers refer to large quantities.

There are lots of gadgets in the shop.

Others refer to small quantities.

There have been a few changes to the prices.

And others are used in questions.

How many people were at the meeting?   How much money did you bring?

	Countable	Uncountable	Both
Large quantity	too many*	too much*	lots of, a lot of
Small quantity	a few, not many	a little, not much	
Questions	How many?	How much?	

* Remember that *too many* and *too much* have a negative meaning. It means that the quantity is bigger than you want or need.

▶ 7.3

7.1

a Circle the best form -ing or to + infinitive to complete the sentences. In one case both answers are possible.

1 **I'm really looking forward** *to going/to go* away this weekend.
2 **I can't afford** *going/to go* on holiday this year.
3 **I love** *doing/to do* jigsaws.
4 **I've decided** *looking/to look* for a new job.
5 **I'd like** *staying/to stay* at home watching the TV this evening.

b Are any of these sentences true for you? Write new sentences about yourself using the words in **bold**.

7.2

a Look at the groups of words. Which one is different? (Tip: you need to decide if the words are countable or uncountable.)

1   health sickness doctor happiness

2   children water enthusiasm food

3   minute hour sleep clock

4   sister father parent love

b Complete the conversation with *some* or *any*.

A So, this is the flat. It's in a great area. There isn't (1)_____ traffic. It's really quiet at night. There are (2)_____ great little bars and cafés nearby. There are (3)_____ local shops too, and a mini supermarket.

B Are there (4)_____ bus stops nearby?

A Yes, there's one just outside. The bus takes you straight to the town centre. So, what do you think? Do you like it?

B Well, I need (5)_____ time to think. Can I call you later?

A Yes, sure, you can call me (6)_____ time.

c Act out the conversation in pairs. Change the information so that it is true for your home.

7.3

a Look at the picture and choose the best quantifier to complete the sentences.

1 There are *a lot of/much/a little* people on the beach.
2 There isn't *a little/much/many* space on the sand.
3 There aren't *much/many/a few* people in the water.
4 There are *a few/much/lots of* clouds in the sky.

b Look around your classroom, or out of the window. What can you see? Write four sentences describing the scene using quantifiers.

8.1 SENTENCES WITH *IF*

Sentences with *if* have two parts, an *if* clause and a main clause. The *if* clause describes a situation, the main clause describes the result of that situation.

If clause (situation)	Main clause (result)
If it rains,	they have their classes indoors.
If I see him,	I'll give him the message.

The *if* clause can also come after the main clause.

I'll give him the message if I see him.

NOTE: there is no comma when the *if* clause comes after the main clause.

If + present simple (1): situations and facts that are always true

Use sentences with *if* + present simple to talk about situations and facts that are always, or generally, true. The verb in the main clause is also in the present simple. In these sentences *if* means the same as *when*.

If clause (situation)		Main clause (result)
+	If I run a lot, (present simple)	I feel tired. (present simple)
–	If I don't run a lot,	I don't feel tired.
? *Wh*	If you don't run a lot,	how do you feel?

NOTE: these sentences are sometime called zero conditional.

If + present simple (2): situations and events in the future

We can also use sentences with *if* + present simple to talk about situations in the future. We usually use *will* in the main clause.

If clause (situation)		Main clause (result)
+	If I run a lot, (present simple)	I'll feel tired. (*will* future)
–	If I don't run a lot,	I won't feel tired.
? *Wh*	If you run a lot	how will you feel?

NOTE: these sentences are sometimes called first conditional. They are often used to give instructions, make recommendations, promises or threats. (See also 9.1.)

▶ 8.1

8.2 MODAL VERBS: *MUST, CAN'T, MAY, MIGHT*

Use the modal auxiliary verbs *must*, *can't*, *may* and *might* to talk about possibilities and to make deductions. (See also 6.1).

Each modal auxiliary verb adds meaning to the main verb. In this case the modal verbs tell us something about the speaker's attitude towards the situation they are talking about.

Attitude	Modal verb
definitely true	**must** *She must be happy.* (she looks happy)
possibly true	**may/might** *He may/might be happy.* (sometimes he smiles)
possibly not true	**may not/might not** *They might not be happy.* (they sometimes look sad)
definitely not true	**can't** *They can't be happy.* (they never look happy).

NOTE: You cannot use *mustn't* to say that you think something is definitely not true.

He can't be at home. NOT *He ~~mustn't~~ be at home.*

▶ 8.2

8.1

a Choose the correct verb form to complete the conversations.

1 A OK, so, what happens if *we combine/ we'll combine* these two chemicals?

   B They explode!

2 A What do you usually do at the weekend?

   B Well, if the weather *is/will be* nice, *we usually go/we'll usually go* to the country.

3 A Have you seen Teo? I need to give him this message.

   B If *I see/I'll see* him, *I tell/ I'll tell* him you're looking for him.

   A Thanks!

4 A *I tell/I'll tell* mum if *you do/you'll do* that again!

   B Oh, please don't! *She's/She'll be* so angry!

b Match conversations 1–4 in **a** to situations a–d.

   a brother and sister playing
   b a Science lesson
   c two workmates in an office
   d two friends chatting

c Work in pairs. Act out the four conversations.

8.2

a Put the words in the correct order to form deductions.

1 be driver the can't She

2 might car his It be

3 may be not driver the She the car of

4 alone the in be She car must

b Match deductions 1–4 in **a** to photos a–d.

c Write one more deduction for each photo.

1 ....

2 ....

3 ....

4 ....

9.1 IF + PAST SIMPLE

Use *if* + past simple to talk about situations in the present that are impossible or stating the opposite of the real situation.

If I had more time, I'd do more sport. (= I don't have enough time)

We also use *if* + past simple to talk about imaginary situations in the future. *If I won the lottery, I'd give up my job.* (but I really don't think I'm going to win the lottery!)

NOTE: these sentences are NOT referring to the past.

We use *would* + infinitive in the main clause to describe the imagined result. (See also 8.1.)

	If clause (situation)	Main clause (result)
+	If I ran a lot (past simple)	I would feel tired. (*Would* + verb)
–	If we didn't live here	we would be happier.
? *Wh*	If you didn't live here	how would you feel?

NOTE: These sentences are sometimes called second conditional.
NOTE: The verb *to be* can have two forms in the *if* clause.

If I was/were you, I would go home.
If he was/were rich, he still wouldn't be happy.

▶ 9.1

9.2 SO & SUCH

Use *so* and *such* to emphasise the quality of something.

He was so nice. It was such a nice day.

so	happy (an adjective, no noun)
such a	happy child (adjective + singular noun)
such	happy children (adjective + plural noun) beautiful sunshine (adjective + uncountable noun)

Use them to make exclamations.

She's so nice! He's such a good person! You're such generous friends!

Use them to join two sentences. Use *that* to link the two sentences. But we can also make the sentences without *that*.

She was so angry (that) she just walked out the door.

▶ 9.2

9.3 SOME-/ANY-/NO- + -ONE/-BODY/-THING

We use *some-*, *any-* and *no-* with *-one*, *-body* and *-thing* to talk about people and objects in general.

Do you have anything I can read? (it doesn't matter what)
I think there's something in my bag. (but I'm not sure exactly what it is)

Use *-one* / *-body* to refer to a person. There is no difference in meaning.
Use *-thing* to refer to an object. The verb is third person singular.

*Nothing exciting ever **happens** here. **Has** anyone seen Alex?*

Use *someone/body/thing* in affirmative sentences, offers and requests.

I saw something nice in that shop. Would you like something to drink?

Use *anyone/body/thing* with *not* or in questions.

I don't know anything. Did anybody come to the party?

Use *anyone/body/thing* also in affirmative sentences. In these sentences *any* = all.

Anyone can come. (= all people can come)

No one/body and *nothing* have a negative meaning. Use them with an affirmative verb without *not* in statements and questions.

Nobody answered my question. Is there nothing in the fridge?

(See also 7.2.)

▶ 9.3

9.1

a Complete the sentences with the verbs in brackets using the past simple or *would*.

1 I _____ money, if I _____ the discipline. *(save / have)*
2 If _____ for it, I _____ in a new computer. *(can pay / invest)*
3 I _____ happier, if I _____ my job/studies. *(be / change)*
4 If _____ concentrate more on work, I _____ less time. *(can / waste)*
5 I _____ on my own, if I _____ it. *(live / can afford)*

b Which sentences are true for you? Give more information to explain why they are true.

9.2

a Complete the sentences using *so* & *such* and match them to the photos.

1 Property in Hong Kong is _____ expensive / is _____ a waste of money.
2 I made a mistake with the figures. I'm _____ stupid / I'm _____ an idiot!
3 Calculating expenses can be _____ complex / _____ a complicated thing.
4 Winning the lottery is _____ unlikely / is _____ an improbable thing.

b What other adjectives (with *so* & *such*) can you use to describe the images?

9.3

a Use indefinite pronouns to complete the text.

(1) _____ asked me the other day, 'what is the main problem facing our society?' I thought, 'we all want to have services, but (2) _____ wants to pay higher taxes to maintain them.'
Is there (3) _____ who likes paying taxes? All we do is complain about the money we have to pay, but at the same time everybody thinks that roads and other services are important.
Is there (4) _____ we can do to make people change their minds about taxes?

10.1 PASSIVE (1): PRESENT SIMPLE

Form the passive in the present simple with *is/are* + past participle. Regular past participles end in *-ed*. Many verbs have irregular past participles.

> *Football **is followed** by millions of people all over the world.*
> *Millions of football shirts **are sold** each year.*

+	I You/We/They He/She/It	am ('m) are ('re) is ('s)	paid every week.
–	I You/We/They He/She/It	'm not aren't isn't	paid very well.
?	Am Are Is	I you/we/they he/she/it	followed by a lot of people on Facebook?

The subject of the passive sentence is the object of the active sentence.

Active: *People play **baseball** in the United States.* (object)
Passive: ***Baseball** is played in the United States.* (subject)

We often use passive verb forms to focus on an action.

> *Football is **followed** by millions all over the world.*

Use *by* if we want to say who or what does the action.

We do not use *by* if the person or object that does the action is unknown, unimportant or obvious.

> *The shirts are made in China.* (we're not interested in who makes them)
> *The shirts are made by children.* (we're using *by* to add important information)

▶ 10.1

10.2 PASSIVE (2): PAST SIMPLE

Form the passive in the past simple with *was/were* + past participle. (See also 10.1.)

+	I/He/She/It You/We/They	was were	paid every week.
–	I/He /She /It You/We/They	wasn't weren't	paid very well.
?	Was Were	I/he/she/it you/we/they	followed by a lot of people on Facebook ?

Use the passive in the past simple to focus on actions in the past.

> *The museum was opened in 2002.*
> *The shoes were made by local people.*

The past simple passive is often used in formal speech, in written reports and news articles.

> *The miners were rescued yesterday.*

▶ 10.2

10.1

a Correct the mistakes in the sentences.

1 Big football matches are watch all over the world.
2 The same brands is sold everywhere.
3 A lot of money spent on designer clothes.
4 English is speak all over the world these days.
5 Many English words use in advertising.

b Add phrases with *by* to the sentences.

1 The thief was arrested by ....
2 Ten million football shirts are sold each year by ....
3 Many of our clothes are made by ....
4 Hundreds of thousands of illegal football shirts are bought every year by ....
5 Millions of pounds are spent on advertising football shirts every year by ....

c Look again at the phrases you wrote in **b**. Which

a add some important, unusual or interesting information?
b aren't necessary because we already know, or understand who did the action?

10.2

a Complete the gaps with the verbs in brackets in the past or present simple passive.

Häagen-Dazs produces ice cream, cakes and frozen yoghurt. The brand (1) .... *(establish)* by Jewish-Polish immigrants Reuben and Rose Mattus in 1961. Starting with only three flavours, its first store (2) .... *(open)* in New York in 1976. Now, *Häagen-Dazs* have dozens of flavours and their products (3) .... *(distribute)* in 55 different countries. Of course, their ice cream (4) .... *(sell)* in supermarkets and grocery stores all over the world, as well.

The name *Häagen-Dazs* has no special meaning. They are just two words which (5) .... *(choose)* because they sound Danish and because Denmark (6) .... *(know)* for its high quality dairy products in the U.S.A. *Häagen-Dazs* ice cream (7) .... *(make)* using quality ingredients to produce high-priced gourmet ice cream.

b Rewrite the sentences about another ice cream company starting with the words in **bold**.

1 Ben & Jerry's opened **their first ice cream parlour** in 1978 in Vermont, USA.
Their first ice cream parlour was opened in 1978 in Vermont, USA.
2 Ben Cohen and Jerry Greenfield created **the brand**.
3 They sell **Ben & Jerry's ice cream** all over the world.
4 They use **quality ingredients** to produce high-priced ice cream.
5 In 1983, they used **Ben & Jerry's ice cream** to build the largest ice cream dessert ever.

c What do the two companies have in common? Write three sentences comparing the two companies using the passive.
Their first ice cream shops were opened in the 1970s.

149

11.1 REPORTED SPEECH: *SAY*

When we report what someone said we usually change the tenses.

Direct speech	Reported speech
'I like you.' (present simple)	She said that she **liked** me. (simple past)
'He's **playing** football.' (present continuous)	She said that he **was playing** football. (past continuous)
'**I'll see** you tomorrow.' (*will/won't* + verb)	He said that he **would** see me tomorrow. (*would/wouldn't* + verb)
'I **can't come** to the meeting.' (*can/can't* + verb)	She said that she **couldn't come** to the meeting. (*could/couldn't* + verb)

Pronoun changes

Sometimes pronouns change too. This depends who said what and to whom.

'I like you,' said Joe. → Joe said **he** liked **me**.

Time changes

We also need to change some of the time expressions we use when we report speech.

Direct speech	Reported speech
today	that day
tomorrow	the next day
at the moment	at that moment
(right) now	(right) then

NOTE: there are a lot of reporting verbs that we can also use in the same way as *say*, including *explain, answer, reply, complain, shout.*

▶ 11.1

11.2 REPORTED SPEECH: *TELL*

When we use *tell* to report what someone has said, we must always say who they were talking to. We need to use a name, a noun or a pronoun. The name, noun or pronoun comes directly after the verb *tell.*

He told **Jane** that he was tired.
He told **his mother** that he was tired.
He told **me** he was tired. NOT He ~~told he was tired.~~ He ~~told he was tired to Jane.~~

NOTE: When we use *say* we can add *to* + the person they're talking to **after** the words that the person said.

He said he was fine **to me**.

▶ 11.2

11.1

a What did the person say? Change the reported speech into direct speech.

1 She said she wanted to meet more people.
2 Luke said he would be at the party on Saturday.
3 Marie said she was feeling good that day.
4 Chris and Soo said they couldn't go to the cinema the next day.
5 Marsha and Juan said they were watching TV at that moment.

b Read the email and summarise it using reported speech.

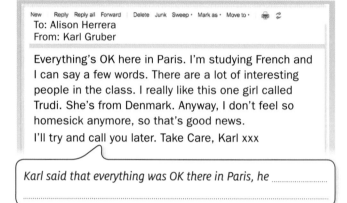

New   Reply Reply all Forward | Delete Junk Sweep · Mark as · Move to ·
To: Alison Herrera
From: Karl Gruber

Everything's OK here in Paris. I'm studying French and I can say a few words. There are a lot of interesting people in the class. I really like this one girl called Trudi. She's from Denmark. Anyway, I don't feel so homesick anymore, so that's good news.
I'll try and call you later. Take Care, Karl xxx

Karl said that everything was OK there in Paris, he _____

11.2

a Report the conversations using *tell*.

I'LL MEET YOU HERE AT 9.
Jan   Paola

YES, WE'RE MEETING AT 9.30.
Hugo

Giulia
EVERYBODY'S GOING TO BE THERE AT 9.15.

WE'RE ALL GETTING THERE AT 9.45.

Franz
OK, I'LL BE THERE ABOUT TEN MINUTES LATER.

Paola told Jan that she'd meet him there at 9.
Jan told Hugo that they _____ .
Hugo told _____ .
Giulia _____ .
Franz _____ .

b What time did each person arrive at the meeting?

c Find and correct the mistakes in each of the conversations.

1 A: He said me he was getting married.
  B: Really?
2 A: She told that she wanted to leave him.
  B: I don't believe that!
3 A: They told to me that they couldn't live together.
  B: I'm not surprised.
4 A: She said me that she didn't need any help.
  B: Yes, I know. She told me the same.

12.1 MODAL VERBS REVIEW

The modal auxiliary verbs that we have looked at include *will, may, might, could, should* and *would*.

All modal auxiliary verbs follow these rules of form:

1 use the modal + infinitive without ~~to~~
2 use the modal to form questions and negatives
   Can you speak Chinese? I might not come tonight.
3 you don't need an *-s* for the third person singular
   He should see a doctor. She can't see you right now.

Use modal auxiliary verbs to add information about the speaker's attitude to the main verb.

I don't swim. (this tells us a fact)
I can't swim. (this adds information about the person's ability)

Modal verb	Use
will	to show that we're talking about the future
may, might, could	to say you think something is possible, but you aren't sure
can	to talk about ability, possibility and permission in the present
should	to make recommendations
would	to talk about imaginary situations
would	to make a request

(See also 5.2, 6.1 and 8.2.)

▶ 12.1

12.2 *USED TO*

Use *used to* + infinitive to talk about habits and routines in the past.
I used to walk to work.

+	I/you/we/they/he/she/it		used to	love fish.
–	I/you/we/they/he/she/it		didn't use to	eat meat.
?	Did	I/you/we/they/he/she/it	use to	live in the country?

Used to & past simple for habits

Use the past simple instead of *used to* without changing the meaning.

I used to have a dog when I was younger. → *I had a dog when I was younger.*

NOTE: We do **not** use *used to* for actions that only happened once.

I went to Africa on holiday in 2005. NOT *I ~~used to go~~ to Africa on holiday in 2005.*

Talking about present habits and routines

We cannot use *used to* to talk about present habits and routines. We use the present simple (often with *usually*).

I usually play tennis twice a week. NOT *I ~~use to play~~ tennis twice a week.*

▶ 12.2

12.1

a Look at the phrases in **bold**. Find and correct five mistakes.

> A **Will you to be** at the concert this evening?
> B I'm not sure. I really want to go but I **might needing** to stay late at work.
> A Oh no, **don't you can ask** your boss if you **can leave early**? Just this once?

> A **Could you do** me a favour, please?
> B Yes, what is it?
> A **Would you looking after** my dog over the weekend?
> B Oh sorry, **I can't**! We're going away!

b Choose the correct modal verb to complete the text.

> I'm going away with some friends this weekend to a music festival. I know we *can/'ll/might* have a great time. All my favourite bands are on. We *might/should/would* stay on for a few days. We haven't decided yet. We *could/'d/might* really like to travel down the coast. If the weather's good, we *might/should/would* do some windsurfing. I *'d/'ll/could* give you a call when I get back.

12.2

a Find and correct three mistakes in the text.

> I used to love school. I didn't used to want to come home at the end of the day. I used to kick and cry and ask to stay with my friends. My mum use to get really embarrassed! She used to have to pick me up and carry me to the car! What about you, did you used to love school too?

b Write a short text describing your early memories of school. Use *used to* and *didn't use to*.

c Complete the sentences using the correct form of *used to*.

1 They .... *(play)* in the local pub, now they play in stadiums.
2 They .... *(travel)* in an old van, now they have a private jet.
3 They .... *(have)* a lot of fans, but now they're famous.
4 They .... *(make)* a lot of money, now they're millionaires.
5 They .... *(love)* making music... and they still do!

d Write three more sentences comparing the band's lives before they became famous with their lives now. Use the verbs in the box to help you.

> drink   eat   enjoy   live   spend   work

WRITING BANK

1 LEARNING JOURNALS

a

Learning Journal

Date:

13th September 2011

Lesson:

Page: 4–5 (Speaking the same language)

What we did:

We talked about languages and countries. We listened to people from Paraguay and Wales talking about languages.

What I learned:

'first/second/official language', 'mother tongue', 'bilingual'

In class I was:

very nervous about speaking in English. 😕

For homework I'm going to do:

the vocabulary exercises in the Workbook

I'd also like to:

learn more about Paraguay. Try the Simple English Wikipedia?

b

> 13/09/11 (p4-5)
>
> Vocab
> first ⎫   Italian is my first language.
> second ⎬ language
> official ⎭   English is an official
>   language in India.
> bilingual   Stefan is bilingual.
>   He speaks Spanish and
>   Portuguese.
> mother tongue   *What does this mean? Check
>   in next lesson!*
>
> Country   Languages
> Wales   Welsh, English
> Paraguay   Spanish, Guarani
> Holland   Dutch
> China   Mandarin, Cantonese
>
> Homework – Wbook vocab exercises

1   Read the journal entries. Which do you find easier to read? Which gives you most information about the lesson?

2   Read the journal entries again. Which entry includes
    1   the activities the student did in the lesson?
    2   the student's feelings about the lesson?
    3   the page in the course book the lesson comes from?
    4   example sentences for new vocabulary?
    5   questions about vocabulary or grammar?
    6   information about the homework?
    7   ideas for extra study at home?

3   a   💬 Work in pairs. Read the advantages of writing a learning journal. Put the advantages in order, 1–8 (1 is the most important).
    a   You have to think about your lesson again.
    b   You can read your journal before a test.
    c   You can compare journals with a partner.
    d   You can see your progress.
    e   You can see which techniques help you to learn.
    f   You can record vocabulary that isn't in your course book.
    g   You can remember questions to ask your teacher.
    h   You practise writing in English.

b   Can you think of any other advantages? Share your ideas with the class.

4   Write a journal entry about your last English lesson. Include:
    ● what you studied
    ● your feelings about the lesson
    ● any questions you have about the lesson
    ● what you will study at home

5   💬 Work in pairs. Compare your journal entries. Are they similar or different?

TIP

Writing a learning journal is a useful way to remember what you have learned and to practise writing in English. You don't need to write full sentences. You just need to make sure you include the important information from your lesson.

2 COMMENTS ON A WEBSITE

a NYblogger Thanks for an excellent article, Germaine. So interesting to read about your experiences.
27/09/11 • 1:52:02 PM

b All Comments (1)
LOL! Really love this video. So funny!
Gretchen321 04/07/2011

Showing first 10 comments | View all comments | Go to latest comment

c StefanK BIG congrats for the new job! Very happy for you ☺
posted at 11:42 AM • Like

d Search:
Post: Messages • Status • Photos • Videos • Links

CameraQueen
12/10/2011 9:16 AM
Lovely image, Milosz! Easily my fave of your album! Looks like you had a great time.
Reply • Forward • Delete

1 Look at the comments. Which comment(s) come(s) from
1 a photo sharing website?
2 a social networking website?
3 a video sharing website?
4 a blog?

2 💬 Work in pairs. Do you ever write comments like these? Where do you write them? Compare your answers with your partner.

3 Read the comments again. Find abbreviations that mean
1 congratulations
2 favourite
3 laugh out loud

4 a What does the writer omit in each comment? Match omitted words 1–4 to comments a–d.

1 I   a Very happy for you.
2 It's   b Looks like you had a great time!
3 I'm   c So interesting to read about your experiences.
4 It   d Really love this video.

b Read three more comments. Cross out all the unnecessary words.
1 I love this photo. It looks like such a beautiful place!
2 Great video, great song! It's definitely the best one from the band's new album.
3 We're so excited to hear you're engaged! It's fantastic news. ☺

5 a 💬 Work in pairs. Choose three photos from this book. Write comments about them for a photo sharing website.

b Visit one of the websites in 1 and leave a comment.

TIP

Comments on websites are generally short and informal. When you write a comment on a website, use short sentences and abbreviations. Remember to use a friendly tone!

3 WRITING TO SAY SORRY

1 Read emails 1–3. Match the emails to photos a–c.

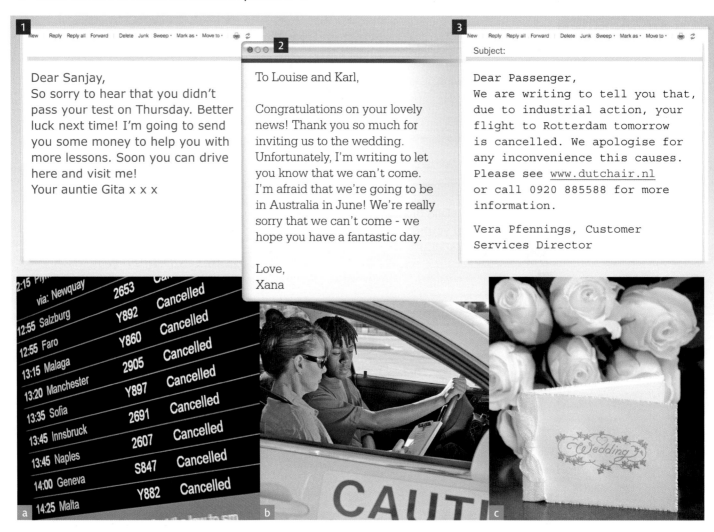

1

Dear Sanjay,
So sorry to hear that you didn't pass your test on Thursday. Better luck next time! I'm going to send you some money to help you with more lessons. Soon you can drive here and visit me!
Your auntie Gita x x x

2

To Louise and Karl,

Congratulations on your lovely news! Thank you so much for inviting us to the wedding. Unfortunately, I'm writing to let you know that we can't come. I'm afraid that we're going to be in Australia in June! We're really sorry that we can't come - we hope you have a fantastic day.

Love,
Xana

3

Subject:

Dear Passenger,
We are writing to tell you that, due to industrial action, your flight to Rotterdam tomorrow is cancelled. We apologise for any inconvenience this causes. Please see www.dutchair.nl or call 0920 885588 for more information.

Vera Pfennings, Customer Services Director

2 Read the emails again. Which email(s)

1 give(s) bad news?
2 respond(s) to bad news?
3 say(s) thank you before saying sorry?
4 is/are sent to more than one person?
5 is the most informal?
6 is the most formal?

3 Complete the phrases from the emails.

a We are w_____ to tell you that…
b So sorry to h_____ that…
c I'm writing to l_____ you k_____ that…
d We a_____ for…
e I'm a_____ that…
f We're really s_____ that…

4 a Which of the phrases in 3 do we use to

1 give bad news?
2 respond to bad news?
3 say sorry?

b Which phrase is only used in formal writing?

5 Choose one of the situations below and write an email to say sorry. Use the expressions in 3 if appropriate.

1 A good friend failed some important exams (decide what kind of exam). Write an email to make him/her feel better (think of something positive that you can say).

2 An old friend has invited you to his/her house for a holiday. Write an email to him/her to say that you can't visit and explain why.

3 You are a member of a club (decide what kind of club). You can't attend club meetings anymore. Write an email to the club secretary to say sorry and explain why.

TIP

Remember to make your emails friendly and sympathetic. Imagine you are the person receiving the email and think about how you feel when you read it.

4 A REVIEW

1 🗨 When you buy a new gadget, what helps you decide which one to choose? Put the reasons in order, 1–6 (1 is the most important).

a the price ....
b the company or brand name ....
c what other people say about it ....
d the appearance (size, colour, etc.) ....
e the special features ....
f how easy it is to use ....

2 Read the review. What gadget is the writer reviewing? How do you know?

3 What information does the review include? Tick the correct options.

1 the name of the gadget ....
2 where the writer bought it ....
3 why the writer chose it ....
4 the best features ....
5 the disadvantages ....
6 who the gadget is suitable for ....
7 how much it costs ....

4 Read the review again. <u>Underline</u> all the adjectives. Which are a) comparative adjectives? b) superlative adjectives?

5 **a** Think about a gadget that you use frequently. Complete the notes about the gadget.

> *Gadget* ....
> *What I like about it* ....
> ....
> *What I don't like about it* ....
> ....
> *Rating* ☆☆☆☆☆

b 🗨 Work in pairs. Compare your gadgets. Would you like to use your partner's gadget? Why/Why not?

6 Write a review of your gadget in a similar style to the review in **2**. Use your notes in **5** to help you.

> **TIP**
> When you write a review, remember to say why you like or dislike the product. Start with the reasons why you chose it and finish by saying what type of person it is suitable for.

Customer Reviews

Sonic 110

Posted by Anna • 29 Nov 2011

GREAT PRODUCT, GREAT PRICE!

Last week I bought the new Sonic 110 – I'm really pleased with it!

At first I wasn't sure which model to buy. A friend recommended the X200. The best thing about that model is the state-of-the-art camera, which takes fantastic photos. The disadvantage? It's one of the most expensive models around!

In the end, I decided to buy the Sonic 110 because I wanted something cheaper and simpler than the X200. I'm really happy with my choice. For me, the biggest advantage of this model is the screen. The colours are so clear and bright, even when you're outside in the sun. It's perfect for surfing the internet or watching videos.

The Sonic 110 is smaller and lighter than the X200. Some people might think that's an advantage. Personally, I disagree – it's the only thing I don't like about this model! The keys on the Sonic 110 aren't very big, which can make typing difficult. This model probably isn't the best option for people who send a lot of emails or text messages.

But for people who want the latest technology, at a lower price than the X200, the Sonic 110 is a great choice!

» See more **5 star**, **4 star** reviews

5 WRITING TO SAY THANK YOU

1 Work in pairs. Think about a few times you said thank you to someone recently. Discuss the questions.

- Who did you thank?
- What did you say thank you for?
- How did you say thank you? In person, on the phone or in a letter or email?

2 a Read the thank you notes. Which note is for

1 a friend?
2 a relative?
3 a person the writer doesn't know well?

b Which note is a) the most informal? b) the most formal?

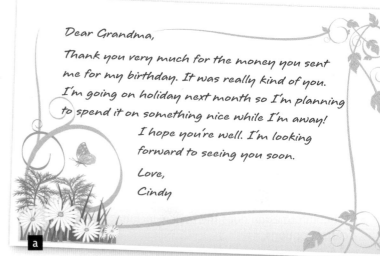

Dear Grandma,

Thank you very much for the money you sent me for my birthday. It was really kind of you. I'm going on holiday next month so I'm planning to spend it on something nice while I'm away! I hope you're well. I'm looking forward to seeing you soon.

Love,
Cindy

a

Hi Karin,
Thanks so much for your support this week. Things have been really difficult with all the revision and everything! Really appreciate all your help. Let's get together after the exams! ☺
See you,
Jon

b

New   Reply Reply all Forward   Delete Junk Sweep · Mark as · Move to ·

Subject:

Dear Mr and Mrs Schutz,

I am writing to say thank you for letting us stay in your property in Austria last month. We were very happy with everything and we thought the flat was beautiful.

We had a lovely holiday in Seefeld. The weather was excellent and we really enjoyed exploring the town and the local area. We will definitely use the 'FindAFlat' website again when we plan our next holiday!

Thank you again.

Kind regards,
Ferrara Costa

c

3 Read the notes again. Identify the three parts of each note.
- greeting   • saying thank you   • ending the letter

4 a Complete the table with phrases from the notes.

	Informal	More formal
Greeting		
Saying thank you		
Ending the letter		

b What other phrases can you use?

5 Choose one of the situations you discussed in **1**. Write an appropriate note to say thank you.

6 Swap notes with a partner. Check that your partner has included the three parts from **3** and used appropriate language.

TIP

When you write, remember that errors of formality are often more obvious to the reader than small errors in grammar, vocabulary or spelling. Be careful not to write too informally to someone you don't know very well.

6 MAKING ARRANGEMENTS

View earlier messages: 1 Year | All

Ling
Hi Bryan, Hi Tao! How are you?

Bryan
Good thanks. ☺ You?

Tao
I'm fine thanks! We're making plans for Saturday – do you still want to come to the beach?

Ling
Yeah, I'd love to! What time are you planning to leave?

Bryan
We're thinking of meeting at my house at 10.

Ling
OK, sounds great. How about I bring a picnic for everyone?

Tao
Sure! There will be about eight of us. Jen and Mati are coming – they're vegetarian.

Ling
Hmm, OK...

Bryan
Why don't we have a barbeque? Then everyone can bring something to cook. It might be easier.

Tao
Good idea! I'll email the others tonight and let them know.

Bryan
Thanks Tao! Right, what else do we need to plan?

1 Read the web chat between Bryan, Ling and Tao. Answer the questions.
   1 What are they organising?
   2 When are they going?
   3 What have they organised so far?

2 Look at the words and phrases in the box. Which are used to
   a make suggestions?
   b respond to suggestions?

   why don't we   sure!   it might be
   I'd love to   good idea!
   we're thinking of   sounds great
   how about

3 a Read the web chat again. Make a 'to do' list for the other things that the friends need to organise.

   b 💬 Work in groups. Continue the web chat between Bryan, Ling and Tao. Make arrangements about the things on your 'to do' lists.

4 💬 Work in pairs. You want to do something with your English class to celebrate the end of your course. Decide what you will do and when.

5 Write a web chat to make arrangements for your event.

TIP

In a web chat, use simple sentences in an informal style. Remember to respond to other people's suggestions in a friendly, polite way!

COMMUNICATION BANK

1.4 Functional language, page 12, Exercise 8

e towels
f bottle opener
g sink plug
h remote control

2.4 Functional language, page 22, Exercise 5a

Student A
You are the passenger. The weather is bad today and there are delays to all of the flights. When you check in, ask about the delays to your flight.

2.4 Functional language, page 22, Exercise 5b

Student A
You are the hotel receptionist. Because of work to renovate the hotel sports facilities, the swimming pool and gym are closed. There is a private sports club across the road which hotel guests can use free of charge. The club is open until 10pm.

3.0 Key Vocabulary, page 25, B

a as a capital city
b for an emperor
c in memory of a loved one
d as a religious monument
e as a defence against invasion
f to hold competitions
g to bury the dead
h to protect an important source of water

3.4 Functional language, page 32, Exercise 7

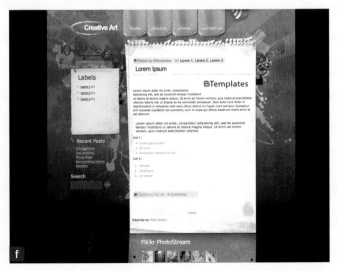

5.5 Speaking task, page 57, Exercise 4

Student A

Part 1

Read the information about the school in photo **a** and answer Student B's questions.

Name of school: **City English**

1	Accommodation?	small, friendly hotel near Dublin (3 kilometres)
2	Courses – which subjects?	English, French, Spanish, Japanese
3	Class size?	1–5 students
4	Activities?	film club, trips around Dublin
5	Price?	€350

Part 2

Ask Student B questions to complete the table about the school in photo **c**.

Name of school: **American Families**

1	Accommodation?	....
2	Courses – which subjects?	....
3	Class size?	....
4	Activities?	....
5	Price?	....

6.2 Vocabulary, page 62, Exercise 4

Student A

2.4 Functional language, page 22, Exercise 5a

Student B
You are the airline check-in assistant. The flight has been cancelled. All passengers are booked on to the next flight tomorrow morning. The airline has booked hotel rooms for all the passengers at the airport. They can get a free dinner at the hotel.

2.4 Functional language, page 22, Exercise 5b

Student B
You are the guest. You want to book in for two nights. You want to know the opening times of the swimming pool and gym.

5.5 Speaking task, page 57, Exercise 4

Student B

Part 1

Ask Student A questions to complete the table about the school in photo **a**.

Name of school: City English	
1 Accommodation?	
2 Courses – which subjects?	
3 Class size?	
4 Activities?	
5 Price?	

Part 2

Read the information about the school in photo **c** and answer Student A's questions.

Name of school: American Families	
1 Accommodation?	students stay with American families in their homes
2 Courses – which subjects?	English, History, Literature
3 Class size?	10–15 students
4 Activities?	walks in the mountains, swimming, cycling
5 Price?	$550

6.2 Vocabulary, page 62, Exercise 4

Student B

8.2 Listening, page 86, Exercise 4b

1

Sue went to meet her birth family. She liked them and they liked her. The Millers were serious, shy people and so was Sue. She was never close to her brother Bob Mcdonald (who was not her real brother) and was worried that she would lose him.

2

Marti met her real brother (Bob McDonald) first and they became good friends, because they were both outgoing and fun. She then met her birth parents, but Marti thought that they didn't want to get close to her, because they thought of Sue as their real daughter.

3

Marti was jealous because she thought she was losing her parents to Sue. Sue and Marti never became friends because they are very different and both felt jealous in some way. However, they now go to the family events of both families.

8.2 Reading, page 87, Exercise 3

He is a human chameleon and because of this unique ability he becomes the patient of a famous psychiatrist (Mia Farrow) who eventually falls in love with him, not before, of course, he also becomes a psychiatrist himself!

The film makes all this believable because it is very clever. It mixes real archive film of news reports from the 30s and 40s with new material that includes Allen. This is done using antique film cameras and lenses, well before digital filmmaking technology made this easy. So, we see Allen superimposed next to real people (not actors!) from history. He even appears next to Charlie Chaplin!

So, who else does Zelig become in the film? Well, in the company of an American Indian, he becomes an Indian himself. Alongside writer Eugene O'Neill, he starts to look like him although he doesn't grow the moustache. When he's with Jack Dempsey, he becomes a professional boxer, only he has glasses and a different physique. In the film, he also becomes a baseball player, a black jazz musician and a gangster!

Like many great comedies, *Zelig* is hilarious but it also makes some very serious points about identity and how we can become different people in different situations. For me, this makes it one of his best ever films, and it must certainly be his most original.

9.5 Speaking task, page 101, Exercise 5

Name: Melanie Fulton	
Income per month	
'take home' pay	800
any other income	100
Total income	900
Expenses per month	
accommodation	250
transport	50
bills (telephone, gas, electricity)	125
subscriptions (magazines, TV, gym)	0
food	100
eating out and entertainment	250
clothes, shoes	200
Total expenses	....
Income minus expenses	....

REVIEW C, Unit 8, page 103, Grammar, Exercise 3b

b) cans

REVIEW D, Unit 10, page 136, Grammar, Exercise 1b

1   c) North America
2   b) England
3   c) 275 million people
4   b) English

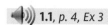 **1.1**, *p. 4, Ex 3*

Ellen

Here in Wales there are two official languages – Welsh and English. Everybody speaks English, but not everybody speaks Welsh – but all road signs and official documents are in both languages. I have two first languages. I speak English and Welsh, and so do all my family. I usually speak Welsh at home, and I studied in both languages at school. I learned French at school as a foreign language, so I speak some French, but I never practise it, so I've forgotten a lot of it. Oh, I also speak a little Japanese – very little! I'm studying it at the moment.

Ernesto

Hi! I'm Ernesto. I'm from Paraguay. My first language is Guaraní – that's the language I learned first. My second language is Spanish. It isn't my mother tongue, but I learned it when I was very small! We have two languages in my country, because Guaraní and Spanish are both official languages in Paraguay. Most government forms and school books are in both languages. Most people here are bilingual, so they speak both languages really well!

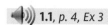 **1.9**, *p. 13, Ex 5*

Sandra

This year I don't have much time to study English, because of my job, but I plan to spend about four hours a week working on English. I like music and films, so I plan to listen to music and to watch films in English once or twice a week. You can learn a lot of vocabulary and slang from this, and it's fun. Sometimes in class I forget what I learned before, so I plan to read my notes before class to help me to remember what we talked about in the last class. I also plan to study my notes from class when I'm doing my homework. Homework usually takes me about two hours a week. I think this is all I'll have time for.

Max

This year I think I can spend about eight hours a week studying English – one hour in the morning every day before work, and three hours at the weekend. I have homework twice a week, and I plan to spend a lot of time outside class studying vocabulary. I like to make lists of vocabulary and test myself – usually I write the words by topic and then I write a translation next to the word. I plan to read whatever I can in English and write down all the new words in my vocabulary notebook. I'm an expert with my electronic dictionary – I'm very fast and I use it all the time to help me to understand new language when I'm reading magazines. I also plan to find exercises to help me practise online.

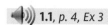 **2.1**, *p. 14, Ex 3*

Roxanne

I don't like cities, especially the one I live in. It's noisy and dirty! When I can, I like to go somewhere wild, in the middle of nature. My favourite place is the rainforest in the south of China. It's wet and rainy, but there's so much to see, you don't care! I took loads of photos of trees and animals. I didn't want to forget anything!

Juan

My favourite place in the world is a river in the north of Uruguay, not far from where I live. It's a really peaceful place, so quiet. I go to the river most weekends and fish... At least, I pretend to fish, but a lot of the time I just relax. OK, so if I'm honest, sometimes I fall asleep!

Sunee

I've lived on the island of Phuket in Thailand my whole life. It's small, but it's very friendly. My family and I often go to this beach on the east coast to meet friends and talk, and sometimes we eat here too. It's a lively place – there's always something happening.

Mohammed

I love walking, which is useful, I guess, because I work as a tour guide! The Moroccan desert can be dangerous, but it's very beautiful too, especially in the mountains in the west. I try to help visitors understand that this place is unique – there's nowhere quite like it.

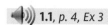 **2.5**, *p. 18, Ex 3*

P = Presenter   S = Steve

P: Welcome to Nature Watch. Our guest this morning is Steve Bolton, who won the World Wildlife Photographer competition a few days ago. Steve, it's a great photo. Was it difficult to take?

S: No, it was very easy! I took it last year, while my girlfriend and I were travelling through Bolivia. I was sitting next to a river and I saw the frog. It was jumping to catch an insect and luckily I had my camera with me... and that was it!

P: Being a photographer is an unusual job. How did it all start?

S: Oh, it started way back, when I was a kid. I got a camera for Christmas when I was eight – no, sorry, when I was seven. I absolutely loved it... When I was nine, I already knew I was going to be a photographer when I grew up. And here I am!

P: What are the best things about your job?

S: Well, I love travelling! I've been to Africa a lot, because my parents live in Nairobi, the capital of Kenya. But I didn't go there last year. For a change, I visited the south, from Australia to Antarctica – well, the

northern part of Antarctica, anyway. Next year I'd like to go somewhere new, maybe North America, to photograph the bears. That'd be exciting!

P: Which animals do you like the best?

S: Butterflies and fish are pretty, but I really love working with big, wild animals, especially lions. I once took a great photo of one when I was working in Africa. It looked amazing while it was running – so beautiful. I don't like snakes, though. They're too dangerous!

P: I imagine working with animals can be difficult...

S: Well, they often surprise you! Once, while I was filming birds in the desert, a monkey ran away with my lunch! On another trip, a crocodile ate my bag – with my mobile inside!

P: How awful!

S: Yeah, it wasn't funny at the time...

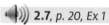 **2.7**, *p. 20, Ex 1*

Jan

A: We had a really great time on holiday. I've got to tell you about the first night, because it was really funny. Something really strange happened...

B: Yeah, what?

A: Well, we spent ages shopping, so we were late getting to the campsite. While we were driving there it got really dark. So we put the tent up quickly, then we went to bed. Anyway, early in the morning, we heard this really strange noise... It woke everyone up, because it was so loud... And that's not all. It didn't sound, well, human...

B: Ooh, frightening!

A: Yeah, it was! Jacek and I wanted to call for help, but Agata told us not to be silly... While we were talking about what to do, she opened the tent door and you won't believe what happened...

B: What?

A: This, uh, cow, put its head right inside the tent! There were cows everywhere!... It seems we were camping in the wrong place!

B: That's crazy!

B: Yep, it was crazy alright, but really funny! We laughed for ages. I'll never forget it.

Lucia

A: It was a fantastic holiday – really great. Well... apart from the last day that is! We had a bit of a scary experience!

B: Oh no, what happened?

A: Well, we were driving through a safari park when some monkeys jumped onto the car! We were driving along, looking at all the animals. Some monkeys were following us when suddenly they jumped onto the roof. We could see them through the windows.

B: Oh no!

A: It was a bit scary! They were making a lot of noise! Then one of them climbed through the window and took my sunglasses!

B: No! I don't believe it!

A: Yes! Then it ran away with them – and they were really expensive! Anyway, then some men came and chased the monkeys away.

B: That sounds... er, interesting, Lucia. The thing is, I've got to go, I've got some friends coming over and... Shall I call you later?

2.9, p. 22, Ex 2

Conversation 1

A: Good morning, can I have your passport, please?

B: Yes, Of course, here it is.

A: Where are you travelling to, sir?

B: Singapore...

A: Do you have your flight reference number with you?

B: Yes, here you are.

A: Thanks very much. How many bags do you want to check in?

B: Just this one...

A: Did you pack the bag yourself?

B: Yes.

A: You didn't leave it unattended at any time?

B: No, no.

A: Ok, thank you. Sir, I'm afraid there is a delay on your flight.

B: Oh dear... How long is it?

A: I'm not sure. They'll inform you at the boarding gate. Please go straight through to passport control now.

B: Oh, that's terrible, I'm going to miss my connection.

A: Here's a free pass to our business lounge, you'll be more comfortable there.

B: Oh, that's great... thank you!

Conversation 2

A: Hi, can I help?

B: Yes, can we check in please. The name's Mantel.

A: Of course, do you have your booking reference number?

B: Yes, here it is, we booked online.

A: What was the name, again?

B: Mantel.

A: Ah yes, here you are, a double room arriving 15th and leaving on the 17th... Is that correct?

B: That's right. Just one question.

A: Certainly...

B: Is breakfast included?

A: Let me check, sir... Yes, that's right. Breakfast is from 7 to 10. And I have some good news for you, you have a suite!

B: Oh, that's a surprise. Thanks very much.

A: Here's your key... room 202... Leave your bags and we'll take them up to your room. Enjoy your stay!

B: Thanks, we will! One more thing...

A: Yes ?

B: Is there Wi-Fi in the rooms?

A: Yes, but there's an extra cost for internet. Here are the details.

B: Oh, that's a shame.

3.1, p. 24, Ex 1

A: So, do you remember The Seven Wonders of the Modern World, Jack?

B: Oh yes, wasn't it some kind of online competition or something?

A: Yes, that's it, quite a few years ago, now... 2007 I think. A Swiss-Canadian, Bernard Weber, set up the project. He asked people to vote on the seven best constructions in the world today, is that right?

B: Yes, I remember – first people from around the world nominated their favourite landmarks – they all had to be man-made – and then everyone voted for the top seven. The winners were announced on July the 7th 2007, the seventh of the seventh of 2007!

A: I don't think I can name all seven though!

B: Well, in alphabetical order they are: Chichen Itza – the Mayan pyramid in the Yucatan Peninsula, Mexico...

A: Oh, yes. I've been there – it's wonderful.

B: The Christ the Redeemer statue in Rio de Janeiro, Brazil...

A: Oh yes, there's a great view of the city from there. I've never been, but I've seen photos. Amazing!

B: The Colosseum in Rome...

A: Of course!

B: The 6,000 kilometre-long Great Wall of China...

A: I'd love to go to China to see that – they say it's the only man-made structure that you can see from space.

B: The Inca city of Machu Picchu, near Cuzco in Peru...

A: Another place I've always wanted to visit.

B: Petra, the city made in rock, in Jordan...

A: Oh yes, that really is such a beautiful place.

B: ... and the Taj Mahal in Agra, India.

A: I have been there. What a great list! But no pyramids? I mean the pyramids in Egypt?

B: No, they were on the original list – the Seven Wonders of the Ancient World...

3.10, p. 32, Ex 2

S = Sal   J = Jake   C = Carly   D = Dave

S: Ok. So what do you think? Which is your favourite, Jake?

J: Well, personally, I prefer the ones that show beautiful scenery, because I really like nature. What do you think, Carly?

C: But that's so boring. I'd rather have something modern. I like this design – it's really abstract and cool.

D: The problem is, you have to change your skin every two weeks if you like things that are in fashion! I'd prefer something more classic, like a piece of art. What about you, Sal? Which do you prefer?

S: I like that one. I'd like to have one that shows one of my hobbies or interests. I'd much rather have one that says something about me and who I am.

J: Well, really, if you want your laptop skin

to say something about you, wouldn't it be better to have a custom design – something that you design yourself?

S: I suppose you're right. Or... what about no design at all? What if you don't want people to know anything about you? Which is better?

D: I hadn't really thought about that.

4.1, p. 38, Ex 2

1
Wow, I look so young in this photo... Many girls in Colombia have what's called a Quinceañera party when they're fifteen. All your friends and family are there. It's a great party. We all dress up in these lovely dresses – it's definitely much more important than a normal birthday party. It's when you become an adult. I remember we danced all night... I met my first boyfriend there! Did I feel like an adult afterwards? Not really. I was still at school. I couldn't drive a car. I didn't leave home till I was 25! But I had lots of fun and lots of presents!

2
We were both 28 when we got married. We were so nervous – and so happy. It really was a very special day. All our friends and family were there. Even my boss came! I don't think I stopped smiling all day! Did it make a difference? Well, yes, it did. I was surprised how big a difference it made. Some people say weddings are just an excuse for a party, but no, it's much, much more. When I look at the ring and think of that day, I know it changed my life for me.

3
This was such a wonderful day. And she's such an incredible lady. It was really hard to believe that she was 100 years old. She spoke so clearly and intelligently. Everybody was there to celebrate with her: her colleagues, her friends, her family. It really was a very special occasion.

4.7, p. 46, Ex 2

Photo A

A: Claudio!

B: Helen! Welcome back! Here, these are for you.

A: They're beautiful, thank you.

B: It's great to see you. I know it was just a week, but I've missed you, Helen.

A: Oh, me too... I mean, I've missed you too. It was a really boring business trip, and I'm glad to be back! So tell me, how are things?

B: Oh, pretty good, yeah. It was fairly quiet at work this week so...

Photo B

A: George! It's great to see you again. It's been a long time since we last met. It must be what, twenty years now?

B: Twenty-two I think..., yes, twenty-two since we retired from the school. It's good to catch up, after all this time. It's a shame we've only got a few hours.

A: Yes, we must meet up again soon. So, what are you doing now?

B: Oh, I moved to Scotland when I stopped teaching... Did I tell you that my eldest son has a business in Edinburgh?

A: Yes, I remember... I'm glad he's been so successful.

B: Yes, we're very proud. How are your sons?

A: They're fine, thanks. They'd love to meet you...

Photo C

A: Oh, it's so good... it's so good to see you. Eight months. It's... it's been so long since I saw you.

B: Yeah, it is, it is... it's great to be back home again. So, Mum... how's it going?

A: Oh, not bad... we've been OK. But you don't want to hear about that! We all want to hear about you!

B: Well, I've got lots to tell you. Is Dad here? And everyone else?

A: Yes, they're all inside. They can't wait to see you.

 **5.1**, *p. 49, Ex 2*

1

My candidate for the Teacher of the Year award is Professor Quarashi. Professor Quarashi teaches university courses in IT, or Information Technology. That's really unusual – not many women teach IT in Saudi Arabia. My family didn't want me to go to university. They wanted me to get married. But Professor Quarashi helped me. She spoke to my parents, and now I'm studying IT too. Professor Quarashi says it's important to choose your favourite subject for your degree, and I love computers! Thank you, Professor – you're my hero!

2

My vote goes to Matthew Sanford! Matthew teaches in the USA. He's disabled and he needs to use a wheelchair. But he doesn't stay at home all day. He teaches yoga! He believes everyone can do something amazing – whoever you are and whatever problems you have. His yoga lessons are great, I really look forward to them. They're certainly much more fun than staying home and watching TV!

3

A & B: Vote for Phil!

A: Phil Higgins is our Science teacher. He teaches us at primary school.

B: Primary school is usually boring, but Mr Higgins makes it fun.

A: Yeah. And he's amazing because he's not just a Science teacher – he's a pilot too!

B: Yeah. Sophie and I, we go to a tiny school in Australia, miles from any towns. We've only got one classroom, and one teacher, Mrs Green. Mrs Green is a great teacher, but she doesn't teach Science. Mr Higgins is our Science teacher. And he's the best!

A: We love learning about science. Mr

Higgins' Science lessons are great.

B: Yes, he flies his plane to our village once a week, and he teaches us Science outdoors. He thinks classrooms are ugly places!

A: And we think he should get the Teacher of the Year award.

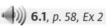 **5.3**, *p. 50, Ex 1*

1 **Ilaria**

Hi, I'm Ilaria. I'm not doing anything exciting this summer, because I need to study. I'm taking my final exam in Forensic Science next month. Forensic Science is really popular now. I chose this course because I love TV police dramas like CSI and Bones, and I want to help the police find criminals. The problem is, thousands of students have had the same idea! I'm working really hard for this exam because I need to get a good grade.

2 **Raushan**

I'm Raushan. Next month, I'm going to start a degree in equine studies. In my home country, Kazakhstan, horses are very important: my family has several horses and we ride them in competitions. There aren't any Equine Studies degrees at my local university, so my family... we're moving to the USA in the new year and I'm going to study there. There are loads of equine courses in the USA – you can even take a course in horse psychology, so you can learn how horses think! But I'm more interested in learning about health and medicine. I want to help our horses be strong, fit – and win lots of prizes!

3 **Lee**

Hi, I'm Lee. At first, I wanted to study Sports Science at uni, 'cause I love football. But I couldn't make my mind up. I didn't know if I'd enjoy studying sport instead of playing it. Then I heard about this new course at Birmingham University, all about social networking – chatting to friends online, that sort of thing. I already spend half my time doing that! I'm starting the course next year, and I'm getting excited about it already. My parents don't think it's a 'real' degree – they want me to study a traditional subject, like, I dunno, Chemistry. But I think the internet – that's the future, isn't it? It might be 'trendy' now, but in ten years' time it's going to be like history or literature – everybody's going to be doing it!

5.9, *p. 56, Intonation*

1 A: Please can I sit here?
  B: Please can I sit here?
2 A: Could you help me, please?
  B: Could you help me, please?
3 A: Would you like to come?
  B: Would you like to come?

5.10, *p. 57, Ex 2*

A: Hello. Adventures in English here. How

can I help you?

B: Er, good morning! I read an advertisement about your school in the *International Times*, and it sounds very interesting. Could I ask you a few more questions?

A: Certainly. What would you like to know?

B: Well, first of all could you tell me where your students stay?

A: Sure. Students stay in a big hotel near the famous Sydney Bridge. Lots of our students like to take photos there!

B: That sounds nice... I'd like to know more about the courses. What subjects do you teach?

A: Well, there's English, of course! But you can also choose extra classes in Literature, Art and Music. Music is always very popular!

B: OK, thanks... I'd also like to know how big your classes are.

A: They're quite small. We usually have between five and ten students in a class. No more than that.

B: Great, thanks. Sorry, I have another question. What activities can students do after school?

A: Oh, there's lots! Students can do sports, walk around the city, or they can go to the cinema. We also take students on trips to the coast.

B: One last question... What does your course cost?

A: It's $600 a week!

B: $600! But the plane ticket's $550! Oh dear, I need to think about this... Could I call you later?

A: Of course, whenever you like.

B: Thank you. Thanks for your help.

6.1, *p. 58, Ex 2*

1

This is a great story. It's about how teenagers are volunteering to help older people learn how to use computers. They don't just help them with technical things. They teach them about fun things too – finding clips from their favourite films, or their favourite singers, scanning and copying old photos, helping them find the news they're interested in... and it's not only about computers. It's about building bridges in the community, bringing the old and the young together, helping them understand each other's worlds. There should be more projects like this.

2

I know this sounds like a joke – but it really did happen. I was there. I saw it. There was a cat stuck in the tree, and its owner called the firefighters – they had to use their ladder and everything. It was very difficult, but in the end they got the cat down. I don't think it was the best possible use of the emergency services! But I suppose it gave them some extra practice for when there's a real emergency!

3

We help out at a local charity – I go out

every Sunday if I can – and we were out one day, handing out food and talking to the homeless people down by the market. It was cold, and we were giving them soup and bread. Anyway, we were there as usual, and this young kid walked over, he was just a passerby, and he walked up to one man and offered him his burger – the burger his dad had just bought for him. His dad was nodding and smiling, and the homeless man smiled too – it was such a nice, generous gesture.

🔊 **6.2**, *p. 61, Ex 2*

N = Natalie   J = Jason

J: Umm Natalie, can I take this afternoon off as holiday?

N: Hmm, I don't know Jason. You should finish that report for the presentation tomorrow.

J: I know, but I can't do any more today. I'm still waiting for the information I need from John Bodley.

N: Well, you should call him and tell him you need it urgently.

J: I know, I've called a few times and left a message. He hasn't called back yet. The thing is... I'm going to play football, to make some money for the local hospital. I can't say no, can I?

N: Well, I suppose it's OK this time. But you shouldn't ask for time off on the same day – you should ask at least a week before.

J: Sorry, Natalie. Thanks. I can finish the report this evening.

🔊 **6.10**, *p. 66, Ex 2*

1 A: I'm not feeling well. I have a headache and a fever.
   B: Why don't you go home and go to bed?
2 A: There's a fire in the kitchen!
   B: You should call the emergency number.
3 A: I'm not doing well in college, because I miss you so much. What should I do?
   B: You should ask someone for help. Why don't you speak to your teacher and see what she says?
4 A: I've got terrible problems at work. I'm so stressed. Do you think I should talk to my boss?
   B: There are people who can help with stress. Why don't you talk to a professional?
5 A: I'm going to be late for class. What can I do?
   B: What about calling your friend? She can let someone know.
6 A: Oh no! This woman has fainted!
   B: Quick, you need to call a doctor.

🔊 **7.1**, *p. 73, Ex 2*

P = Presenter   J = Jan   T = Tanya

P: On today's programme, we're visiting two unusual restaurants. The first one

is called the Restaurant of the Future, and it's at Wageningen University in the Netherlands. We spoke to science correspondent Jan Walters to learn why it's so unusual. ... Hi, Jan. Well, it doesn't look like a futuristic restaurant. So, what's so special about this place?

J: Well, it looks like a normal university canteen – and in fact it is a normal university canteen. The interesting thing is that it's also a laboratory.

P: What do you mean, a laboratory?

J: Well, there are ten cameras in the canteen, which film people as they eat and drink. Here on these screens, the researchers watch how people make a choice about what to eat and drink. Scientists are studying the science of food, doing research into why people eat and drink the way they do. And they're getting a lot of very interesting data. More than 250 students at the university are taking part in the project. Of course, the students don't know what the scientists are looking for, but they do their best to co-operate. The scientists have already made progress, in fact they've made some surprising discoveries.

P: For example...?

J: Well, they've discovered that, on average, women spend longer deciding what to eat than men. And they make changes – very small changes – in the lighting, the decoration, etc. and they've noticed, for example, that people eat more food when there are flowers on their table.

P: That's interesting... And what kind of food do people eat?

J: Oh, all sorts! Manufacturers often ask the researchers to do work on new food in the restaurant, so the menu is always changing. They also do tests on all kinds of things: how much food people leave on their plate, how quickly they make a decision about what to eat... lots of things...

P: Now, our second destination is a very different kind of restaurant of the future. We're in London's Soho, in an oriental fusion restaurant called Inamo. I spoke to restaurant critic, Tanya Ballesta. ... Hi Tanya.

T: Hi there. How are you?

P: So, tell us, how is this the restaurant of the future, then?

T: Well, the first thing to notice is the lighting and the decoration. The interior designers did lots of different experiments before they chose this. They have created a special atmosphere, like a science-fiction movie. I think it's great!

P: And they've invented a new system for ordering food, is that right?

T: Yes, as you can see, the tables are touch-sensitive and interactive. Each table has a projector and a track pad, so you can see the food flash up on the table top in front

of you. Then while you are waiting, you can watch the chef making food on a live web cam, and even play a video game on your table.

P: So, there are no people serving?

T: There's no one taking your order, but the waiter brings the food to your table. That way it's much quicker, and there are no mistakes! And when you've finished, you can order a taxi to take you home by simply clicking a button.

P: It all seems a bit too high tech for me.

T: Well, they're experimenting with new ideas all the time, and most people love the novelty value. One day all restaurants might be like this!

🔊 **7.4**, *p. 78, Ex 1*

1 Fontez

How much technology do I use? Not much! I want to help the environment, so I try not to use lots of energy. It helps me to save a little money too, which is great. I hate shopping, it's so boring! I don't have a lot of things. I don't have a TV, an MP3 player, or even a fridge, nothing like that. Do I ever miss technology? Um, if I'm honest, yes, I do, sometimes. A computer would be great – I love surfing the net, there's a lot of fascinating information out there. At first I didn't use to have any gadgets or electric items at all, but a few years ago I bought myself a small electric fire. Where I live, it can get cold in winter – really cold! But I try not to use it for too many hours a day.

2 Bella

When I use technology, I feel really ill. I get a terrible headache, and then I have to go to bed. It isn't much fun! My doctor told me that technology can make a few people feel sick. This is a huge problem for me! Just look around you the next time you're in town: how many gadgets do you see? Nearly everyone seems to have mobile phones, MP3 players ... there aren't many places I can visit without getting a headache, so I usually stay in! I think, some day, I'll have to move. There are still lots of countries where people don't use much technology, like parts of Africa. I'd like to go there – it would be good to feel well again.

3 Kerim

I live in a place which doesn't have any electricity, so there isn't much technology. I don't care – it isn't a problem for me. I don't need a lot of gadgets to be happy – I think people spend too much time watching TV and playing computer games anyway. I'd rather spend more time having fun with my friends and family! I'm not really interested in science and technology, and I get bored when we have to study it at school. I'm much more interested in music. I want to be a musician when I leave school, like my dad. I'd like to be like him.

🔊 7.5, *p. 80, Intonation*

1 **A:** Young people know more about technology than their parents.
   B: I completely agree with you.
2 **A:** I think everyone should eat organic food.
   B: No, I don't agree.
3 **A:** Science programmes on TV are boring. Do you agree?
   B: Absolutely not.
4 **A:** The environment is our biggest problem today.
   B: I definitely agree with that.

🔊 8.1, *p. 82, Ex 3*

A: These photos are great aren't they?
B: Let's see. What are they exactly?
A: Well it's this new website I've found – it has a collection of fake photos. Look – and an explanation about how they faked them.
B: What do you mean?
A: Well, look at this one for example. It's a really old photo, and it was really famous at the time. It's supposed to be a photo of the Loch Ness Monster.
B: It doesn't look very realistic to me!
A: Well, no, but at the time a lot of people believed it was real.
B: So how did they fake it then?
A: Well, it was taken before the days of computer-generated images – they used a toy submarine and a model, a simple plastic model... but it worked, the photo's still really well-known.
B: So's this one! I love it! The first time I saw it I thought it was genuine. And so did a lot of other people too. It was from a video for a prototype of a new mobile phone. It was shown online. Lots of people commented on it and wanted to know where to buy it. But it didn't actually exist. It was a fake, I mean, it was just a concept, you know, an idea, for a phone of the future. They just used a piece of white paper, got the actor to look like she was using it as a phone and added the images in later.
B: That's really clever! It had me fooled! The final result is pretty impressive though isn't it? I'd want to buy it too!
A: And what about this one then? This photo looks authentic to me.
B: Yes, you're right, the photo is, but what about the trick? Do you think that's real? I mean, do you really think he's lifted the girl up into the air? There must be some kind of trick to it!
A: Well, it's magic isn't it? I mean, you just have to believe, don't you?
B: And you believe in it?
A: No, but it's really clever – I've got absolutely no idea how they do it! No matter how carefully I look, I really can't see how they do it.

🔊 8.6, *p. 90, Ex 1*

T = Teacher   E = Emma

T: Now listen, Emma, I'm a little worried about you this term. If you don't work harder, you'll fail this course and I don't want that to happen. Your grades are very low. Be careful!
E: Can I redo my essay?
T: Well, usually I don't let students rewrite, but if you give me your essay by tomorrow, I'll give it back to you by Monday.
E: Thank you.
T: OK – off you go now, and get on with your essay.

🔊 9.1, *p. 92, Ex 2*

1 **A:** Can you lend me some money? I need to pay for the dog's haircut.
   B: Sure. How much do you need to borrow?
   A: About 30. Give me 50, and I'll save the rest for the weekend.
2 **A:** It was a great idea to spend the money on this trip!
   B: I know – we deserve it. We worked hard, and, well, we earned a lot of money this year. I don't feel guilty!
   A: And, of course, we won all that money, too... in the lottery.
   B: Here's to us!
3 **A:** It's too much money to invest in a painting.
   B: It's a good price, let's make an offer...
   A: I'm not sure we should, I don't want to waste our money.
   B: Come on, let's see what happens.
4 **A:** How much does this handbag cost, please?
   B: $400.
   A: Oh, I can't really afford it, but I really like it.
   B: It really suits you, madam.
   A: I could just use my credit card!
   B: Yes, of course, cash or card, whichever you prefer, madam.
   A: Ok, I'll have it.

🔊 9.2, *p. 93, Ex 5*

1 Well, I think even if I was rich, I wouldn't invest in art, it's too risky. I think property is a better investment. I think having a mortgage and paying interest to the bank is ok, because you can get the money back from rent. It's a good way of planning for the future.
2 I agree with them, it's good to spend money on a luxury holiday. We do the same every summer. Sometimes we get a loan from the bank, or pay for it by credit card, and forget about it for a couple of months, but it's worth it! The trouble is, you get the bill for your summer holidays at Christmas!

3 Shopping is one of the greatest pleasures in life. But I don't think you should spend all your salary on expensive clothes and handbags. It's ok from time to time, if you've got a bit of spare cash. But don't pay for it on credit...
4 Spending money on dogs, now that's crazy! I know somebody who spent a fortune on them; there are lots of hidden costs with animals – their food, vet's fees, they're almost as expensive as having children.

🔊 9.4, *p. 95, Ex 1*

1 If you saved more money, you wouldn't have this problem.
2 I'd help you if I had more time.
3 If you lived in a smaller place, you'd be able to live more cheaply.
4 Would you be happier if you had less money?

🔊 9.11, *p. 101, Ex 4*

Well, Steve. As you can see, you spend more than you earn, which is why you can't pay off your credit card bills. So, what we need to do is look at how you can spend less money. First of all, you say you buy a sandwich for lunch. Why don't you make your own lunch at home and take it to work? That would be much cheaper. Then, the second thing that would save you money is not eating out as much. This is very expensive. Why don't you cook at home and share the expenses with your housemates? It seems you could also cut down on your entertainment expenses. You could go out one night a week instead of two. Why not ask your friends to come to your house to watch TV or to have dinner instead of going out? OK – the next thing is the gym. You say you're paying £40, but you only go once a month. That's an expensive trip to the gym! Why not give up the subscription and pay each time you go, or even better, do some exercise that doesn't cost money, like going running around where you live. The final area where you can save money is on clothes and shoes. You need to cut this down to half. Look for things in sales that cost less. So... what do you think?

🔊 10.1, *p. 106, Ex 3*

1 I hate the way they show the same adverts over and over on TV. Sometimes you're flicking through the channels and it's the same ad on all of them. Car adverts in particular annoy me – I don't really know why. I don't like the way they're selling a 'lifestyle'– and the slogans are so exaggerated, like 'it must be love' or 'the power of dreams'... I mean, come on, it's just a machine!
2 I hate it when I get ads on my mobile phone. I hear the beep beep and I know I've got a message and it turns out that it's the mobile phone company saying you

have x number of points and telling me what I can do with these points, they have a promotion or special offer or something. So annoying! There's so much advertising out there, and I don't mind that we see posters and billboards everyday but the last thing I want is more advertising in my pocket! C'mon, guys!

3   I saw this guy walking around in the town centre, advertising a new clothes store. What I liked was the fact that the advert was on his T-shirt! The T-shirt was a bright colour, and he was attractive, and I thought, 'That's a very original campaign!' So I thought I'd go and have a look. They had an opening sale and I bought some clothes there – I got a few real bargains… so I told all my friends to go. So I'm a good advert too!

10.2, *p. 108, Ex 1*

What does a football shirt represent? Well, of course, it is a symbol of a football club. But big football clubs are sponsored by other companies – they get money from companies who want their logo to appear on the shirt. So the shirt advertises two things at the same time: its own club and another company. It's a big business, and huge profits are made from the shirt sales.

The football shirt is also a fashion item. To keep making more money, new shirts are designed every year, for both 'home' and 'away' games. The fans keep buying the new ones because everyone wants the latest shirt, not one from last year. But it's not just the fans who buy them. Football shirts are now seen everywhere. Walk down any tourist street and you'll see hundreds of different football shirts for sale. And of course, the shirt says something about you and your identity. That's why football shirts are so popular!

Thanks to global media, football is now followed all over the world, in countries where nobody supported it before, such as Japan or China. When European clubs visit Asia for promotional tours, their shirts are worn by everybody. So there is a big market for imitation shirts because the official shirts are incredibly expensive. Thousands of fake football shirts are sold at bargain prices.

Unfortunately, like many clothes these days, most football shirts are manufactured in the developing world by factory workers on very low salaries, who often work in terrible conditions. They are then sold at huge profits by the clubs. So for me, the football shirt is a symbol of globalization – the good and the bad. It helps brings the world together through the love of football, but it's also an example of exploitation – how big industries exploit the poorer countries in the world.

10.7, *p. 114, Ex 2*

A: What's that?
B: Jollof rice.
A: Jollof rice?
B: Yes, basically it's rice cooked with tomatoes and spices. It's a traditional West African dish.
A: And what's this?
B: That's moinmoin. It's a kind of bean paste. It's made with steamed brown beans and vegetables. It's often served on a banana leaf, or wrapped up in a banana leaf. It tastes great with fried chicken. You should try it!
A: Mm… I don't know. Is it spicy?
B: Yes, a little bit, but not too much… I think you'll like it.
A: OK, I'll have some.
B: Me too.

11.1, *p. 117, Ex 3*

1   We first met at university. We were living in the same students' residence. It was a flat with four bedrooms and we shared a kitchen and a living room. On our first night in the flat we all got together to cook a meal. It was fun, and we got on really well from the very beginning. We weren't studying the same subjects – she was studying medicine and I was studying languages – but that didn't matter. In fact I think it helped – it meant we didn't talk about work all the time!

2   We first met about five years ago. I was new to the town, and I wanted to make friends. I love playing football, and one day I saw a sign up at work saying that they were looking for players on a Monday night. So I signed up. There were a lot of great people there, and Martin was one of them. We had a lot in common; we'd studied the same things, we worked in the same field… and last year we started a business together.

11.5, *p. 121, Ex 5*

J = John   A = Angela   G = Guest

J: Where's the bottle opener?
A: It's in the drawer, John, where I always put it.
J: Well, it's not here now. I always put it back when I use it and you always move it.
A: No I don't!
J: Yes, you do. You never put anything back in the right place.
A: How can you say that? You're the one who always loses everything.
G: Well, we should go now.
J: No, don't go, just because Angela's getting angry. She's such an angry person.
G: Thanks for a lovely evening, see you, I'll call you tomorrow…
A: Now see what you've done!
J: I didn't do anything – it was you… your

mother always argues in front of people too, you're…

11.11, *p. 125, Ex 3*

A: Hey Lee! How's Rosie?
B: She's fine. I saw her the other day and she said she was doing really well at university. She told me that she liked her classes this term.
A: What about her boyfriend – Pete, is it?
B: She said he was living closer to her now. She also said that her mum and dad still had the book shop and her brother was working in a shoe shop now.
A: That's nice.

12.1, *p. 126, Ex 4*

1   A: I found this great clip on YouTube last night. Have you seen it? The one about the shark attack?
     B: Oh yeah! It's great, isn't it, really funny! My brother sent me the link. Of course, it's a fake.
     A: Really? Oh no – I thought it was real!
2   A: How was the concert last night? Did a lot of people go?
     B: Yeah, it was really full. I mean the venue's small, but it was full, and the atmosphere was great. Stefan played really well and everyone seemed to enjoy it.
     A: I'd like to see him next time.
     B: I'll let you know when he's on.

12.6, *p. 134, Ex 4*

1   A: We were in the park yesterday, and they've got this great photo exhibition on. You'd absolutely love it. The photos are huge – they show all kinds of scenes of park life – really good.
     B: Sounds interesting. When is it on until?
     A: Next Saturday, I think. You really should go. It's just the kind of thing you like.
     B: Really? I'll have to take a look.
2   A: Did you see Dee on TV last night?
     B: Dee? On TV? Are you sure?
     A: Yeah, on one of those documentaries that show real life stories…
     B: What was she doing?
     A: She was talking about her job. You have to see it. It'll make you laugh.
     B: I had no idea! I'm so sorry I missed it!
     A: It's OK. It's on again next week.
     B: When's it on? Let me make a note of it. I really don't want to miss it this time!
3   A: Are you going to the concert tonight?
     B: What concert?
     A: The one on the beach – at sunset – you know, down at Jaume's bar. Siva and his band are playing. You must go.
     B: Mm, I'm not sure. I went to one last year – it's not really my kind of thing.
     A: Really? You surprise me! Oh well, I'll ask Maria to come along instead – she'll love it!

IRREGULAR VERBS

INFINITIVE	PAST SIMPLE	PAST PARTICIPLE
be	was, were	been
become	became	become
begin	began	begun
bite	bit	bitten
break	broke	broken
bring	brought	brought
build	built	built
buy	bought	bought
choose	chose	chosen
come	came	come
cost	cost	cost
do	did	done
dream	dreamt/dreamed	dreamt/dreamed
drink	drank	drunk
eat	ate	eaten
fall	fell	fallen
feel	felt	felt
find	found	found
fly	flew	flown
forbid	forbade	forbidden
forget	forgot	forgotten
forgive	forgave	forgiven
get	got	got
give	gave	given
go	went	gone, been
grow	grew	grown
have	had	had
hear	heard	heard
hide	hid	hidden
hold	held	held
keep	kept	kept
know	knew	known
learn	learnt/learned	learnt/learned
leave	left	left
let	let	let
lose	lost	lost

INFINITIVE	PAST SIMPLE	PAST PARTICIPLE
make	made	made
meet	met	met
pay	paid	paid
put	put	put
read /riːd/	read /red/	read /red/
ride	rode	ridden
ring	rang	rung
rise	rose	risen
run	ran	run
say	said	said
see	saw	seen
sell	sold	sold
send	sent	sent
set	set	set
shake	shook	shaken
show	showed	shown
shut	shut	shut
sing	sang	sung
sit	sat	sat
sleep	slept	slept
speak	spoke	spoken
spend	spent	spent
stand	stood	stood
steal	stole	stolen
stick	stuck	stuck
swim	swam	swum
take	took	taken
teach	taught	taught
tell	told	told
think	thought	thought
throw	threw	thrown
understand	understood	understood
wake	woke	woken
wear	wore	worn
win	won	won
write	wrote	written